Col. (Dr) Rajesh Kumar is conferred the Doctorate (Ph.D.) by H.E. MOH Farook the Chancellor and Governor of Jharkhand State, presenting the thesis and the book under publication on *E-governance and Disaster Mitigation.*

Photo at Rajbhawan, Ranchi (Jharkhand) on 20 Aug 2011.

Disaster Management

Disaster Management

BY

COL. RAJESH KUMAR

ISBN: 978-93-5324-113-1

First Published, 2017

Published by

GenNext Publication
5, Ansari Road
Daryaganj, New Delhi-110002
Phone: 9811692060
E-mail: gennextpublication@hotmail.com

Printed at: G. Print Process, Delhi.

Contents

Acknowledgements 13
Preface 15

1. Disaster Management: An Introduction 17

• Introduction • Term of Reference • Aim • Layout • Types of Natural Disasters • Relevance of Disaster Management Study • Conclusion.

2. Factors and Significance of Disasters 29

• Introduction • India's Vulnerability to Disasters • The Problem • Justification of the Study • Limitations of the Study • India: A Country Profile Millennium Challenge • Background • The Disaster Management Information System • Disaster Mitigation and Emergency Preparedness • Trauma Management • Rescue International • Natural Disasters • Disaster Mitigation Tool Kit • Health Kit • First Aid Medicine Kit • School Kit • Kit for Kids • Domestic Kit • Sewing Kit • Cleaning Utilities • Baby Items • Cleaning Supplies • Miscellaneous • Paper Products • Personal Items • Forecasting of Natural Disasters • Disaster Mitigation and Vulnerability Atlas of India • World-Wide Earthquake Locator • World Earthquake Information from USGS National Earthquake Information Centre • Earthquake Data • Predicting an Earthquake • EQNet: Earthquake Information Network • UC Berkley Seismological Laboratory • Flood • Cyclone • National Hurricane Centre • Canadian Hurricane Centre • National Weather Service Disaster Survey Reports • Purdue University Hurricane and Tropical Data • Drought • Current Drought Status in Queensland, Australia • The Canadian Climate and Water Information • Weekly Global Climate Highlights from CPC • The Greater Horn Information Exchange (GHIE) • Drought Monitor • How can you help? • You can help • Information Technology Tools for Natural Disaster Risk Management • EIIP Virtual Forum • NASA's Disaster Finder • Doctors Without Borders • Virtual Hospital at University of Iowa Health Centre Virtual Hospital (VH) • References • Notes.

3. Disasters: Causes and Effects 63

• Existing Institutional Arrangements • National Level • State Level • District and Local Level • Other Stakeholders • External Linkages • Disaster Management Policy • State Level • District Level • Legal and Techno-legal Framework • Financial Arrangements • Initiatives for Disaster Mitigation • Disaster Preparedness • Indian Armed Forces in Management of Natural Disasters • Conclusion • References.

4. Typology and Profile of Regional, Seasonal, Social and Accidental Disasters 85

• Operational Definitions • Types of Disasters • Man-made Disasters • Natural Disasters • Policy Disasters • Floods • Cyclones • Earth Quakes • Effects of Disaster • Special Features of Disaster Management • Stages of Disaster Management • Road Map to Improve Disaster Management Organisation in India • Introduction • Recommended Measures – Organisational • Recommended Measures – Institutional • Recommended Measures – Infrastructure Support • Recommended Measures – Preparedness for Disasters • Recommended Measures for Quick Response • Recommended Measures – Strategic Aspects • Recommended Measures – Training • Testing of Hypothesis • However there are certain threats that plague the system • Bibliography • Refernces • Notes

5. Case Studies: E-governance 113

• Technology-led Strategy • A Case Study of Karnataka, Kerala and Odisha : Strategies in Good Governance • The World Bank in its Document • E-Governance • Khajane • E-Lottery • Mukhya Vahini • Other Initiatives • Friends Project of Kerala • Project Application • The Philosophy • An Innovative Approach • Dramatic Impact on People • Orissa Gramsat Pilot Project • Infrastructure and Functioning • Computerization/E-governance Initiative of Panchayati Raj Department • Case Study: Gujarat • e-Governance in Gujarat • Vision • Change Management • GSWAN – the Backbone of e-Governance Applications • SICN – State-of-the-art connectivity • IWDMS – Streamlining Documentation for Knowledge-led Governance • Digital Signature Certificates – For a secure digital world • Citizen Convenience Centres – Setting Standards in One-Day Governance • e-Nagarpalikas – One-Day Governance for Everyone • Gyan Ganga – The River of Knowledge • e-Gram – e-Governance at the Panchayat Level • e-Dhara – Land Records Online • Talim Rojgar • SWAGAT – An epitome of transparency • SWIFT - State Wide Information on Financial Transactions • CCIS - Comprehensive Case Information System at High Court of Gujarat • IDS - Integrated Disease Surveillance System (IDS) • e-PRIMA (Panchayati Raj Institutes – Maintenance of Accounts) • HMIS – Health Management Information System • Government's Futuristic Plan for IT Savvy Manpower • Industry-Institute Linkages – College to Career Programme • The Final Analysis • End Note • References • Bibliography • Internet Sites • References.

6. Global View in Indian Context 139

• General • Role of Government • Role of International Agencies • Role of UNO2 • The Role of Voluntary Agencies • Other Organisations • The Role of the Media • Problem Areas • Disaster Management in Some Foreign Countries • General • Australia • USA • The Global Perspective in Indian Scenario • United Nations in Disaster Management • Disaster Management Programme (DMP) • Disaster Management Training Programme (DTMP) • United Nations Disaster Management Team (UN DMT) • Deployable UN Co-ordination Support Mechanisms • Non Deployable UN Coordination Entities • UN Organisation for Disaster Management • UN's Role in Some Recent Disasters • Recommendations • Disaster Management in Australia • Path of Request for Assistance • Disaster Management in the USA • Disaster Management in Europe • Conclusion • References • Emergency Management • Flooding • Landslides/ land subsidence • Meteorological Hazards • Seismic Hazards • Tsunami • Volcanic Hazards • Notes.

7. Preparedness and Mitigation in Restoration of E-Governance 181

• National Policy on Disaster Management • General • Disaster Management Planning • Primary Relief Functions • Secondary Relief Functions • Coordination and Control • National Level • Contingency Action Plan • Financial Aspects • Procedure for Extending Financial Assistance to States • Arrangement for Financing Relief • Ninth Finance Commission's Recommendations • Warning Systems • State Level Mechanism • Model Showing Disaster Relief Cycle at State Level • Role of Armed Forces • Role of Police and Home Guards in Rescue and Relief Operation • Home Guards • Role of Voluntary/ Non Governmental Organisation (NGOs) • Disaster Management in India: Need and Recommended Integrated Approach • General • Current Concerns • Disaster Relief Execution Capability • Preparedness Aspects • Sustainability Aspect • Development Thrusts • Other Concerns • Approach to Disaster Management • General • Comprehensive Emergency Management • Definition and Applicability • Commended Organisation for Disaster Management in India • National Policy • National Disaster Organisation • Basic Components • Functional Component • National Institute of Disaster Management (NIDM) • State Level Organisation • Role of Armed Forces • Financial Implications • Conclusion • Reference • Notes.

8. Conclusion 217

• General • Global Trends • The Transition in India • The Disaster Management Act 2005 • National Vision • Centre-staging Communities • National Disaster Response Force (NDRF) • Mitigation Measures and Role of Science and Technology • Techno-Legal and Techno-Financial Regime • Earthquake Risk Mitigation in India • Background • Critical Gaps • NDMA Guidelines for Management of Earthquakes • Proposed National Earthquake Risk Mitigation Project (NERMP) • Cyclone • Urban Flood Disaster Management • Background • Urban Flooding is Different • Running Urban Centres 24x7 • National guidelines from NDMA • Flood Management – An Overview • The Flood Hazard • Past Initiatives by the Government of India • Institutional Mechanism • Flood Management Measures • Flood Response • Flood Management Plans • Strengthening Disaster Response in India • Disaster Management: Shifting Axis from Visible to Invisible • Medical Preparedness for Disaster Management • Role of Laboratory in Disaster Management • Setting up Laboratory Support to Disease Surveillance Post Disaster Situations • Laboratory Support for Disaster Management • Networking of Laboratories under Integrated Disease Surveillance Programme (IDSP) • e-Governance Suggestions • Major Areas of Implementation • Commercial • Suggestions • Weaknesses • Threats • Conclusion.

Index **249**

Dedication

This book is dedicated to my loving son Yashashvee who is right now undergoing the military training at Dehradun, India and sporty and chirpy daughter Ambalee who has been participating in national level sports.

Acknowledgements

No creation in this world is a solo effort, neither is this research-work. I, have enjoyed the encouragement, cooperation and support of many people to whom I owe a deep sense of gratitude while writing this book. My heartfelt thanks to my supervisor Dr Vijay Bahadur Singh whose precious suggestions, calm patience and deep concern have helped me to keep constant and in good stead throughout my work.

Being an Army Officer and owing a profile of Communication Engineering and Landmarks in adventure sports, opportune me to be posted at various interesting war theatres in India. Unforgettable one was an assignment of commanding the Infantry Brigade Signal Company of Technical and GD soldiers in defensive role at largest/highest battle field on Indo-China-Borders at Chushul in Laddakh. Two years tenure of managing disasters of troops at freezing-lake "Pangong-Tso" and fighting info warfare in the snow-desert terrain have been excellent exposure and learning to me. The average subzero temperature compelled me to remain near the Bukhari and confinement in the Basha (wooden house). The Central Buddhist Institute at Choglamsar (Ladakh) and its librarian Mr Tashi Namgiyal who took personal interest in contributing books and apprising me the Ladakhi Buddhist culture and Disasters right from ancient days till present in this region. The Fire and Fury Library of HQ 14 Corps of Indian Army at Leh has contributed a lot to my research work for which I am thankful to Lt Gen R B Singh, AVSM, YSM the Corps Commander who made the library available to me 24 hrs a day all through the summer season.

I would specially thank Shri KM Singh, IPS member of NDMA, who have been my source of inspiration and who extended the indeed guidance on my work.

Actually, I find no appropriate words to express my deep sense of gratitude to my better half Dr Arunima Singh who has been contributing her selfless cooperation and being together even in the hostile climatic condition and in sub-zero temperature.

From the deepest core of my heart I am thankful to the people from Bihar and Jharkhand who inspired and supported me to carryout the research work.

Finally, I thank all the members of my family, well wishers and friends who directly or indirectly contributed in the completion of my book.

Colonel Rajesh Kumar
(Colonel Rajesh Kumar)

Preface

Disaster management- Disasters can be man-made or natural. The major issues of disaster management with greater focus, the knowledge, resources, managing skills and technological advancement have to be incorporated. Its scope to study of natural disasters and early warning system may play a great role to save and rehabilitate the civil society.

Significance of managing and mitigating Disasters- It would be presumptuous to comment that disasters can be totally forecasted and managed by technology. However, a well oiled disaster management machinery, if in place, will help save a number of costly lives and property. It is essential that the capacity of the South and the SE region be built so that they are able to assess the risk, identify risk reduction measures and plan and implement these risk reduction measures in a coordinated fashion.

This dissertation consists the knowledge and brings out the fact as under:-

- Chapter-I elaborates the introductory portion of the Disasters in Indian region.
- Chepter-II deals with types of Disasters affecting civilisations and its significance.
- Chapter-III explains causes and effects on Indian society in modem world.
- Chapter-IV says about regional, seasonal, social and accidental disasters.
- Chapter-V enlighten with the remedial measures on Case studies.
- Chapter-VI exhibits global opinion in Indian context.
- Chapter-VII brings out alarm and preparedness to mitigate and restore e-govemance.

- Chapter-VIII summarise the book work with suggestions to society, NGOs and Government.

Let us face the fact that our future is not safe and the world is bound to be enveloped by disaster risks if we do not address the issue in time. If we monitor risks and risk reduction on a daily basis we will find that, rate of increase in disaster risk is much higher than the rate of risk reduction. Urbanisation climate change population boom, environmental degradation, industrialisation, unsafe development etc coupled with terrorism and other blasphemous activities are gradually adding to the existing risk.

Disaster Management: An Introduction

> *"Lives of all mankind are regulated by the rhythm of the seasons. We are accustomed to rhythm, to regulated change; but not to the extraordinary, the departure from the normal, and even though we are aware of the almost regular irregularities of the earth's natural forces, they nearly always catch us unawares."* —**Anon**

Introduction

1. Man may think that he is the master of the world, but every now and then Nature unleashes her might to remind him who the prime mover is. In normal times, Nature is our benefactor, we get our food, housing, and energy from it, and indeed we owe our existence to her. And then, at other times, nature is our greatest adversary - when the tectonic plates shift, when hot magma forces its way to the surface of the earth, when severe cyclones storm, and when avalanches strike, there is nothing we can do to it. When earthquakes hit, there is often no warning and the damage can be worse than by a nuclear bomb. In 1976, an earthquake devastated Tangshan, China killing 242,000 people. In fact, unofficial counts put the death toll at 655,000 and that earthquake may not have been the biggest in history. Earlier, in 1556, an earthquake had hit China which may have killed over 800,000 people. The recent earthquake that devastated POK and parts of J&K has caused human miseries and loss that is no lesser than the worst disaster of the same kind. And who can forget the juggernaut of the Tsunami and the rapacious assault of Katrina during 2005? Disasters, of course, can be

man-made or natural. But to examine the major issues of disaster management with greater focus, this MRP shall limit its scope only to the study of natural disasters.

Term of Reference

2. Disasters can be man-made or natural. But to examine the major issues of disaster management with greater focus, the MRP shall limit its scope only to the study of natural disasters.

Aim

3. To study and analyse various facets of management of natural disasters, with special reference to India and its adjoining region.

Layout

4. The research paper is divided into the following parts:-

(a) Overview.

(b) Disaster Management in India.

(c) Disaster Management Systems in Developed Countries.

(d) India's role in Disaster Management in South and South-East Asia.

(e) Road Map for the future.

This part will examine the following issues:-

(f) Definitions.

(g) Classification of disasters.

(h) Types of natural disasters.

(i) Effects of disasters.

(j) Background.

(k) Relevance of disaster management study.

Definitions

(a) *Disaster.* The Concise Oxford Dictionary defines disaster as "sudden or great misfortune", "calamity or complex failure". It may be defined as an unexpected happening causing a huge loss of life and property. It may be natural or man-made. Some organisatoins have a more quantified definition of disasters e.g. the natural hazards research group at the University of Colorado (US) defines disaster as a calamity that causes more than one million Dollar damage or leaves more than 100 people dead or injured.

(b) *Disaster Prevention.* This may be described as measures designed to prevent natural phenomenon from transforming into emergency situations. Prevention concerns the formulation and implementation of policies and programmes to prevent or eliminate the occurrence of disasters.

(c) *Disaster Preparedness.* Disaster preparedness may be described as action designed to minimise loss of life and damage, and to organise and facilitate timely and effective rescue, relief and rehabilitation. Preparation is concerned with forecasting and warning, education and training of the population, organisation for management of disaster situation, including preparation of operational plans, training of relief groups, stockpiling of supplies and earmarking of necessary funds.

(d) *Disaster Management.* The calm, deliberate, judicious and controlled mechanisms instituted by a government or other organisations to avert, if possible, and if not, isolate and prevent further escalation of the impact of disaster and thereafter adopt measures to restore normalcy in the available time frame.

(e) *Disaster Legislation.* It is the law describing the responsibilities of a government in the case of disaster. It specially authorises the relief organisation to prepare its task with full cooperation to all concerned.

Classification of Disasters

5. There are different ways to classify disasters. Classification dictates preparedness, response and risk reduction measures as well as the specialists and agencies involved. Disasters are often classified according to their cause, their speed of onset (sudden or slow) and whether or not they are due to "acts of nature" (natural) or "acts of humans" (man-made). The same is briefly enunciated as under:-

(a) *Classification Based on Causes.* Disasters may be classified on the basis of the hazard which causes the disastrous economic and social consequences. Thus, this classification includes earthquakes, flash floods, cyclones, tornadoes, landslides, mud flows, droughts, pest and insect infestations, chemical exploitation, etc.

(b) *Classification Based on Speed of Onset.* The speed of the disaster's onset is another way to distinguish between disasters and the types of responses that may be required.

(i) *Rapid Onset.* A rapid onset disaster refers to an event or hazard that occurs suddenly, with little or no warning, taking the lives of people, and destroying economic structures and material resources. Rapid onset disasters may be caused by earthquakes, floods, storm winds, tornadoes, or mud flows. The recent disasters triggered by tsunami in South East Asia and India and hurricane Katrina in the US are examples of the same.

(ii) *Slow Onset.* Slow onset disasters occur over time and slowly deteriorate a society's and a population's capacity to withstand the effects of the hazard or threat. Hazards causing these disaster conditions may include droughts, famines, environmental degradation, desertification, deforestation and pest infestation.

(c) Classification based on Acts of Nature or Acts of Humans.

Disasters could be natural or man-made. Disasters caused by floods, droughts, tidal waves and earth tremors are generally considered "natural disasters." While those caused by chemical or industrial accidents, environmental pollution, transport accidents and political unrest are classified as man-made.

Types of Natural Disasters

8. *Avalanche.* Avalanche is a slippage of built-up snow down an incline, possibly mixed with ice, rock, soil or plant-life. Avalanches are categorised as either slab or powder avalanches. Avalanches are a major danger in the mountains during the winter as a large one can run for miles, and can create massive destruction of the lower forests and anything else in its path. For example, in Montroc, France, in the year 1999, about 300,000 cubic metres of snow slid on a 30 degree slope, achieving a speed of 100 kilometers per hour, taking hundreds of lives.

9. *Drought and Famine.* A drought is a long lasting weather pattern consisting of dry conditions with very little or no precipitation. During

this period, food and water supply can run low, and can result in conditions such as famine. Droughts can last for several years and are particularly damaging in areas in which the residents depend on agriculture for survival. Famine is a natural disaster characterised by a widespread lack of food, agriculture foodstuffs and livestock.

10. *Earthquake.* An earthquake is a sudden shift or move of the tectonic plate in the Earth's crust. On the surface, this is manifested by a moving and shaking of the ground, and can massively damage poorly built structures. The most powerful earthquakes can destroy even the best built up structures and thus cause wide-spread loss of life. In addition, they can trigger secondary disasters, such as tsunamis and volcanic eruptions. Earthquakes occur along fault lines, and are unpredictable.

11. *Fire.* A fire is a natural disaster that may destroy ecological systems like grasslands, forests, causing great loss of life, property, livestock and wildlife. Bush fires, forest fires and mine fires are generally started by lightning, but also by human negligence or arson, and can burn thousands of square kilometers. Some of the biggest city fires are The Great Chicago Fire, The Great Fire of London, and The San Francisco Fire.

12. *Flood.* A flood is a natural disaster caused by too much rain or water in a locality, and could be caused by many different sets of conditions. Floods can be caused by prolonged rainfall from a storm, including thunder storms, rapid melting of large amount of snow, or rivers which swell from excess precipitation upstream and cause widespread damage to areas downstream, or less frequently the bursting of man-made dams. The recent flood in Mumbai in 2005 claimed approximately 500 lives.

13. *Hurricane.* A hurricane is a low-pressure cyclonic storm system which forms over the oceans. It is caused by evaporated water which comes off the ocean and becomes a storm. The Coriolis Effect causes the storms to spin, and a hurricane is declared when this spinning mass of storms attains a wind speed greater than 74 mph or nearly 120 kmph. In different parts of the world hurricanes are known as cyclones or typhoons. The former occur in the Indian Ocean, while the latter occur in the Eastern Pacific Ocean. One of the most damaging hurricanes in recent memory was Hurricane Katrina, which hit the United States East Coast in 2005.

14. *Landslide and Mudslides.* A landslide is a disaster closely related to an avalanche, but instead of occurring with snow, it involves rocks, trees, parts of houses and anything else which may happen to be swept up. Landslides can be caused by earthquakes, volcanic eruptions, or general instability in the surrounding land. Mudslides, or mud flows, are a special case of landslides, in which heavy rainfall causes loose soil on steep terrain to collapse and slide downwards.

15. *Tsunami.* A tsunami is a giant wave of water which rolls into the shore of an area with a height of over 15 m (50 feet). It comes from Japanese words meaning harbor and wave. Tsunamis can be caused by undersea earthquakes as in the 2004 Indian Ocean Earthquake, or by landslides such as the one which occurred at Lituya Bay, Alaska. The tsunami generated by the 2004 Indian Ocean Earthquake currently ranks as the deadliest tsunami in recorded history.

16. *Volcanic Eruption.* This natural disaster is caused by the eruption of a volcano, and eruptions come in many forms. They range from daily small eruptions which occur in Hawaii, or extremely infrequent supervolcano eruptions in places like Lake Toba. Recent large volcanic eruptions include that of Mount St. Helens and Krakatoa, occurring in 1980 and 1883, respectively.

Effects

17. 'No two disasters are alike' is a common saying amongst specialists in the field. What comes to the mind when one hears the word disaster is the cataclysmic physical dimension of the event, the images of the numerous tragedies, conveyed and replayed to us by the print and electronic media. However, there are other effects of disasters, the knowledge of which is essential to undertake the post-disaster operations. The effects could be one or a combination of the effects discussed in the succeeding paragraphs.

18. *Environmental Effects.* These include destruction and damage to life and property, decreased quantity and quality of water, destruction of crops and food stocks.

19. *Medical Effects.* The study of disaster epidemiology lists four possible medical effects of disasters, i.e. traumatic injuries, emotional stresses, epidemic diseases and indigenous diseases. The threat of epidemic arising out of a disaster is the foremost. Cholera and plague

are known to have affected population after floods in various parts of the world. The effect of trauma depends on the degree of exposure and the profoundness of personal impact on the victim, the socio-economic status of the victim and whether the person has had to deal with such incidents earlier.

20. *Socio-Economic Effects.* A disaster often highlights the social struggles in a society and underscores the inherent inequalities within a political system. Earthquakes and hurricanes, affect a disproportionately high percentage of poor in the developing countries and this can lead to profound political and social changes within the society. Many governments have been destabilised immediate after a disaster. The case often cited is the chain of events leading to the independence of Bangladesh. In 1970, a tropical cyclone generated a massive storm and the failure of the then Pakistani government to deal with the situation highlighted the second grade treatment of the East Pakistan by West Pakistan. As far as economy is considered, disasters disrupt rather than destroy economies, as was the case during the Gujarat earthquake which resulted in a daily production loss of 400 crores to trade and industry.

Background

21. *Global.* While man has always lived with the spectre of an impending disaster, it is only in the last fifty years or so that the alarming frequency and ferocity of such disasters have risen significantly. At the global level, there has been considerable concern over natural disasters. Even as substantial scientific and material progress is made, the loss of lives and property due to disasters has not decreased. In fact, the human toll and economic losses have mounted. It was in this background that the United Nations General Assembly, in 1989, declared the decade 1990-2000 as the International Decade for Natural Disaster Reduction with the objective to reduce loss of lives and property and restrict socio-eco damage through concerted international action, especially in developing countries. Ironically, it was during this very period that the world witnessed some of the worst loss of human life and economy. Hurricanes and cyclones took large tolls in South Asia, the Philippines, Central America, the Caribbean and the United States. There was unprecedented flooding in Europe, China, Venezuela and the United States. Earthquakes in Turkey, Japan, China

and the United States killed many and cost billions. The numbers of people affected by natural disasters in last two decades are given as under:

People Affected by Natural Disasters in the Last Two Decades

Category of Natural disaster	*Number of people affected (millions)*	*Percentage of Total*
Droughts	185.5	9.9
Earthquakes	11.7	0.6
Floods	1,418.2	75.5
Landslides	0.5	0.0
Volcanoes	1.5	0.1
Wild fires	3.3	0.2
Windstorms	238.5	12.7
Others	20.1	1.1
TOTAL	**1,879.2**	**100.0**

Note: Share of Total Damage Caused by Different Categories of Natural Disasters During Last Two Decades.

22. *Indian Context.*

(a) *India's Natural Disaster Profile.* Floods and droughts significantly impact the majority of India though they are most prevalent in the North West and Eastern regions respectively. Geo-physical hazards affect the Himalayan region in the North and North East portions of the country where they rank in high deciles for mortality. Cyclones influence a relatively small area of the country but have high-ranking mortality impacts. Lastly, the multi-hazard mortality demonstrates that almost the entire country is significantly impacted by at least one hazard and mortality impacts are particularly concentrated in the north and North East regions. The profiles of the regions affected by cyclones, earthquakes and floods are enormous as below:

(b) *Effect on India.* India has been traditionally vulnerable to natural disasters on account of its unique geo-climatic conditions. Recurrent phenomena include floods, droughts, cyclones, earthquakes and landslides. About 60 per cent of the landmass is prone to earthquakes of various intensities; over 40 million hectares is prone to floods; about 8 per cent of the total area is prone to cyclones and 68 per cent of the area is susceptible to drought. In the decade 1990-2000, an average of about 4344 people lost their lives and about 30 million people were affected by disasters every year.

Sl. No.	*Disaster*	*No. of Events*	*Total Killed*	*Total Affected*
1.	Cyclone	133	16,2986	91 Million
2.	Drought	21	42,504,30	1391 Million
3.	Earthquake	24	60,396	11 Million
4.	Floods	158	51,020	663 Million

Relevance of Disaster Management Study

23. As long as natural disasters continue to wreak havoc on human lives and property, mankind will wage its crusade to manage them better. Therein lies the answer to the question: Why study Disaster Management? The key word in the phrase 'disaster management' is obviously 'management'. The world has always understood that nature can only be better 'managed' and never mastered. As long as this axiom forms the bedrock of all thought in this direction, we can only improve our philosophy of disaster management.

24. *Global Relevance.* When it comes to disasters, everyone is at risk. Natural hazards strike with little or no warning and unimaginable ferocity and can affect not just cities and provinces but even entire continents. An analysis of past disasters indicates that 3.4 billion people, (more than half the world's population), live in areas where at least one hazard could significantly impact them. The World Bank report titled, 'Natural Disaster Hotspots: A Global Risk Analysis' which presents a global view of disaster risks associated with some major natural hazards—drought, floods, cyclones, earthquakes, volcanoes and landslides throws up some startling findings. Some key statistics are summarised below:-

(a) Approximately 20 per cent of the Earth's land surface is exposed to at least one of the natural hazards.

(b) 160 countries have more than one quarter of their population in areas of high mortality risk from one or more hazards.

(c) In 35 countries, more than 1 in 20 residents live at relatively high mortality risk from three or more hazards.

(d) More than one-third of the United States' population lives in hazard-prone areas, but only one per cent of its land area ranks in the highest disaster-related mortality risk category.

(e) Taiwan is one of the most vulnerable countries to natural hazards, with 73 per cent of its land and population exposed to three or more hazards.

(f) More than 90 per cent of the populations of Bangladesh, Nepal, the Dominican Republic, Burundi, Haiti, Taiwan, Malawi, El Salvador, and Honduras live in areas at high relative risk of death from two or more hazards.

(g) Poorer countries in the developing world are more likely to have difficulty absorbing repeated disaster-related losses and costs associated with disaster relief, recovery, rehabilitation and reconstruction.

25. *Relevance to India.* With its vast territory, large population and unique geo-climatic conditions, Indian sub-continent is exposed to natural catastrophes traditionally. A total of 1879.2 million people were affected by natural disasters alone between 1990 and 1999. Among the 35 States/Union Territories in the country, 25 are disaster-prone. Out of a total of 443 districts, 271 are disaster-prone. On an average 4,888 people are killed and 59 million affected annually from various types of disasters. Some statistics supporting these facts are as under:

(a) Indian Subcontinent is amongst the world's most disaster prone areas.

(b) 55 per cent of land is vulnerable to Earthquakes, as follows:

  (i) 12 per cent land is liable to severe earthquakes (intensity IX or more).

  (ii) 18 per cent land is liable to intensity VIII (similar to Latur/ Uttarkashi).

  (iii) 25 per cent land is liable to intensity VII (similar to Jabalpur quake).

  (iv) Earthquakes contribute to 31 per cent disasters in India.

(c) Eight per cent of land is vulnerable to Cyclones.

  (i) From 1891-1990, 262 cyclones (92 severe) have struck in a 50 km wide strip on the East Coast.

  (ii) Less severe cyclonic activity on West Coast (33 cyclones in the same period).

(iii) In 19 severe cyclonic storms, the death toll has been over 10,000 lives.

(iv) In 21 cyclones in Bay of Bengal, 1.25 million lives have been lost.

(d) Five per cent of land is vulnerable to floods.

(i) Floods contribute to 34 per cent disasters in India.

(ii) As much as an average of 67 million hectare of land is flooded annually. On an average, 800 lives are lost annually and millions are rendered homeless.

(iii) About 20 lakh hectares of crops are damaged every year.

(e) 16 per cent of country's total area is drought-prone.

(i) Drought contributes to three per cent disasters in India.

(ii) 50 million people are affected by droughts annually.

(iii) About 68 per cent of total sown area of the country is drought-prone.

26. *Relevance to Armed Forces.* A few decades ago, referring to armed forces and disaster management in the same context would have been viewed as an ironic paradox since the role of armed forces was essentially that of waging war and defending nations from adversaries rather than from the fury of nature. With the changing definition of classical wars having altered radically in today's uni-polar world, nations have begun to look at assigning a more holistic role for their armed forces during peacetime. Thus, the hitherto neglected humanitarian facet of employing armed forces has come into sharp focus. In fact, post the tsunami of Dec 2004, development of a credible marine expeditionary force has received impetus in many countries as a result of the quick, efficient and hitherto unheard of scale of relief operations undertaken by the armed forces of many nations. The armed forces have some very obvious pros in their favour as an automatic choice to assist in managing disasters. They are a massive pool of young, fit manpower governed by a disciplined and responsible command structure, as well as an arm of the government. The armed forces are considered 'well-suited' for employment during disasters due to the following reasons:

(a) *Availability of Manpower.* One of the key pre-requisites of credible disaster management is the requirement of people to undertake the operation. The Armed Forces of a nation, especially one as populated as India, offer a ready-made pool of young, healthy, fit and most importantly, motivated men and women to draw from. The sense of national pride and responsibility instilled in these men and women makes them extremely proactive in such operations.

(b) *Structure and Organisation.* The armed forces are considered an example of discipline. This virtue in such a large organisation ensures that orders are followed in letter and spirit, in accordance with a single higher directive – a boon at the scene of a disaster where it is the chaos and panic that creates the maximum hurdles in providing assistance than the actual calamity itself.

(c) *Ease and Speed of Deployment.* Mobility with ease and speed are the very essence of what an army trains for. Disaster management requires coordinated swift responses with maximum efficiency. The armed forces are spread all across the country and can be deployed with speed to any part by land, sea and air. This unique ability to be omnipresent at short notice is invaluable for relief operations.

(d) *Availability of Special Resources.* As a rule the forces operate in trying conditions, difficult terrain. The ability to sustain themselves in the most hostile natural conditions is almost second nature to every defence personnel. In addition, the armed forces boast of every conceivable resource that one could require in any contingency, be it land, sea or air. In this ability, the armed forces are unique and definitely a boon to any government faced with a natural calamity.

Conclusion

27. After studying, the effects of disasters, its repercussions on mankind in context of all countries of the world, especially India. It is crucial to study the disaster management and the systems followed in different countries around the world and to come up with pertinent recommendations in Indian context.

Factors and Significance of Disasters

"I am compelled to utter a truism-in asserting that physical catastrophes have their inevitable and exclusive origin in certain combination of physical facts." —**Rabindranath Tagore**

Introduction

1. The man has made tremendous technological progress in his relatively brief existence on the earth; he is still virtually helpless against vagaries of nature. Natural disasters such as floods, cyclones, landslides and earthquakes ravage man's domain at will and causes much loss to life and property. In addition to natural disasters, man has contrived to add to his miseries by waging wars and creating other man-made emergencies such as riots, conflicts, refugee situations and others like freak accidents, epidemics, industrial accidents, and environmental fall outs. Often the difference between them is marginal.

2. Disaster management has become a major theme of our times. The advancement in communications has brought to us much more rapidly and vividly the untold miseries and dissolution suffered by human beings in the wake of cataclysmic events. As per WHO data there has been marked increase in disaster situation over the years. Globally, natural disasters account for nearly 80 per cent of all disaster-affected people. The insurance industry estimates that natural disasters represent 85 per cent of insured catastrophe losses globally. In 1996, 40 million disaster affected people depended on humanitarian assistance, a 60 per cent increase over the average figure of 25 million in the 1980s. In the first half of this decade, over US$ 30 billion was spent on humanitarian assistance. Over the past 25 years, the cost of

natural disasters stands at over US$ 87 billion a year. The average amount spent on humanitarian response in US$ 3 billion a year. Compared to expenditure on disaster mitigation, the average annual global military spending is around US$ 780 billion. The number of disasters in the first 60 years of the twentieth century totaled 4098 whereas in much shorter period of 30 years from 1962 to 1989 the number was 3380. Rightly so, the UN has declared 1990s as the international decade of natural disaster reduction (IDNDR), to enhance disaster management capabilities all over the World.[1]

3. Despite everyone's concern for disasters and technological developments in the world, the response to disasters has been knee jerk and uncoordinated at international, national and state levels. The problem is more acute in developing countries rather than in developed ones. The United Nations and its specialised agencies have always had an interest in and commitment to disaster relief. Therefore, there are now disaster relief, preparedness, prevention and mitigation programmes being carried out by various United Nations Organisations.

India's Vulnerability to Disasters

4. The disturbing fact is that even in a region like South Asia, where poverty, deprivation and death due to disasters are common enough feature of life, India remains the worst affected country. In fact, the frequency of all categories of disasters, varying from epidemics to road accidents and perennial droughts and floods, is escalating, resulting in a multifold growth of injuries, disabilities, diseases, and deaths disrupting life supporting systems, and adding to the health, social, and economic burden of an already impoverished people. In India, between 1988 and 1997, disasters killed 5,116 people and affected 24.79 million every year in India. In 1990, 9,846 people died and 34.11 million people were affected by disasters. 'Experience and study tell us that the actual figures greatly exceed the documented once'.[2]

5. India a country with one-sixth of the human population of our globe, comprises an area of 32,87,263 sq. km. It extends from snow covered Himalayas to tropical rain forest of the South. Bounded by the great Himalayas in the North, it stretches southwards and at Tropic of Cancer; it tapers off into the Indian Ocean between the Bay of Bengal in the East and Arabian Sea on the West. Lying entirely in the Northern

Hemisphere, it covers 29 longitudes and 31 latitudes and has coastline of over 7500 km.

6. India's physical geography and climate, pattern of rainfall make it prone to a range of natural disasters such as floods, storms, cyclones, earthquakes and epidemics. Being densely populated and industrialised it is liable to experience a variety of manmade disasters. These could include industrial accidents such as Bhopal Gas Tragedy, major fire, transportation accidents such as Ferozabad Railway accident in 1995, or even hostile acts either in peace or war. Be it an 'act of God' or 'act of Man' a mind boggling spectrum of disasters wreck havoc in Indian subcontinent.

7. The record of Indian society as a whole has been quite dismal as far as disaster relief and managing the situation arising in the wake of a calamity is concerned. The national and state governments carry out most of the brunt and co-ordination for disaster relief. It is in this area that India needs improvement in its approach and handling of disaster like situations.

The Problem

8. This paper examines the process of Disaster Management in India, its structure, establishes need for an Integrated Approach.

Justification of the Study

9. The Contingency Action Plan for Natural Calamities, the government's blueprint for disaster response, is more reactive than proactive. It emphasises relief, not reduction. This flies in the face of the new international trend, which has been marked by a radical shift towards disaster preparedness and reduction in a national workshop on the psychosocial consequences of disasters, held at NIMHANS, Bangalore in 1998, the participants concluded: that band-aid relief alone cannot meet the challenge, long-term commitments must be planned for.[3]

10. Crisis management and subsequent relief distribution must not be seen as the primary function of disaster management. It is increasingly evident that there is a need for an integrated approach which incorporated building disaster mitigation contents into the overall development plans, with a view to minimise the impact of disasters. The relief to development continuum must be the impact of disaster

management endeavour, as we seek to break free from the restrictive focus of only alleviation and restoration measures. The NGOs and the media have an exceedingly important role to play. They must take a lead in helping translate this transition in thinking from the conceptual level to the formulation of concrete developmental plans.[4]

11. A multi-sector approach, involving the government, NGOs, academics and the affected communities is slowly gaining currency in India. To united meet the challenge of preparing, responding to, and equipping the community to deal with a cocktail of disasters will be the greatest humanitarian challenge for India in the new millennium. The country profile of India vis-à-vis disasters and the challenge it poses in the new Millennium.[5]

12. In view the above it is evident that India needs to evolve policies, procedures and methods to reduce the sufferings of its masses. The subject matter will be discussed so as to analyse as to how the World in general handles disasters and how do we in India deal with it at the National, State and district levels as also suggest need for and an integrated approach.

Limitations of the Study

13. The study has following limitations:

(a) Disaster relief and management procedures and organisations differ from state to state and cannot be covered in its entirety.

(b) Response of various organs of the government can be only analysed in broader terms due to constraints of space.

(c) Focus of study is primarily on disasters caused by natural calamities.

India: A Country Profile Millennium Challenge

14. India is one of the world's major theatres of disasters, both natural and human-made. Floods, droughts, cyclones and earthquakes pound it end to end every year. Communal riots, conflicts, fire, epidemics, and other disasters compound the country's chronic troubles.

15. In the decade 1988-97, disasters in India affected on an average over 2.4 million people and killed 5,116 each year, in 1998, disasters affected 34,112,566 people in India and killed 9,846. Between 1985

and 1995, disasters caused an annual economic loss of about US$ 1,883.93 million.

16. Meeting the challenge of the UN's International Decade for Natural Disasters Reduction appeal to put scientific disaster response mechanism in place on a priority basis has been attempted by various government bodies with mixed results. In India, at the policy level, the apex body to deal with disaster exigencies is the National Crisis Management Committee (NCMC).

17. Natural disaster is the bounden responsibility of the Union Ministry of Agriculture and Animal Husbandry. Specialists say that the basic criteria for the Ministry's intervention are loss and damage accrual on cultivable land, which need not necessarily include livestock death and incapacitation.

18. The condition of the natural disaster response mechanism, such as it is, is the job of the Natural Disaster Management Division of the Agriculture Ministry. The Health Ministry is to chip in its bit through its Emergency Medical Relief Division.

19. Human-made disasters, such as communal and ethic riots, other conflicts and refugee situations are dealt with by the Home Ministry, which responds with its law and order artillery rather than from humanitarian concern for the riot or conflict affected.

20. The Contingency Action Plan for Natural Calamities, the government's blueprint for disaster response, is more reactive than proactive. It emphasises relief, not reduction. This flies in the face of the new international trend, which has been marked by a radical shift towards disaster preparedness and reduction in a national workshop on the psychosocial consequences of disasters, held at NIMHANS, Bangalore in 1998, the participants concluded: that band-aid relief alone cannot meet the challenge, long-term commitments must be planned for.

21. Disaster preparedness and reduction mean appropriate development planning with disasters as a key action node. In actual practice, it would include drought management mechanism, response material, traffic control and planning for measures such as extensive earthquake-resistant housing in seismic zones, careful construction and layout of roads, railway lines, and of other drainage structures on the flood plains.

22. The omnibus disaster situation in the country is worsening. The Central Water Commission, a nodal government agency, has noted that 11.2 per cent of India is flood-prone. In 1998, floods inundated 37 per cent of India.

23. In a human-made prevention of the natural courses of things, flash floods intruded in the desert state of Rajasthan in 1996. Scientists blamed the phenomenon on development planning gone haywire. A study shows that human-made structures, including canals, dams, and embankments, have worsened the flood situation all over the country.

24. India is a land of geographical and climatologically extremes, so it comes as no surprise that of its total cultivable area an estimated 28 per cent is drought-prone.

25. The country's 7,516 km coastline is continuously whipped by high-velocity winds that pummel the east-coast states of Odisha and Andhra Pradesh every year, causing incalculable damage. Despite a battery of coastal weather radar and early warning systems that facilitate early evacuation, cyclones, still kill hundreds and destroy entire fishing fleets and communities every year.

26. Earthquakes raze the northern Himalayan region and the Deccan plateau in southern and central India. An earthquake in the Decca in 1993 killed over 10,000 people. Another earthquake that hit Jabalpur in central India in May 1997 showed up the dismal inadequacy of relief and shelter, despite the potential for resource mobilisation. Legal activists point out the need to relate to relief as a right than as charity. It is estimated that 57 per cent of India is earthquake-prone.

27. Compounding the variety of natural disasters is the heterogeneity of human-made disasters. Communal and caste riots pepper the country. The virtual militant- security forces siege in the Kashmir valley and the northeastern states has left entire generations of ordinary people as collateral damage.

28. In India, number of the internally displaced caused by developmental projects was over 21.3 million in 1990 and is probably 30 million today, according to Dr Walter Fernandes of the Indian Social Institute. This figure is a third higher than the number of conflict-induced Internally Displaced People (IDP) world wide, estimated to be between 20-22 million.

29. As for non-conventional disasters: the cost of road accidents is equivalent to one per cent of a country's GNP, and India is no exception. The transport enable-and- control mechanism in India is about to crack. Four-wheeled vehicle increased by 23 per cent to 4.5 million between 1990 and 1993 and it has been forecast that 267 million vehicles will be on the road by AD 2050.

30. The country is, on the face of it, a dismal picture. With a mounting human cost and barrage of criticism, even government experts agree today that a shift of emphasis towards disaster preparedness and better advance work at the grass roots is imperative to stem the rot.

What is DMIS....

31. The Disaster Management Information System, is a civil society initiative supported by socially conscious institutions and individuals, companies and organisations. The system was launched by SRISTI, (Society for Research and Initiatives for Sustainable Technologies and Institutions) on the 18th of January 2002 at Indian Institute of Management, Ahmedabad, Gujarat, India.

Background

32. Natural disasters impart lessons at a very high cost of life and property. But if those lessons do not lead to learning and knowledge generation then it is a very heavy cost to bear. This lack of learning from the past hurts most at the recurrence of disasters. The earthquake in Gujarat (*26th January 2001, an earthquake of 7.9 magnitude on Richter scale struck Gujarat, India, with its epicenter in Kutch, causing destruction of three towns and death of more than 20,000 people*) and the subsequent chaos was an indicator of how crucial disaster planning is to manage relief and rehabilitation during disasters.

33. SRISTI participated in the relief and rehabilitation work in Kutch. But the relief work suffered immensely due to lack of information and proper planning. When we tried to get answers to important questions that were cropping up – for instance, whether there exists a database on the distribution of available resources and expertise with individuals, institutions and corporations – all we got in response was a blank. This pointed to the urgent necessity of building a system for disaster mitigation and for documenting experiences of individuals and organisations, which might act as a knowledge resource and help in better coordination in case of future disasters.

The Disaster Management Information System

34. Thus, SRISTI initiated an effort to build a "Disaster Management Information System". Through this initiative we are trying to develop a database-driven information system for Disaster Management Authorities (DMA) in various states, NGOs and other organisations. We appealed to NGOs, relief workers, DMAs and individuals to share their experiences and volunteer services and resources to the online database maintained at our website. The database currently contains more than a thousand volunteers who have offered to volunteer their services and resources in time of emergency. About 700 organisations and institutions are also listed on the site, besides other resources and web links.

The DMIS is a wholly voluntary activity run with contributions in terms of time and services by SRISTI volunteers, NGOs and above all civil society institutions across the world. All the information shared with us is accessible to all, except where the volunteer has chosen to limit accessibility only to the relevant authorities.

Disaster Mitigation and Emergency Preparedness

35. Emergency preparedness is crucial for coming out from disasters with least damage. Just the knowledge of what to do, may help save lives of you and your family. Here are collection of studies and links of documentation related to disasters preparedness also as per the type of disaster. Besides these, links to resources for forecasting disasters are also provided here. The source of the reference is also given along with them.

Trauma Management

36. Disaster stress may revive memories of prior trauma, as well as possibly intensifying pre-existing social, economic, spiritual, psychological, or medical problems. Trauma management is crucial and rescue workers as well as family members should prepare themselves to handle trauma hit members in the family.

37. Disaster Preparedness: Preparedness Questionnaire, ask yourself how prepared you are in the event of a disaster. This is a step towards getting yourself ready to meet eventualities which might save you, your families life in the event of disasters. Also you may be able to help your community to come out better during disasters. After going

through this questionnaire explore resources listed above for preparedness in the event of disasters as mentioned.

1. Do you think that your family is relatively well-prepared for a disaster such as an earthquake, tornado, cyclones, winter storm, fire, flood and other such incidents?

   This small step to understand and equip yourself about knowledge related to disaster preparedness would help you come out from a disaster unscathed. Your well-prepared family could help save the lives of others, not just yourselves. Are you and your family prepared, ask this question to yourself first?

2. Do you believe that the community you live in is relatively well-prepared for a disaster?

   Do you know about your community/ Panchayat/District, Disaster Management Plan? Is there any source of community Information system that you know of? Are you aware of any source of information to prepare yourself for disasters?

   Has your District/State DMA (Disaster Management Authority) coordinator worked with local hospitals, nursing homes, day care centres, shopping malls, schools, etc. to make sure they have a plan for what to do during an emergency?

3. Have you discussed disaster preparedness with your family?

   If you have a plan of what you will do during a disaster but you haven't shared it with your family ahead of time, your plan may not work! Each family member needs to know how to phone for help, escape out of the house, and seek safe shelter in the house. Each family member needs to know how to be safe when they are out of the home (at work, school, play). Each family member needs to know how the family plans to reunite if it becomes impossible to return to the home.

4. Do all members of your family know how to call for help?

   If you have kids, do they know how to phone for help? Do they know to dial 100 (if it is available where you live)? If you don't have 100, do you have the number of the Police, Fire, Ambulance, responsible friend/relative, etc. near the phone? Do your kids know what sort of information they will need to give over the phone (i.e., the address of the home, their last name, etc.)? Do they know to phone from outside of the house if the house is on fire? Do they know to stay off the phone during an electrical storm?

5. Have you conducted a home hazard hunt and fixed potential hazards?

   Many disasters at home can be averted with a simple hazard hunt. Is the home fire-safe - no frayed electrical cords, no overloaded outlets, working smoke detectors, if any, working carbon monoxide detectors, no flammable liquids near sources of heat or flames? Are working fire extinguishers easily available? Is the home earthquake safe—no unsecured heavy objects (mirrors, bookshelves, etc.), the water heater bolted to the wall? If there is a water tank on the top of the house, then how much water should be stored in earthquake prone zones?

6. Do you have a Family Disaster Supply Kit?

   In your supply kit you will need ALL of the things it will take to survive 72 hours. This will include food and water of course, but also medicines, blankets, flashlights, etc. Even if you don't put together an actual kit (although we encourage you to do so), think about having at least enough food, water and medicine at home with you to last 72 hours.

7. Do you have a Disaster Supply Kit for each car?

   A small box in the trunk of your car, other vehicle with blankets, a first-aid kit, cash, food, flashlight, radio, etc. could literally mean the difference between life and death. Every car should have a kit (atleast a first aid kit). You might want to change the contents of the kit for the different seasons of the year.

8. Are you trained in First-Aid (within the last three years)?

   Basic first-aid, for example how to stop bleeding by applying pressure, can be crucial, even life saving knowledge. First-aid courses are often offered by and local hospitals and charitable hospital for nominal charges. Think how happy you (and the victim) will be if you are able to make use of current training in an emergency situation.

9. Are all responsible family members current in First-Aid?

   Unfortunately, there is the possibility that YOU might be the victim! Does everyone in your family know basic first-aid?

10. Are you current in CPR (trained in the last three years)?

    CPR - Cardio Pulmonary Resuscitation is a simple technique that has saved many folks who would have otherwise been choking, drowning, smoke inhalation, or heart attack victims. When you think about a few hours of training saving a loved one's life, isn't it worth it?

11. Are all responsible family members current in CPR?

    Again, there is the possibility that YOU might be the victim! Or, you might not be home when the incident occurs. Be sure that everyone in your family is trained.

12. Do you have operational smoke detectors and carbon monoxide detectors?

    Having a smoke detector and/or a carbon monoxide detector in your home is NOT good enough! You need to make sure they are operational, that is, they must have working batteries. An operational smoke detector more than doubles your chance of escaping from your home alive. Two good rules of thumb are check your detectors once a month (pick a day of the month, say the 1st, and make a habit of checking the detectors every month on the 1st); when you change your clock for daylight savings/standard time, change the batteries of detectors too.

13. Do you have a charged ABC fire extinguisher?

    There are three basic classes of fires. All fire extinguishers are labeled using standard symbols for the classes of fires they can put out. A red slash through any of the symbols tells you the extinguisher cannot be used on that class of fire. A missing symbol tells you only that the extinguisher has not been tested for a given class of fire.

    Class A: Ordinary combustibles such as wood, cloth, paper, rubber and many plastics.

    Class B: Flammable liquids such as gasoline, oil, grease, tar, oil-based paint, lacquer, and flammable gas.

Class C: Energized electrical equipment - including wiring, fuse boxes, circuit breakers, machinery, and appliances.

Many household fire extinguishers are *"multipurpose"* A-B-C models, labeled for use on all three classes of fire. If you are ever faced with a Class A fire and don't have an extinguisher with an *"A"* symbol, don't hesitate to use one with the *"B:C"* symbol.

WARNING: It is very dangerous to use water or an extinguisher labeled only for Class A fires on a Class B or Class C fire.

Do you know where your fire extinguisher is? Do you know if it is still fully charged (they can lose their charge over time)?

14. Do you know how to use the fire extinguisher?

    Using a fire extinguisher is not completely straightforward and the time to learn how to operate one is NOT during a fire. Follow the four-step PASS procedure. Pull the pin: This unlocks the operating lever and allows you to discharge the extinguisher. Aim low: Point the extinguisher nozzle (or hose) at the base of the fire. Squeeze the lever above the handle: This discharges the extinguishing agent. (Some extinguishers have a button instead of a lever.) Sweep from side-to-side: Moving carefully toward the fire, keep the extinguisher aimed at the base of the fire and sweep back and forth until the flames appear to be out. A good practice might be to purchase two fire extinguishers—one to keep and one to let each family member practice on.

15. Do you know how to turn off all utilities (gas, electricity, water, etc.)?

    For a variety of reasons, it may be necessary to turn off the utilities in your home. Do you know where the water main is? Do you know where the circuit breaker box or main switch is? Does everyone in your family know NOT to turn off the electricity if you have to stand in water to do so?

16. Do you know where your family records are?

    If your house burned down today would your insurance papers, household inventory, receipts, other important papers etc. burn too? A great place to keep your valuable papers (marriage certificate, birth certificates, passports, insurance papers, household inventory, etc.) is in a safe deposit box. It is probably not wise to keep your will in a safe deposit box though. A will is best kept with your lawyer or a close friend (if you die it will become difficult for others to access your safe deposit box, making it difficult for them to find your will).

17. Do you know where your family will meet outside your home in case of an emergency?

    If your family is separated during an emergency you should have two contingency plans in place. The first plan should be a place to meet near your home (such as across the street at a neighbour's) if the emergency is something like your house burning down. The second plan should be a place to meet in your community, away from your home, (such as a local business or friend's house) if the emergency is something like your neighbourhood being evacuated. By knowing ahead of time where to rendezvous, family members can avoid needlessly worrying about members that are fine and concentrate on family members that are unaccounted for.

18. Do you know at least two exits from every room in your house in case of a fire?

    Most rooms have a door and a window. If the window is a second story window, do you have a way to escape safely (i.e., a fire ladder)?

19. Have you practiced an emergency drill in your home within the past year?

    Drills are a terrific way of making sure that everyone in the family (kids and adults) understands and has the physical/mental ability to carry out the plan your family has developed. If kids get confused about whether to stay inside or leave the house during a fire for example, the time to get them straight about it is BEFORE anything happens.

20. Do you have an out-of-area phone contact?

    Believe it or not, long distance phone calls are often easier to make immediately following a disaster than are local phone calls. Does everyone in your family knows to phone the contact to inform about there safety.

21. Do you know about disaster plans at your workplace, at your children's school or day care, etc.?

    Few of us spend 100 per cent of our time at home, so we need to know about the disaster plans at the other places we (and our loved ones) spend time. Be sure that you know what the plan is and that it is a sound plan.

22. Can you list the actual cash value of EVERY item in your home?

    You may be asked to create such a list after a fire, cyclone or flood! Obviously, a wise choice is to make that list (often times called a household inventory) well before a disaster occurs. A household inventory can provide you with some excellent information for deciding how much insurance to purchase as well.

23. Some family members have special needs, for example the elderly, mobility impaired or sick. Do you have a plan for making sure these members will be safe during a disaster?

    Check your family disaster plan and make sure it will work for everyone. For example, if the family plan is to seek shelter in the basement or community shelter during a cyclone warning, be sure everyone in the family is able to negotiate the stairs to the basement/shelter. If some members are unable to go to the basement/shelter, make sure you have a second plan in place for them (i.e., seek shelter in an interior room, under a heavy piece of furniture).

24. Do you have a plan for your pets?

    A simple sign on your door, alerting the fire department to the fact that you have pets inside, could save your pets' lives. Bringing a pet to a temporary shelter may pose health risks that the local shelter may not be willing to cope with. It's a good idea to arrange for a place ahead of time (maybe a friend or relative) where your pets could stay temporarily in case of an emergency.

    There are lots of places to go for more information about disaster preparation and planning.

Rescue International

38. Formed in 1985 Rescue International (RI) is a nonprofit organisation of people and companies that provide special search, rescue, and recovery services and products to requesting agencies free of charge. RI's educational programmes are based on a foundation of experienced instructors teaching students skills and providing information derived from hands on experience and backed up with a written programme guide and/or manual. RESCUE Training Resource and Guide:

Free rescue training site with a wealth of information including reference articles, online quiz's, links database, photo galleries, slideshows and much more. Created by a volunteer rescuer in Australia.

EPIX - Emergency Preparedness Information eXchange

39. The purpose of EPIX is to facilitate the exchange of ideas and information among Canadian and international public and private sector organisations about the prevention of, preparation for, recovery from and/or mitigation of risk associated with natural and socio-technological disasters.

Search and Rescue Institute

The Search and Rescue Institute offers search and rescue, first aid and disaster preparedness and operations training.

Stanford University Disaster Preparedness and Response

40. Disaster preparedness and response resources from various parts of the world with things organised by organisation/author, disaster plans, bibliographic resources, etc. Very useful links to a lot of information. Safety for Everyone.

Natural Disasters

41. This is a very useful instructional website on the basics of safety associated with day-to-day life scenes such as at home, or on the road, industry, office, etc with a special page on natural disaster. Although very fundamental, sometimes people lack even the most fundamental knowledge and hence this website can be very handy to teach kids and adults.

42. I am focusing on preparing a template for disaster management including following seven issues:

(a) *Database:* On various resources, skills, and services required for relief at short notice. It will have information on safety equipments, oxygen cylinders and various other equipments, skills and other information required to deal with emergency.

(b) *Logistics:* One of the most difficult problems to be handled is the organisation of supply chain for relief. Several colleagues at IIMA also developed logistics system for Collectorate at Bhuj. This system could not be integrated with the GIS system so that supplies could be tracked right upto the village. This needs to be done. Likewise, other elements of logistics need to be put in place.

(c) *Technological Needs:* Whole range of technical questions regarding buildings, cutting concrete slabs, rescue and relief emerged which needed to be solved on the spot. The best practices have to be put in use.

(d) *Self Reliance:* The community self-reliance, lot of aid led to excessive inventory at the household level leading to reduced incentives for work and self-help. Likewise, there were areas where communities came together to help each other. The lessons of community self-help need to be put together. A database of volunteers who can move at short notice will need to be developed.

(e) *Communication Infrastructure:* This is a serious problem and has to be resolved once for all. It will require network of ham radios, use of All India Radio, setting up helplines, etc. We will also have to create information dissemination system and develop mechanism for capacity building.

(f) *Emergency Preparedness:* Drills will have to be organised to keep society prepared for dealing with such emergencies. One will have to learn from the experience of other similar drills.

(g) *Forecasting:* Wherever possible, disasters which can be anticipated over time or space need to be looked into. For instance, buildings erected on land fill areas which were wet lands or low lying areas were more likely to get damaged, as was borne out by the recent evidence.

Disaster Mitigation Tool Kit

43. *Kits to Sustain Everyday Life in the event of a disaster:* We are giving information for an ideal kit that might be useful to disaster affected people. However, preparation for this should be done before hand. The following kits are suggested in places where people might not have ready access to many essential supplies for everyday life as preparation to a disaster:

Health Kit

- 1 hand towel
- 1 washcloth
- 1 hair comb, regular size (not pocket)
- 1 nail file or nail clipper
- 1 bath-size bar of soap in wrapper
- 1 toothbrush in sealed package
- 1 large tube of toothpaste
- 6 adhesive bandages (such as Band-aids)

Wrap the brand new items in the new hand towel tie it with string or yarn, and place inside a sealed, one-litre plastic bag with a zipper closure.

First Aid Medicine Kit

- Sterile Gauze Pads: (4x4) 50 Pads
- Adhesive Tape: 6 Rolls, 1/2" or 1" x 10 yds or more
- Triple Antibiotic Topical Ointment: 4 Tubes (1 oz tubes) Example: Neosporin Ointment
- Aspirin: 325 mg (5 gr) tablets

1. Ferrous Sulfate Tablets 500 Tablets of 325 mg
2. Children's Multivitamins with Iron Chewable Tablets 500 Tablets
3. Adult Multivitamins with Iron Tablets 500 Tablets
4. Children's Acetaminophen Chewable Tablets 300 Tablets of 80 mg.

*Where possible, purchase tablets in bottles of 100 or more. No samples are permitted. For example, if the required number of tablets is 1,000, then collect:

- 1 bottle of 1,000 tablets each, or
- 2 bottles of 500 tablets each, or
- 4 bottles of 300 or 250 tablets each, or
- 8 bottles of 130 tablets each, or
- 10 bottles of 100 tablets each

5. Acetaminophen for Adults —pain reliever
6. Antacid—for treatment of upset stomach/heartburn
7. Mebendazole or Thiabendazole—for intestinal worm infection
8. Sulfamethoxazole/Trimethoprim—antibacterial for adults and children
9. Tetmosol Soap—for treatment of scabies for adults and children
10. Oral Rehydration Salts—to combat dehydration for adults and children
11. Promethazine—for treatment of nausea
12. Metronidazole—for treatment of intestinal amebiasis (amebic dysentery)
13. Chlorhexidine—antiseptic for adults and children
14. Tolnaftate 1 per cent Antifungal Cream—for skin infections for adults and children
15. Rolled Bandages —for first aid applications

School Kit

In many countries, there are no books, or even classrooms. Classes are mobile or held in the open air. School kits may be the only educational resources available. Often students must write down everything the teacher says or writes on a board. Their teacher's knowledge and their own notes are their only textbooks. They have difficulty learning without the basic tools in this kit, which is designed for a variety of ages.

- 1 blunt scissors
- 2 pads of 8 ½ "x 11" ruled paper

- 1 30-centimeter ruler
- 1 pencil sharpener
- 6 unsharpened pencils with erasers
- 1 eraser, 2 ½"
- 12 sheets of construction paper
- 1 box of 8 crayons

Prepare a 12"x14" (finished size) cloth bag with handles and a closure (Velcro, snap, or button) and place the items in the bag.

Kit for Kids

Kits with the basic supplies every baby needs. Please be sure that all items are NEW!

- 6 cloth diapers
- 2 shirts
- 2 baby wash cloths
- 2 gowns
- 2 diaper pins
- 1 sweater
- 2 receiving blankets

Bundle the items inside one of the receiving blankets and secure it with diaper pins.

Domestic Kit

The following kits are recommended following a natural disaster. Bedding Pack

- 2 flat double-bed sheets
- 2 pillow cases
- 2 pillows

Other necessities:

Linen (new only)

- Sheets
- Towels
- Blankets
- Pillows

Sewing Kit

Sewing kits foster interdependence rather than dependence. Women can make clothing in their own size and in the style of their culture. Cottage industries often grow out of the sewing classes where women use these kits to practice valuable income-generating skills.

- 3 yards of cotton or cotton-blend solid-colour or print fabric (there must be 3 uncut yards of fabric or the kit is not usable)
- 1 pair of sewing scissors
- 1 package of needles
- 1 spool of thread
- 6 matching buttons

Wrap sewing notions in the fabric and tie it with a string or strip of cloth. Place items in a sealed one-gallon plastic bag.

Cleaning Utilities

44. These resources enable people to begin the overwhelming job of cleaning up after a flood or hurricane.

- 5 gal. bucket with resealable lid
- Bleach ½ gal.
- Scouring pads, 5
- Scrub brush
- Cleaning towels, 18 each
- Sponges, assorted size-7 pack
- Laundry detergent, 50 oz.
- Household cleaner, 12 oz.
- Disinfectant dish soap, 28 oz.
- Clothes pins (50)
- Clothesline, 100 ft.x3/16
- Dust masks, 5 packs
- Latex gloves, package of 2 pr.
- Work gloves, 1 pr.
- Trash bags, 24 bg. roll
- Insect repellant, 14 oz.
- Air freshener, 9 oz.

Please purchase all liquids in plastic bottles. Be sure to send all new materials that are unopened when they are sealed or in packages. Put all items in the plastic bucket and seal lid.

Individual Items Needed for Disaster Response

Though all of the following items are needed at some time, some are in heavier demand than others.

Baby Items

- Disposable diapers
- Baby wipes

Cleaning Supplies

- Dry laundry detergent
- Dish detergent
- Dry disinfectant
- Mops
- Shovels
- Rubber gloves
- Buckets
- Plastic garbage bags (30 gallon)
- Squeegees
- Pressure water sprayers
- Power scrubbers
- Scoop shovels

Miscellaneous

- Generators
- Tarps
- Tents
- Cots

Paper Products

- Paper plates
- Paper cups
- Paper towels

- Toilet paper

Send all new paper goods that are unopened.

Personal Items

- Soap
- Toothbrushes
- Hand lotion
- Feminine hygiene produces
- Large (adult) diapers
- Insect repellent
- Surgical masks and gloves
- Sun block (rated 15 or higher)

Forecasting of Natural Disasters

45. Forecasting of natural disasters is not possible but awareness of calamity (earthquake / flood / cyclones) prone areas is also crucial.

Disaster Mitigation and Vulnerability Atlas of India

46. A combination of local hazard intensity and vulnerability of existing house types has been used for carrying out risk analysis given in the district-wise tables. The Vulnerability Atlas, thus, provides ready macro-level information for use by the authorities for natural disaster mitigation and preventive actions. Recognising the usefulness of the Vulnerability Atlas for formulating pro-active policies to face the threat of natural hazards, is being brought to the notice of the development planners, decision-makers, professionals and householders.

International Research Institute for Climate Prediction

47. The IRI Forecasting Research Group provides a seasonal climate forecast. This forecast is a net assessment (or distillation) of information from a variety of climate prediction tools, including dynamical models of the atmosphere, statistical models of climate variability related to sea surface temperature variability, and knowledge of the current state of the climate system.

Interactive Weather Information Network (IWIN)

48. This system is located at the National Weather Service Headquarters in Silver Spring, Md. It obtains raw data from a

telecommunications gateway, satellites, and other multilayered redundant links.

Earthquake

World-Wide Earthquake Locator

49. The World-Wide Earthquake Locator is an interface developed by Bruce Gittings of the Department of Geography at the University of Edinburgh in 1995, very much as an illustration of what is possible using the World-Wide Web and the internet. It develops the networking aspects of work we have done building an earthquake analysis system using data dynamically obtained over the internet. Select an earthquake's *Description of Location* to show the location of that earthquake on a map. The data displayed reflect the contents of the USGS earthquake database.

World Earthquake Information from USGS National Earthquake Information Centre

50. National Earthquake Information Centre - World Data Centre for Seismology Earthquake information and observation station: The site hosts one of the most comprehensive systems. Earthquake Maps and answers to your questions ABAG.

Earthquake Maps and Information

51. Information links on modeling of houses, publications related to earthquake, maps information, disaster preparedness information. Recent Earthquake Activity information centre. CFROST is located at the Harbour Centre campus of Simon Fraser University (SFU) in Vancouver, British Columbia Canada. It hosts a Emergency Preparedness Information Exchange (EPIX) providing information about recent earthquake activity in different seismic zones of the world.

Earthquake Reporting Service

52. US Geological Survey and UC Berkeley service for earthquake reporting. Earthquake basics and educational material; geological and historical information; links to professional and amateur organisatoins; online access to earthquake data. Current research activities and results in seismology, crystal structure and deformation, geology and borehole physics.

Earthquake Data

53. Data Global /composite earthquake information, research or special services Seismo-surfing the Internet. The following are known Internet type connections where original seismic data or seismic research information is available. See the end of the list for several other indexes to related fields.

Seismicity Maps of Recent Earthquake Activity in the World

54. Earthquake Activity, Earthquake Notification E-mail. Earthquake Hazards Programme- Present Earthquake Activity across world. Maps of probable hazards from future earthquakes including shaking intensity, liquefaction, landslides. Links to websites and organisations for information about how to prepare for an earthquake.

Predicting an Earthquake

55. Although a great deal is known about where earthquakes are likely to occur, there is currently no reliable way to predict the days or months when an event will occur in any specific location.. The USGS is thus focusing its research efforts on developing long-range earthquake probability forecasts in seismically active urban areas. The only on-going USGS research in earthquake prediction is the Parkfield Prediction Experiment.

EQNet: Earthquake Information Network

56. This website provides a common ground for all kinds of information about earthquake disasters. The site is a information store house for valuable data and information services related to earthquakes and similar disasters. The site also contains some information about earthquakes in other countries such as Peru, India, Turkey, etc.

UC Berkley Seismological Laboratory

57. Where can I find information on earthquake preparedness and safety? These links offer a variety of useful information on how to prepare your family and your home for a damaging earthquake. An information centre for emergency preparedness. Listservs/Newsgroups/Newsletters on earthquake warning and management: Organisations and Web Sites for Listservs/Newsgroups/Newsletter. An alphabetical listing of a large number of newsletters and listservs.

European-Mediterranean Seismological Centre (EMSC)

58. EMSC runs an Early Warning System for any potentially damaging earthquake in the European-Mediterranean region (and worldwide for M > 7). It works as a network of seismic networks by merging in near real-time information sent over the Internet by about 30 contributing institutes. It generates between 70 and 100 warning messages each year within an hour of the earthquake occurrence.

Flood

Effectiveness of Geographic Information Systems (GIS) Applications in Flood Management

59. Quick Response Report # 130 from Natural Hazards Centre titled "Effectiveness of Geographic Information Systems (GIS) Applications in Flood Management during and after Hurricane Fran" by Ute J. Dymon. Federal Emergency Management Authority: FAQs to prepare flood mapping:

Floods and hazards mapping using Geographic Information Systems (GIS) for better management of disasters related with floods and dam bursts.

Cyclone

Cyclone watch online: For Indian Ocean

60. The image provided depicts the latest JTWC forecast positions for the current Tropical Storm/Typhoon in the West Pacific. Presented are the current position (the large, red Tropical Storm/Typhoon symbol), intensity (the number within the symbol, as listed above), and forecast positions for 12, 24, 36, and 48 hours (the small, white symbols). Track forecast uncertainty (based on JTWC 5-year average forecast track errors (1990-1994)) is represented by the thin yellow line surrounding the white track forecast positions.

More Cyclone, Hurricane, Information centre

61. The word "hurricane" probably comes from the Mayan storm god Hunraken, or other Caribbean terms for evil spirit and big wind. And the terms "hurricane", "typhoon" and "tropical storm" all describe the same type of swirling wind activity. They are giant whirlwinds where air moves around a centre of low pressure - the eye of the storm-

reaching high speeds in circular waves extending 20 or 30 miles from the middle.

Latest Joint Typhoon Warning Centre (JTWC) Forecast Positions

62. The image provided depicts the latest JTWC forecast positions for the current Tropical Storm/Typhoon in the West Pacific. Presented are the current position (the large, red Tropical Storm/Typhoon symbol), intensity (the number within the symbol, as listed above), and forecast positions for 12, 24, 36, and 48 hours (the small, white symbols). Track forecast uncertainty (based on JTWC 5-year average forecast track errors (1990-1994)) is represented by the thin yellow line surrounding the white track forecast positions.....

More University of Wisconsin, Cooperative Institute for Meteorological Satellite Studies:

63. Tropical cyclones resource centre: Satellite Derived Winds and Analyses of storm related data.

National Hurricane Centre

64. Tropical Hurricane awareness centre. Learn about the hazards of hurricanes and what you can do to help protect yourself, your family, and your property. Early cyclone warning system in Andhra Pradesh (India) from 1977–1997 – A case study: India has a very long coast line of 5700 km which is exposed to tropical cyclones arising in the Bay of Bengal and the Arabian Sea. The present paper deals with a case study of Andhra Pradesh, a state situated on east coast of India and being most vulnerable for cyclones and hurricanes.

Canadian Hurricane Centre

65. Provides information about the hurricanes, genesis, sequences along with precautions to be taken. Along with educational information for the kids and students interested in studying the hurricanes. The centre also provides latest hurricane data in the region. Hurricane and Tropical Storm Info, Southern Regional Climate Centre, Louisiana State University: The centre provides information about tropical storms and hurricane. Latest data of tropical storm imagery, observations, satellite data, and predictions based on the trajectory taken is provided on the website. Hurricane Hunters Home Page: The 53rd Weather

Reconnaissance Squadron, known as the Hurricane Hunters of the Air Force Reserve, is one-of-a-kind: the only Department of Defence organisation flying into tropical storms and hurricanes on a routine basis.

Lowes Storm 2000 Hurricane Tracking Site

66. The website host a Storm Warning Centre, which provides latest information on storms in the region, along with information about regional weather, preparedness for disaster resulting from storms. The centre also provide email updates about latest storm predictions.

National Weather Service Disaster Survey Reports

67. National Weather Service teams document the impact of major weather systems. Reports include chronology of forecasting and storm tracking along with related events in the path of the storm.

Purdue University Hurricane and Tropical Data

68. This page provides access to a wealth of hurricane information including charts on the track of the storm plus a text based table of tracking information. The table includes position in latitude and longitude, maximum sustained winds in knots, and central pressure in millibars. Starstone's Eye of the Storm Tracking Software: Features a CD ROM based hurricane tracking program for the PC. Also a free version for basic tracking and mapping, and a 3D hurricane tracking screen saver.

Drought

Global VCI Imagery

68. Satellite data on vegetation and temperature and drought information and paper on Monitoring vegetation condition from NOAA operational polar-orbiting satellites. The site also provides historical data on droughts in various parts of the world.

Bureau of Meteorology Australia

69. The website provides extracts and summaries from the climate archive, weather predictions up to seven days ahead, alerts of dangerous weather up to two days ahead. Includes wind and storm warnings, fire weather warnings and flood warnings. Besides numerical weather

prediction output from computer models (text, gridded data files, maps). A special service called "SILO: Meteorological and agricultural information for rural interests" contains a rich source of meteorological and agricultural information/products for Australia.

Current Drought Status in Queensland, Australia

70. This web site is produced by the Queensland Centre for Climate Applications (QCCA). QCCA is a collaborative initiative of the Department of Primary Industries and the Department of Natural Resources to enhance climate applications research and climate extension activities for our rural industries. NCDC's SSM/I Monthly Image Products allows for global analysis of land surface temperature, wetness, and snow cover. The products presented on the site include full and anomaly fields for wetness and snow cover, and anomaly fields for blended surface temperature for the period January 1992 to the latest available month. These climate products are derived from the Special Sensor Microwave Imager (SSMI), a polar orbiting satellite with global coverage. Drought Watch on the Prairies is a product of Agriculture and Agri-Food Canada. A great source for current information on drought and its impacts across Canada. The impact of climatic variability on the environment is of great importance to the agricultural sector on the Canadian Prairies. Monitoring the impacts on water supplies, soil degradation and agricultural production is essential to the preparedness of the region in dealing with possible drought conditions.

The Canadian Climate and Water Information

71. This site provides information on the national climate and surface water (hydrometric and sediment) data archives for which Environment Canada has responsibility. The National Archives and Data Management Branch, Atmospheric Monitoring and Water Survey Directorate of the Meteorological Service of Canada maintains these Internet pages on behalf of Environment Canada's various partners and clients, and the Canadian public. Sahel Weather and Crop Situation reports from FAO: The "Sahel Report" is issued every month throughout the growing season, which lasts from June to October. The report describes weather conditions, pest infestations and crop prospects in this drought-prone zone. A synthesis report is published at the end of

the season containing first harvest estimates, based on a series of Crop Assessment Missions which are undertaken jointly with national and regional authorities. FAO's Global Information and Early Warning System on Food and Agriculture (GIEWS) for Africa: GIEWS has been answering questions like these, providing regular bulletins on food crop production and markets at the global level and situation reports on a regional and country-by-country basis. The system aims to provide policy-makers and policy-analysts with the most up-to-date information available on all aspects of food supply and demand, warning of imminent food crises, so that timely interventions can be planned.

CPC's Global Precipitation Monitoring information

The monthly and seasonal outlooks provided are based primarily on climate phenomena that exhibit a relatively large degree of predictability such as the El Niño/ Southern Oscillation (ENSO) cycle, as well as decade-to-decade variability and trends.

Weekly Global Climate Highlights from CPC

72. The Weekly Global Climate Highlights (WGCH) provides a quick, but not necessarily comprehensive, look at current climate anomalies and episodic events. The product is designed to alert the user to significant situations that warrant further examination or study.

The Greater Horn Information Exchange (GHIE)

73. The Greater Horn Information Exchange is dedicated to sharing regional and national data, studies, activities, and analyses for projects in the Greater Horn of Africa with the broadest possible range of GHAI stakeholders, together with providing a variety of resource materials including geographic and thematic maps, data sets, and monitoring and evaluation results which contribute to the holistic, regional perspectives needed to achieve the GHAI goals.

USAID's Famine Early Warning System (FEWS)

74. The Goal of the Famine Early Warning System (FEWS NET) is to strengthen the abilities of African countries and regional organisations to manage threats of food security through the provision of timely and analytical early warning and vulnerability information.

Drought Monitor

75. Tracking drought blends science and art. No single definition of drought works for all circumstances, so people rely on drought indices to detect and measure droughts. But no single index works under all circumstances, either. That's why we need the Drought Monitor, a synthesis of multiple indices, outlooks and news accounts, that represents a consensus of federal and academic scientists.

How can you help?

76. You can help us build this resource by joining DMIS. We are looking toward creating a online database of resources and volunteers accessible in times of disaster. Volunteers would be contacted by respective Disaster Management Authorities of various state governments or NGO's in times of disasters only. The database would be accessible to all, however if the volunteer has chosen not to be accessible to all, his/ her information would not be revealed.

You can help

1. By volunteering your services for the relief and rescue operations at the time of a disaster.
2. By volunteering resources for the relief, rescue and rehabilitation efforts.
3. By sharing your experiences, research, publication, databases etc.
4. By providing expert advice as to how to deal with this disastrous situation, sharing your experiences, publications etc Areas of expertise could be: In Structural Engineering, Trauma specialists, Rehabilitation planning, Physicians and paramedics, Rescue professionals ....
5. By spreading this message all over the world and asking for joining the effort and volunteering services and resources.
6. By adopting a village or an activity in disaster hit areas. NGO's, Corporate, trusts, Individuals could adopt villages or can take up an activity in the disaster hit areas. SRISTI would also help your contributions reach the affected people by channeling the same through various NGO's and coordinating with Government Agencies.

77. This sections contain links to papers, websites, databases, links to organisations, and website address of Disaster Management Authorities (DMAs). These resources helps you to provide crucial studies of experiences of quakes, storms, cyclones and other disasters. These provide insight into developing a better disaster mitigation plan. Pl. get in touch with us on any information on any disaster management information known.

Information Technology Tools for Natural Disaster Risk Management

78. Over the last few decades the importance of effective management of information is being recognised in the disaster management sector. Several countries are setting up disaster management information system for effective management of disaster. The applications of these systems range from emergency response planning to short range early warning to long range mitigation and prevention planning.

EIIP Virtual Forum

79. The Emergency Information Infrastructure Partnership (EIIP) Virtual Forum is designed to encourage emergency professionals to explore the use of current information technology to support emergency management and disaster response.

NASA's Disaster Finder

80. A searchable index of disaster-related web sites. Provides information about, Mitigation, Preparedness, Warnings, Response, Recovery, Relief, Education and Training, Research, Observing Systems, Emergency Management Systems, GIS Software etc. Which help you to monitor, predict and locate disasters.

Doctors Without Borders

81. Medicines sans Frontiers is a private, non-profit, international organisation, whose objective is to provide medical aid to populations in crisis, without discrimination. World's largest emergency medical aid organisation, whose humanitarian missions provide relief to victims of disaster, conflict and hardship throughout the world.

Virtual Hospital at University of Iowa Health Centre Virtual Hospital (VH)

82. A project of the Electric Differential Multimedia Laboratory, Department of Radiology, University of Iowa College of Medicine. It is a continuously updated medical multimedia database and available over high speed networks 24 hours a day. The VH may be used to answer patient care questions.

References

- Ahmed, Akbar. 1980. 'The impact of Afghan refuges on ethnicity and politics in Baluchistan', Central Asian Survey, 9(3).
- Allan, N. 1974. 'The Modernization of Rural Afghanistan: A Case Study', in Afghanistan in the 1970s, ed. L. Dupree and L. Albert, New York, pp. 113-25.
- Balland, D. and Benoist, A. 1982. 'Nomades et semi-nomades Baluc d'Afghanistan', Revue Geographic de l'Est, 22 (1982), pp. 117-144.
- Balland, D. 1974. 'Vieux sédentaire tadjik, les immigrants Pachtoun dans le sillon de Ghazni (Afghanistan oriental)', Bulletin de l'Assoc, des géographes français, Vol. 51.
- Beattie, H. 1982. Kinship and Ethnicity in the Nahrin Area of Northern Afghanistan Afghan Studies, Vol. 3-4, pp. 39-51.

- Beattie, H. 1982. Kinship and Ethnicity in the Nahrin Area of Northern Afghanistan Afghan Studies, Vol. 3-4, pp. 39-51.

- Boeson, Inger W. 1980. 'Women, Honour and Love: Some Aspects for the Pashtu Woman's Life in Eastern Afghanistan', Afghanistan Journal, 7(2): pp. 50-59.
- Boyajian, Vahe. 2000. 'On Baluchi Separatism', Iran and Caucasus, 3-4. Jetly, Rajshree. 2004. 'Baluch ethnicity and nationalism (1971-81): an assessment', Asian Ethnicity, Vol. 5, Issue 1.
- Burleson, William E. 2008. 'The Kinsey Scale and the Pashtun: The Role of Culture in Measuring Sexual Orientation', Journal of Bisexuality, Vol. 8, No. 3.
- Caron, James M. 2007. 'Afghanistan Historiography and Pashtun Islam: Modernization Theory's Afterimage,' History Compass, 5/2 (2007): 314-329.
- Centlivres, Pierre and Micheline Centlivres-Demont. 1998. 'Tajikistan and Afghanistan: the ethnic groups on either side of the border' in Tajikistan: the Trials of Independence. Mohammad-Reza Djalili, F. Grare and Shirin Akiner (editors). Richmond: Curzon.
- Christensen, A. 1980. 'Organisation, variation and transformation in Pukhtun society: review article', Ethnos, 46, pp. 96-108.

- Christensen, Asger. 1980. 'The Pashtuns of Kunar: Tribe, Class and Community Organization', Afghanistan Journal 7(3): pp. 79-92.
- Christensen, Asger. 1982. 'Agnates, affines and allies: patterns of marriage among Pakhtun in Kunar, North-East Afghanistan', Folk, Vol. 24, pp. 29-63.
- Dorronsoro, Gilles. 1994. 'Politique et ethnicite en Afghanistan: le cas Tadjik,'CEMOTI, 18 (1994), pp. 131-147.
- Dupree, L. 1956. 'The Changing Character of South-central Afghanistan Villages', Human Organization, Vol. 14, pp. 26-29.
- Dupree, L. 1966/1970. 'Aq Kupruk: A Town in North Afghanistan', 2 parts, American University Field Staff (AUFS), Fieldstaff Reports 10/9-10, Hanover, N. H., 1966; repr. in Peoples and Cultures of the Middle East, ed. L. Sweet, II, New York, 1970, pp. 344-87.
- Dupree, Louis. 1978. 'Pushtun', in Richard V. Weeks (editor), Muslim Peoples: A World Ethnographic Survey. Westport CT and London: Greenwood Press.
- Dupree, Louis. 1978. 'Tajik', in Richard V. Weeks (editor), Muslim Peoples: A World Ethnographic Survey. Westport, CT and London: Greenwood Press.
- Edwards, David B. 1986. 'Charismatic leadership and political process in Afghanistan,' Central Asian Survey, Volume 5, Issue 3/4, pp. 273-299.
- Edwards, David. 1998. 'Learning from the Swat Pathans: political leadership in Afghanistan, 1978–1997', American Ethnologist, Vol. 25, No. 4.
- Ethnology, and History. London: Elibron Classics. Unabridged reprint from 1877.
- Ferdinand, K. 1962. 'Nomad Expansion and Commerce in Central Afghanistan', Folk, Vol. 4, pp. 123-59.
- Ferdinand, K. 1969. 'Nomadism in Afghanistan', in Viehwirtschaft und Hirtenkultur, ed. L. Föeldes and B. Gunda, Budapest, pp. 127-60.
- Ferdinand, Klaus. 1982. 'Marriage among Pakhtun nomads of Eastern Afghanistan', Folk, Vol. 24, pp. 65-87.
- Gafferberg, E. 1975. Perezhitki religioznykh predstavleniu Beludzhe-. Moscow.
- Ghani, M. A. 1976. 'A Critique of Sir Olaf Caroe. Towards an Anthropological Understanding of Tribalism and Centralism in Afghanistan,' Afghanistan, Vol. 29, No. 2.
- Glatzer, Bernt. 2002. 'The Pashtun tribal system', in Concepts of tribal society. Georg Pfeffer and Deepak Kumar Behera (editors). Delhi: Concept Publishing Co.
- Hughes, A. W. 2007. The Country of Balochistan: Its Geography, Topography.

- Orywal, Erwin. 2006. 'Krieg und Kampf in Afghanistan', in B. Chiari (Hg.), Wegweiser zur Geschichte Afghanistans. Militärgeschichtliches Forschungsamt, Schöningh.
- Pehrson R. and F. Barth. 1966. The Social Organization of the Marri Baluch. Chicago.
- Salzman, Phillip Carl. 2000. The Black Tents of Baluchistan. Washington and London: Smithsonian Institution Press.
- Uberoi, J. 1971. 'Men, Women and Property in Northern Afghanistan', India and Contemporary Islam, ed. S. Lokhandwall, Simla, pp. 388-416.
- Uberoi, J.P.S. 1964. Social Organisation of the Tajiks of Andarab Valley, Afghanistan. PhD dissertation, Australian National University. 1.7 Baluch.
- Wirsing, R.G. 1981. The Baluchis and Pathans. London: Minority Rights Group.

  Poulton, Michelle. 1979. Un Village taik dans le nord de l'Afgha-nistan: traditions sociales et économiques face au développement. Dissertation: Thèse 3ème cycle Sciences sociales du développement, Paris, E.H.E.S .S.

Notes

1. Parasu Raman S and Unnikrishnan PV, Disaster Response in India: pp. 3. An over view. India Disasters Report Towards a Policy Initiative.
2. *Ibid.,* p. 2
3. *Ibid.,* p. 6.
4. Army Training Command (ARTRAC) Doctrine on Disaster Management pp. 5.
5. Parasu Raman S and Unnikrishnan PV, Disaster Response in India: pp. 6. An over view. India Disasters Report towards a policy initiative.

Disasters: Causes and Effects

We have never put resources, tools, equipments, skills, know-how in the hands of the people who are affected or are at risk. In fact our efforts take away or often slow dawn the local community, co-operatives and businesses in responding, rescuing and rehabilitating. The recent Tsunami Evolution coalition's evaluation of six countries shows that local capacities are for more effective and sustainable over outside in capacities or top-down efforts. Decentralised disaster risk reduction is our direction for a safer India."

— **Mihir R. Bhatt, Director,**
All India Disaster Mitigation Institute,
Ahmadabad

1. The facts and figures outlined in Part I make it amply clear that India has been traditionally vulnerable to natural disasters on account of its unique geo-climatic conditions. The loss in terms of private, community and public assets has been astronomical.

2. The approach to disaster management, as formulated by Government of India now, has been translated into a National Disaster Framework, a roadmap, covering institutional mechanisms, disaster prevention strategy, early warning system, disaster mitigation, preparedness and response and human resource development. The expected inputs, areas of intervention and agencies to be involved at the National, State and district levels have been identified and listed in the roadmap. This roadmap has been shared with all the State Governments and Union Territory Administrations and they have been advised to develop their own roadmaps.

Existing Institutional Arrangements

3. The subject of disaster management does not specifically find mention in any of the three lists in the Seventh Schedule of the Indian Constitution, where subjects under the Central and State Governments as also subjects that come under both are specified. It has been the norm that the basic responsibility of undertaking rescue, relief and rehabilitation measures in the event of natural disasters is considered that of the State Governments concerned. The Central Government supplements the efforts of the States by providing financial and logistic support.

National Level

4. *Response.* The response by the Central Government is determined by the following factors:-

(a) The gravity of a natural disaster.

(b) The scale of the relief operation necessary.

(c) Augmentation of financial resources and logistic support existing with the State Government.

5. *Decision Making.* The following are responsible for decision-making on occurrence of a disaster:-

(a) Union Cabinet, headed by the Prime Minister.

(b) Empowered Group of Ministers.

(c) National Disaster Management Authority (NDMA) under the chairmanship of the Prime Minister, to lay down the policies and plans.

(d) National Crisis Management Committee (NCMC), under the chairmanship of the Cabinet Secretary.

(e) Crisis Management Group (CMG) under the chairmanship of the Central Relief Commissioner to review contingency plans, measures to deal with the disaster, and to co-ordinate the activities of the Central Ministries and the State Government in relation to disaster preparedness response and relief.

(f) Technical Organisatoins, such as the Indian Meteorological Department for cyclone/earthquake, Central Water Commission for Floods, Defence Research and Development Organisation for nuclear/biological disasters and Directorate

General Civil Defence provide specific technical support for coordination of disaster response and management functions.

6. *Nodal Ministry.* Ministry of Home Affairs is the nodal ministry for coordination of relief and response and overall natural disaster management, and the Agriculture Ministry is the nodal agency for drought management. Ministries responsible to deal with other disasters are given in the table below:-

Ministries Responsible for Various Categories of Disasters

Type of Disaster	*Nodal Ministry*
Natural Disasters less Drought	Ministry of Home Affairs
Drought Relief	Ministry of Agriculture
Chemical Disasters	Ministry of Environment and Forests
Biological Disasters	Ministry of Health

State Level

7. The responsibility to cope with natural disasters is essentially that of the State Government. The State Governments are autonomous in organising relief operations in the event of natural disaster and carrying out long-term preparedness/rehabilitation measures. The State Crisis Management Group (SCMG) under the Chairmanship of Chief Secretary/Relief Commissioner formulates the action plans. A State Level Control Room is set up whenever a disaster situation develops. The Chief Secretary of the State heads a state level committee and is in overall charge of the relief operations in the State. The Relief Commissioners are responsible for relief and function under the state level committee.

District and Local Level

8. The Collector/District Magistrate/Deputy Commissioner coordinates and supervises the powers over all departments at the district level through a district level relief committee. The local bodies can be effective instruments in tackling disasters through early warning system, relief distribution, providing shelter to the victims, medical assistance etc.

Other Stakeholders

9. Other than the national, state, district and local levels, there are

various institutional stakeholders who are involved in disaster management at various levels in the country. These include the police and para-military forces, civil defence and home-guards, fire services, ex-servicemen, Non Government Organisations (NGOs), public and private sector enterprises and media.

External Linkages

10. The Government of India is a member of various international organisations in the field of disaster response and relief. While, as a policy, no requests for assistance or appeals are made to the international community in the event of a disaster, assistance offered suo moto is accepted. Linkages exist with the following organisations:-

(a) UN Office for Coordination of Humanitarian Affairs (UN OCHA), which is responsible, for all international disaster response.

(b) United Nations Development Programme (UNDP), which is responsible for mitigation and prevention aspects of disaster management.

(a) UN Disaster Assessment and Coordination (UNDAC) System for streamlining institutional arrangements for disaster response.

Disaster Management Policy

11. Disaster management is a multidisciplinary activity involving a number of departments/agencies spanning across all sectors of development. It is essential to have a policy in place, to serve as a framework for action by all the relevant departments/agencies. A National policy on disaster management has been formulated, and is in the process of implementation. In line with the changed focus, the policy proposes to integrate disaster mitigation into development planning. The broad objective of the policy are to minimise the loss of lives and social, private and community assets because of natural or man-made disasters and contribute to sustainable development and better standards of living for all. The policy mandates that the Central Government will, in conjunction with the State Governments, seek to ensure that a coordination mechanism is laid down through an appropriate chain of command so that mobilisation of resources is facilitated.

12. **National Level**

(a) *Holistic Approach.* A holistic and pro-active approach towards prevention, mitigation and preparedness will be adopted for disaster management.

(b) *Funding.* Each Ministry/Department of the Central/State Government will set apart an appropriate quantum of funds under the Plan for specific schemes/projects addressing vulnerability reduction and preparedness.

(c) *Mitigation*

(i) Where there is a shelf of projects, the projects addressing mitigation will be given priority. Mitigation measures shall be built into the on-going schemes/programmes.

(ii) Each project in a hazard prone area will have mitigation as an essential term of reference. The project report will include a statement, as to how the project addresses vulnerability reduction.

(d) *Community Involvement*

(i) Community involvement and awareness generation, particularly that of the vulnerable segments of population and women has been emphasised as necessary for sustainable disaster risk reduction. This is a critical component of the policy since communities are the first responders to disasters and, therefore, unless they are empowered, any amount of external support cannot lead to optimal results.

(ii) There will be close interaction with the corporate sector, non governmental organisations and the media in the national efforts for disaster prevention and vulnerability reduction.

(e) *Capacity Building*

(i) Institutional structures/appropriate chain of command will be built up and appropriate training imparted to disaster managers at various levels to ensure coordinated and quick response at all levels; and development of inter-State arrangements for sharing of resources during emergencies.

(ii) A culture of planning and preparedness is to be inculcated at all levels for capacity building measures.

(iii) Standard operating procedures and disaster management plans at state and district levels as well as by relevant central government departments for handling specific disasters will be laid down.

(f) *Prevention*

(i) Construction designs must correspond to the requirements as laid down in relevant Indian Standards.

(ii) All lifeline buildings in seismic zones III, IV and V i.e. hospitals, railway stations, airports/airport control towers, fire station buildings, bus stands, major administrative centres will need to be evaluated and, if necessary, retro-fitted.

(g) *Relief Codes.* The existing relief codes in the States will be revised to develop them into disaster management codes/manuals for institutionalising the planning process with particular attention to mitigation and preparedness.

(h) *International Cooperation.* Promote international cooperation in the area of disaster response, preparedness, and mitigation in tune with national strategic goals and objectives.

13. National Disaster Management Authority (NDMA). The Disaster Management Bill, 2005, which was passed by the Rajya Sabha on 28 Nov 2005, was considered and passed by the Lok Sabha on 12 Dec 2005. The government decided to enact a central legislation on disaster management in the aftermath of the Tsunami disaster on 26 Dec 2004. The salient features of the Bill include setting up of a NDMA under the Chairmanship of the Prime Minister; State Disaster Management Authorities in the States/Union Territories under the chairmanship of Chief Minister or Lt. Governor or Administrator, as the case may be; and the District Disaster Management Authority under the District Magistrate in each district.

14. The Prime Minister, Dr Manmohan Singh, approved the constitution of the NDMA in Feb 2006. The Authority will be serviced by the Ministry of Home Affairs and will be chaired by the Prime Minister. Gen NC Vij, former Chief of Army Staff is the Deputy

Chairman of the Authority which has three other eminent personalities with experience in disaster management.

15. *Charter of Duties*

(a) The NDMA will have the responsibility for laying down the policies and plans for disaster management The Authority will also approve the National Disaster Management Plan.

(b) The Authority will also coordinate the enforcement and implementation of the policies and plans for disaster management and arrange for, and oversee the provision of funds for mitigation measures, preparedness and response.

(c) It will frame guidelines for the minimum standards of relief to be provided to persons affected by disaster and give directions regarding relief in loan repayment.

(d) The Authority will initiate all measures for prevention of disaster and for mitigation of its effects.

State Level

16. The authority at State level will be chaired by the Chief Minister with Ministers of relevant departments i.e. Water Resources, Agriculture, Drinking Water Supply, Environment and Forests, Urban Development, Home, Rural Development etc as members. Ten States and Union Territories – Tamil Nadu, Arunachal Pradesh, Uttaranchal, Odisha, Gujarat, Kerala, Nagaland, Delhi, Andaman and Nicobar Admini-stration and Chandigarh Administration have notified the authority. The other States are in the process of setting up similar authorities. Gujarat and Madhya Pradesh have formulated State Policies for Disaster Management while other States are in process of doing so.

17. Re-structuring of the Relief Department in the States. The Government of India is working with the State Governments to res-tructure the Departments of Relief and Rehabilitation into Departments of Disaster Management with an enhanced area of responsibility to include mitigation and preparedness in addition to the present responsibilities of relief and rehabilitation. To pursue a holistic approach to disaster management, four functional groups have been formed within the departments whose tasks are as indicated below:-

(a) Functional Group 1: Hazard Mitigation.

(b) Functional Group 2: Preparedness and Capacity Building.

(c) Functional Group 3: Relief and Response.

(d) Functional Group 4: Administration and Finance.

District Level

18. The District Magistrate is the chief coordinator who will coordinate all activities related to prevention, mitigation and preparedness in addition to his existing responsibilities pertaining to response and relief. The District Coordination and Relief Committee is being reconstituted/re-designated into Disaster Management Committee. Such committees have already been constituted in 256 districts and are in the process of being constituted in the remaining districts.

19. *Village Level.* At the village level Disaster Management Committees and Disaster Management Teams are being constituted. Each village in multi-hazard prone district will have a Disaster Management Plan. The Disaster Management Committee consists of elected representatives at the village level, local authorities, government functionaries including doctors/paramedics of primary health centres, primary school teachers etc. The teams at the village level will consist of members of youth organisations as well as able-bodied volunteers from the village. The teams are provided basic training in evacuation, search and rescue, first aid trauma counselling etc.

Legal and Techno-legal Framework

20. *Disaster Management Act.* The States have been advised to enact Disaster Management Acts. These Acts provide for adequate powers for authorities coordinating mitigation, preparedness and response as well as for mitigation/prevention measures required to be undertaken. Two States Gujarat and Bihar, have already enacted such a law. Other States are in the process of enacting the law.

21. *Disaster Management Code.* The State Governments have also been advised to convert their Relief Codes into Disaster Management Codes. Some States have constituted committees to revise the codes as per GOI guidelines. The revised codes will ensure that the process of drawing up disaster management plans and mitigation and preparedness measures get institutionalised.

Financial Arrangements

22. *Relief Expenditures.* The policy arrangements for meeting relief expenditure related to natural disasters are, by and large, based on the recommendations of the Finance Commission. The two main windows presently open for meeting such expenditures are the Calamity Relief Fund (CRF) and National Calamity Contingency Fund (NCCF). These have been described in succeeding paragraphs.

23. *CRF.* This Fund is used to meet the expenditure on immediate relief to victims of cyclone, drought, earthquake fire, flood and hailstorm. The amount of annual contribution to the CRF of each State for each of the financial years 2000-01 to 2004-05 is indicated by the Finance Commission. A total of ₹ 11,007.59 crore was provided for the Calamity Relief Fund from year 2000 to 2005.

24. *NCCF.* Pursuant to the recommendations of the Eleventh Finance Commission, a National Calamity Contingency Fund (NCCF) Scheme came into force with effect from the financial year 2000-01. NCCF is intended to cover natural calamities like cyclone, drought, earthquake, fire, flood and hailstorm, which are considered to be of severe nature requiring expenditure by the State Government in excess of the balances available in its own CRF. The initial corpus of the National Fund is ₹ 500 crore, provided by the Government of India. An amount of about ₹ 2,300 crore has already been released to States from NCCF.

25. *Five Year Plans.* Under the Five Year Plans, the Government of India utilises a portion of the funds for mitigating natural disasters. There are also facilities for rescheduling short-term loans taken for agriculture purposes upon certification by the District/State administration. On occurrence of a calamity of great magnitude, funds flow from donors, both local and international, for relief and rehabilitation, and in few cases for long-term preparedness/ preventive measures. Funds for the latter purposes are also available from multilateral funding agencies such as the World Bank. These form part of the State Plan.

Initiatives for Disaster Mitigation

26. The measures that have been instituted and those under implementation to mitigate the effects and increase the level

of preparedness to deal with disasters in the country are highlighted below.

27. **Floods.** In order to respond effectively to floods, Ministry of Home Affairs has initiated National Disaster Risk Management Programme in all the flood-prone States. Assistance is being provided to the States to draw up disaster management plans at the State, District, Block/Taluka and Village levels. Awareness generation campaigns are being implemented to sensitise the stakeholders on the need for flood preparedness and mitigation measures. Elected representatives and officials are being trained in flood disaster management under the programme.

Bihar, Odisha, West Bengal, Assam and Uttar Pradesh are among the 17 multi-hazard prone States where this programme is being implemented with assistance from UNDP, USAID and European Commission.

28. **Earthquakes**

(a) *National Core Group for Earthquake Risk Mitigation.* This Core Group has been assigned with the responsibility of drawing up a strategy and plan of action for mitigating the impact of earthquakes; providing advice and guidance to the States, developing/organizing the preparation of handbooks/pamphlets/type designs for earthquake resistant construction; working out systems for assisting the States in the seismically vulnerable zones to adopt/integrate appropriate Bureau of Indian Standards codes in their building byelaws.

(b) *Hazard Safety Cells in States.* The States have been advised to constitute Hazard Safety Cells (HSC) headed by the Chief Engineer, State PWD with necessary engineering staff so as to establish mechanism for proper implementation of the building codes in all future government constructions, and to ensure the safety of buildings and structures from various hazards. Rajasthan, West Bengal, Delhi and Chhattisgarh have already constituted these cells and other States are in the process.

(c) *National Programme for Capacity Building of Engineers and Architects in Earthquake Risk Mitigation.* Under two such programmes 10,000 engineers and 10,000 architects in the

States will be given training in seismically safe building designs and related techno-legal requirements. Assistance is being provided to the State/UTs to build the capacities of more than 125 State Engineering Colleges and 150 Architecture Colleges to be able to provide advisory services to the State Governments to put in place appropriate techno-legal regime, assessment of building and infrastructures and their retro-fitting.

29. **Cyclones**

(a) *Core Group on Cyclone Mitigation.* A National Core Group on Cyclone Monitoring and Mitigation with experts from Indian Meteorological Department, National Centre for Medium Range Weather Forecasting, Central Water Commission, National Remote Sensing Agency and Indian Space Research Organisation has been constituted. The Group is responsible for looking at warning protocols for cyclones; coordination mechanism between different Central and State Departments; mechanism for dissemination of warning to the local people and; cyclone mitigation measures required to be taken for the coastal States.

(b) *National Cyclone Mitigation Project.* A project for Cyclone Mitigation (estimated cost Rs1050 crore) has been drawn up in consultation with the cyclone prone States. This project envisages construction of cyclone shelters, coastal shelter belt plantation in areas which are prone to storm surges, strengthening of warning systems, training and education etc.

30. **Tsunami**

(a) Statistics indicate that the coastal region of Gujarat is vulnerable to tsunamis from great earthquakes in the Mekran coast. All earthquakes do not generate tsunami; earthquakes of magnitude 7 or more may trigger off tsunamis. Research is still being undertaken in this field. For the Indian region, two potential sources have been identified, namely Mekran coast and Andaman to Sumatra region.

(b) *The Present status of Tsunami Warnings in India.* Tsunami is one of the least probability events in India. There are no proper provisions of tsunami warnings in India as yet, though;

there is a good seismological network in India to record any earthquake within the country and its neighbourhood. The need of a Tsunami Warning Centre (TWC) in India is now being conceptualised at the Government of India level. The Department of Ocean Development in Cooperation with Departments of Space and Science and Technology is evolving a plan of Tsunami Warning System in the Bay of Bengal and the Arabian Sea.

31. **Landslides**

(a) *Landslide Hazard Mitigation.* A National Core Group has been constituted for drawing up a strategy and plan of action for mitigating the impact of landslides, provide advice and guidance to the State Governments on various aspects of landslide mitigation, monitor the activities relating to landslide mitigation including landslide hazard zoning and to evolve early warning systems and protocols for landslide risk reduction. The government has designated Geological Survey of India (GSI) as the nodal agency.

Disaster Preparedness

32. The Bhuj earthquake in January, 2001 brought out several inadequacies in the system. Professionally trained search and rescue teams were not available; specialised dog squads to look for live bodies under the debris were not available; and there was no centralised resource inventory for emergency response. Although army played a pivotal role in search and rescue and also set up their hospital after the collapse of government hospital at Bhuj, the need for fully equipped mobile hospitals with trained personnel was acutely felt. Precious time was lost and it was not possible to cover all severely affected areas as quickly as the government would have desired. It was, therefore, decided that we should remove these inadequacies and be in a stage of preparedness at all times.

33. **Traditional Methods.** If tribes in the Andamans could survive the tsunami, it was because their existing warning systems worked well in comparison to our non-existent modern systems. The fact that traditional houses of wood and stone survived the Uttarkashi earthquake not so long ago while modern buildings collapsed offered a similar lesson. In the flood-prone rural North-East, one can find houses on

bamboo stilts that allow flood waters to flow under them rather than through or over. Native intelligence is significant and technical expertise needs to treat this as complementary asset. This intelligence needs to be tapped for devising approaches to management of disasters.

34. **Specialist Response Teams (SRT).** The Central Government is now in the process of training and equipping eight battalions of CRPF as SRTs. Each team consists of 45 personnel including doctors, paramedics, structural engineers etc. Eighteen teams have been trained so far. These teams are being trained in collapsed structure search and rescue, medical first response, rescue and evacuation in flood and cyclone, under water rescue etc. It is proposed to group together the eight battalions to form a 'National Emergency Response Force'.

35. **State Search and Rescue (SAR) Teams.** The States have been advised to set up their own specialist teams for responding to disasters. Ministry of Home Affairs will provide assistance for the training of the State trainers. Many States/UTs have initiated action for setting up of specialised SAR units. Ten States have identified the Training Centres for training in SAR in the States.

36. **Regional Response Centres (RRC).** Fourteen RRCs are being set up across the country to enable immediate response to floods, cyclones, earthquakes, landslides etc. Standard cache of equipment and relief materials will be kept in these RRCs and Specialist Response Teams will be stationed during the flood/cyclone seasons for immediate assistance to the State Governments. Caches of equipments are being procured and all RRCs will be operational soon.

37. **Health Preparedness.** A fully equipped 200-bed mobile hospital is being set up and attached to a leading government hospital in Delhi. Three additional mobile hospitals with all medical and emergency equipments are proposed to be located in different parts of the country. They will be airlifted during emergencies with additional doctors/paramedics taken from the hospitals with which the mobile hospitals are attached to the site of disaster.

38. **Hospital Preparedness and Emergency Health Management.** Hospital preparedness is crucial to any disaster response system. Each hospital needs to have an emergency preparedness plan to deal with mass casualty incidents and the hospital administration/

doctor trained for this emergency. It has been proposed to include health emergency management in the undergraduate and post graduate medical curricula.

39. **Incident Command System.** In order to professionalise emergency response management, it is proposed to introduce the Incident Command System in the country. This system provides for specialist incident command teams with an Incident Commander and officers trained in different aspects of incident management – logistics, operations, planning, safety, media management etc. The LBSNAA Mussoorie has been designated as the nodal training institution.

40. **Emergency Support Function Plans.** It is seen that the relevant departments start constituting teams/mobilising resources only after the crisis/disaster has struck, leading to delays. The relevant departments/agencies have been asked to draw up Emergency Support Function (ESF) Plans and constitute response teams and designate resources in advance so that response is not delayed. Ministries/ Departments have drawn up their ESF Plans and communicated it to MHA. States have been advised to finalise pre-contract/ agreement for all disaster relief items so as to avoid delays in procuring relief items after disaster situations.

41. **India Disaster Resource Network (IDRN).** A web-enabled centralised data base for the India Disaster Resource Network has been operationalised. The IDRN is a nation-wide electronic inventory of essential and specialist resources for disaster response both specialist equipment and specialist manpower resources. Entries into the inventory are made at district and State level. About 69,329 records in 545 districts throughout the country have already been uploaded since September 1, 2003 when the India Disaster Resource Network was formally inaugurated. The system will give, at the touch of the button, location of specific equipments/specialist resources as well as the controlling authority for that resource so that it can be mobilised for response in the shortest possible time. The data base will be available simultaneously at the district, state and national levels.

42. **Emergency Operation Centres (EOC).** The States are being assisted to set up control rooms/emergency operations centres at the State and district level. Assistance for this is being given under the GOI – UNDP project in the States covered by the project. Assistance

under the Modernisation of Police Scheme is also available for setting up EOCs. The control rooms, which will function round the clock, will be composite control rooms to look after law and order issues as well as disaster management.

43. **National Emergency Operation Centre (NEOC).** To coordinate the entire disaster/emergency operations effectively, the existing Control Room at the national level has been being upgraded as NEOC. It is equipped with satellite phones, GPS, computers, emergency lights, GIS information system etc. in five on-site emergency coordination kits in ready-to-use mode. A state-of-the-art underground and all-hazard resistant, NEOC with superior structural features and communication facilities is being set up. A Committee of CPWD/BARC/DRDO has been constituted to finalise the design parameters. It is likely to be commissioned by 2006.

44. **National Emergency Communication Network.** In emergency response and management, it is extremely important to have the communication links operational between decision-makers at various levels and operational response teams/personnel on the site. Unfortunately at the time of emergency situations such as natural or man-made disasters, the first casualty is the regular telecommunications infrastructure of public wired and wireless (GSM/CDMA) telephones. Considering the crucial role of MHA during such emergencies, it is essential to set-up reliable information and communication network employing both terrestrial and satellite-based communication technologies with redundancies to establish a network for emergency communications.

45. **GIS-based National Database for Disaster Management.** The Geographical Information System (GIS) data base is an effective tool for emergency responders to access information in terms of crucial parameters for the disaster affected areas. The crucial parameters include location of the public facilities, communication links and transportation network at national, state and district levels. The GIS data base already available with different agencies of the government is being upgraded and the gaps are proposed to be bridged. A project for this purpose is being drawn up with a view to institutionalise the arrangements.

46. **Strengthening of Fire Services.** In order to further strengthen the capacity for response, the fire services are proposed to be developed into multi-hazard response units as is the normal practice in several other countries. A project for this (with an estimated cost of Rs 2457 crores) has been drawn up. It is proposed to provide rescue tenders in addition to fire tenders to each fire unit and fill up all gaps up to sub-divisional level.

47. **Strengthening of Civil Defence.** India has a large network of Civil Defence and Home Guards volunteers. The existing strength is about 1.2 million. However, this organisation has not so far been associated with disaster mitigation, preparedness and response functions. It is proposed to revamp the Civil Defence organisation to enable them to discharge a key responsibility in all the facets of disaster management including preparedness. A proposal in this regard has been finalised and is under consideration of the government.

48. **Utility of HAM Operators.** HAM radio services have proved very useful in remote areas, especially during disasters. This was more than evident after the recent tsunami struck the Andaman and Nicobar Islands. The HAM operators on the islands were the first to establish contact with the outside world. There is a subscript to this tale. The defence ministry had all these years forbidden HAM radio operators from the islands, citing their strategic location. Permission was finally granted on December 15, 2004 and two HAM operators from Chennai landed on the islands within a week, just days before the tsunami struck. Had the HAM operators not been there, it might have taken longer for the world to learn about the disaster or the extent of damage. With its own HAMSAT satellite, India is now hoping to rope in and involve the amateur radio operators' community into its integrated disaster management plan.

Indian Armed Forces in Management of Natural Disasters

49. An IAS officer, Mr B Someshwar Rao has been quoted to say, "One state, I was told, prepared a 'contingency plan' to deal with flood situations. The plan, kept secret under the outdated Official Secrets Act, aroused the curiosity of a friend of mine who is an eminent person in the field of disaster management. Using his own channels he obtained a copy of the plan and it boiled down to just one sentence: CALL THE ARMY." A few questions that emerge are; what is the role of the Army?

Is it adequately geared up to meet these challenges? What is the training given to army personnel to respond efficiently to such disaster situations? Is there a genuine requirement for the Army to be called out for such duties time and again?

50. **There are differences of opinion on this issue.** Despite having an elaborate disaster management set-up in our country, what is the necessity of having to employ the Armed Forces time and again for the management of Natural Disasters? Another point of view is that since the army is available, one might as well employ it.

51. **Procedure for Provision of Aid.** General Assistance during disaster situation is to be provided by the Defence Services on orders of the central government. In case it is of such an immediate nature that reference to central government is not practicable, local military authority may comply with a request at their discretion. This is to be reported immediately to respective service headquarter (operations directorate) and normal channels taken recourse to, as early as possible. Any state unable to cope with a major disaster situation on its own and having deployed all its resources will request government of India for additional assistance. Ministry of Defence will direct respective service headquarters to take executive action on approved requests.

52. **Co-ordination.** The responsibility for co-ordination of disaster relief operations at various levels is as follows:-

(a) *Inter Services Co-ordination at Central Level.* Cabinet secretariat (Military Wing).

(b) *Service Headquarters*

(i) Military Operations Directorate (MO 6) at Army Headquarters.

(ii) Director of Naval Operations at Naval Headquarters.

(iii) Directorate of Operations (Transport and Maritime) at Air Headquarters.

(c) Command and Lower Formation Headquarters. Senior General Staff Officer (Operations)/ Chief Operational Officer.

(d) *State Level.* Service liaison officer deputed to form part of Joint control Centres.

(e) *Local Level.* Nominated commander of troops and senior civil administrator in charge of relief.

53. **Organisation for Disaster Relief in Indian Armed Forces.** All formation and units located in various places in the country have the instructions to be ready to move in case required for aid to civil authorities. All formation headquarters prepare detailed contingency plans to meet any eventuality, which may arise due to any natural or other disaster situation. All units located in areas which are prone to the recurring natural disasters like floods etc; have detailed relief plans worked out which are frequently rehearsed. The task of co-ordinating aid to civil authority is generally given to static headquarters like Area and Sub Area Headquarters who report to the theatre commands.

54. **Assistance Rendered by the Armed forces in Disaster Management**

(a) Infrastructure for Command and Control involving provision of communications both telephone, radio and specialist manpower.

(b) Provision of medical care with the help of the medical teams including treatment at the nearest armed forces hospital.

(c) Provision of logistic back-up vehicles such as aircraft/helicopters/ships/boats for transportation of relief material to the affected areas.

(d) Setting up and running of relief camps can be effectively carried out by the armed forces.

(e) Army engineers can undertake construction and repair of roads and bridges to enable relief teams/material to reach affected areas.

(f) Repair, maintenance and running of essential services may have to be undertaken in the initial stages of disaster relief.

(g) Assisting in evacuation of people to safe places before and after the disaster.

(h) Stage management of handling of international relief can be undertaken by the services in case requested to do so by the civil administration.

55. **Preparedness of Indian Armed Forces for Disaster Management.** The primary role of the army is to defend the sovereignty and integrity of our country. Its organisation, training and equipment

are tailored to meet this. It would not be practicable to change the basic structure in order to handle an additional task such as disaster management. Disaster management as we know is a highly specialised subject. At the same time, one should also view the overall picture as to whether our country can really afford a separate agency to look after disaster management. The various advantages of the employment of the armed forces have already been highlighted. In case the army is to be employed for disaster relief and the need is accepted that the Army should be utilised, the next question that emerges is whether the army is organised, trained and equipped for disaster relief.

56. **Organisation.** Keeping in view the primary role of the armed forces, it would be impracticable to change the organisation of the army. Disaster management plans should incorporate the armed forces at all levels from Headquarters Integrated Defence Staff downwards, so that the armed forces know what is expected from it and are prepared to do meet the challenge effectively and efficiently.

57. **Training.** There is no institutionalised training in disaster management or relief. It would be beneficial to train selected officers in aspects of disaster management. Although the Faculty of Nuclear, Biological and Chemical Protection in the College of Military Engineering conducts a course, it is only a beginning and mainly deals with NBC disasters. Probably, its scope could be enhanced or alternately officers could be sent for courses to various institutes, which run these courses. Interaction and participation in seminars would also enhance awareness of the subject.

58. **Equipment.** It may neither be economically viable nor feasible to equip armed forces units across the board with equipment for handling disaster situations. However, certain disaster prone areas such as Assam, Bihar (Floods), Uttarkashi, Gujarat, J & K (Earthquakes), Andhra Pradesh, Odisha (Cyclones) could be identified. The static formations and units at these areas could be given some specialised equipment keeping in mind the nature of disaster, from funds specially allocated for this purpose. These could be utilised by the local units as and when required.

Conclusion

59. Disaster Management requires multi-disciplinary and pro-active approach. Besides the initiatives being taken by the Central and

State Governments, the community, civil society organisations and media also have a key role to play in achieving our goal of moving together, towards a safer India. The message being put across is that, in order to move towards safer and sustainable national development, development projects should be sensitive towards disaster mitigation.

60. The Government's mission is vulnerability reduction to all types of hazards. It has taken the first few but significant steps towards vulnerability reduction, putting in place prevention and mitigation measures and preparedness for a rapid and professional response. With a massive awareness generation campaign and building up of capabilities as well as institutionalisation of the entire mechanism through a techno-legal and techno-financial framework, the country is gradually moving in the direction of sustainable development.

61. The various prevention, mitigation measures outlined above are aimed at building up the capabilities of the communities, voluntary organisations and government functionaries at all levels. Particular stress is being laid on ensuring that these measures are institutionalised considering the vast population and the geographical area of the country. This is a major task being undertaken to put in place mitigation measures for vulnerability reduction. This is just a beginning. The ultimate goal is to make prevention and mitigation a part of normal day-to-day life. We have a firm conviction that with the measures in place, we could say with confidence that disasters like Odisha cyclone and Bhuj earthquake will not be allowed to recur in this country; at least not at the cost, which the country has paid in these two disasters in terms of human lives, livestock, loss of property and means of livelihood.

References

- Adelekan, M. 2005. 'Paradox in the evaluation of a unique drug control effort in a non-western country', International Journal of Drug Policy, Vol. 16, Number 2.
- Allen, Nigel J. R. 2004. 'Opium Production in Afghanistan and Pakistan', in Dangerous Harvest: Drug Plants and the Transformation of Indigenous Landscapes. Edited by Michael K. Steinberg et al (eds) Oxford University Press.
- Blanchard, Christopher M. 2007. 'CRS Report for Congress Afghanistan: Narcotics and U.S. Policy', CRS.
- Blanchard, Christopher M. 2009. 'Afghanistan: Narcotics and U.S. Policy', Congressional Research Service.

- Breckle, S. and M. Koch. 1982. 'Afghanische Drogen und ihre Stammpflanzen. Teil3: Haschisch und Hanf', Afghanistan Journal, Vol. 9, Issue 4, pp. 115-123.
- Byrd, William and Christopher Ward. 2004. 'Drugs and development in Afghanistan', Conflict Prevention and Reconstruction, Paper no. 18. World Bank.
- Anand, Bhuvana. 2004. 'Replacing Narco-Usurers With Micro-Lenders: The Agricultural Finance Component of Opium Substitution Programmes in Afghanistan', MA Thesis. Tufts University.
- Breckle, S. 1979. 'Afghanische Drogen und we Stammpflanzen. Teil 2: Sußholz' , Afghanistan Journal, Vol. 6, Issue 3, pp. 87-91.
- Breckle, S. and W. Unger. 1977. 'Afghanische Drogen und ihre Stammpflanzen. Teil 1: Gummiharze von Umbelliferen', Afghanistan Journal, Vol. 4, Issue 3, pp. 86-95.
- Brown, Allison. 2009. 'Why Buy Something We Hate? Subsidize Other Crops, Not Poppy', Small Wars Journal, December.
- Buddenburg, D. and W. Byrd (eds). 2006. Afghanistan's Drug Industry: Structure, Functioning, Dynamics, and Implications for Counter-narcotics Policy. UNODC/World Bank.
- Bureau of International Narcotics and Law Enforcement Affairs. 2008. 'International Narcotics Control Strategy Report - 2008', US State Department. Brown, Allison. 2009. 'Poppy is Not the Most Profitable Crop, It's the Only Crop', Small Wars Journal, June 2009.

Typology and Profile of Regional, Seasonal, Social and Accidental Disasters

The source of man's unhappiness is his ignorance of Nature.

— **Paul Henry Thiry d'Holbach**

Operational Definitions

1. **Disaster**

(a) The Concise Oxford Dictionary defines disaster as "sudden or great misfortune; calamity or complete failure". To take a simple example, the sudden loss of four family members in a road accident, would probably be described by that family as a disaster, but professionals involved in a counter-disaster activities would probably describe this as an 'accident', 'incident', 'occurrence' or 'emergency'.

(b) The World Health Organisation (WHO) defines disaster as any occurrence that causes damage economic destruction, loss of human life and deterioration in health services on a scale sufficient to warrant an extraordinary response from outside the affected community or area.

(c) Therefore, a 'disaster'[1] occurs when there is a serious disruption to community life arising with little or no warning; which threatens to or causes injury in that community and/or damage to property, which is beyond the day-to-day capacity of the prescribed government or statutory authorities and which requires the special mobilisation and organisation of resources, other than those readily (normally) available to these authorities.

(d) The term 'disaster' evokes extraordinary response from the outside the community or affected area. The disaster agent is a catalyst, which has a potential to create or produce disasters. For example, earthquake, cyclone, floods are disaster agents. Disaster is basically about vulnerability, susceptibility of a potential victim to the life threatening impact of disaster agent. For example, a drought or an earthquake in uninhabited land will not necessarily cause a disaster. It is only when an agent exposes the vulnerability of people that the disaster agent can lead to a disaster.

2. **Crisis Management.** The calm, deliberate, judicious and controlled mechanisms instituted by a government to avert, if possible and if not isolate and prevent further escalation and thereafter adopt measures to restore normalcy in available time frame.[2]

3. **Disaster Preparedness.** It may be described as action designed to minimise loss of life and damage, and to organise and facilitate timely and effective rescue, relief and rehabilitation in cases of disaster. Preparedness is supported by the necessary legislation and means a readiness to cope with disaster situations.[3]

4. **Disaster Prevention.** It may be described as measures designed to prevent natural phenomenon from causing or resulting in disasters or other related emergency situations. Prevention concerns the formulation and implementation of long-range policies and programmes to prevent or eliminate the occurrence of disasters.[4]

5. This chapter deals with general features of some of the common disaster situations, which frequently occur in India.

TYPES OF DISASTERS

6. A wide variety of forces can cause disasters. These forces may be either natural or artificial or combination of both.

Man-made Disasters

7. Within this category of disasters, there are a variety of conditions resulting disaster[5]:-

(a) *Civil Disturbances.* Riots. e.g.: Bombay Riots of 1992.

(b) *Warfare.* Conventional, NBC warfare, LICO, terrorism, and mass movement of people from one place to another.

(c) *Refugees.* Forced movements of large numbers of people, usually across frontiers; example: refugees of Rwanda, recently in Zaire.

(d) *Accidents.* Collapse of buildings, mine disasters; example: Bhopal Gas Tragedy of 1994 in India.

Natural Disasters

8. Within this category of disasters, a variety of forces that may result in disaster[6]:-

(a) *Meteorological Disasters.* Cyclones, hurricanes, cold wave, heat wave and droughts (possibly causing famines).

(b) *Topological Disasters.* Earthquakes, avalanches, landslides, and floods.

(c) *Biological Disasters.* Epidemics of communicable diseases; example, Plague in Surat, Malaria in Rajasthan.

9. The division between natural and man-made is to some extent an over simplification, as many disasters are actually caused by more than one or combination of various forces. Some disasters set a chain reaction of disasters. For example, a flood, which may eventually result in an epidemic of cholera, can follow Cyclone.

10. The cumulative effects of several of these factors have caused some of the worst disasters. For example, in November 1970, a cyclone was followed by one of the worst tidal waves, which led to death of 50,000 people. The occurrence of this natural disaster came at a time of civil strife, followed by Indo-Pak War of 1971 leading to liberation of Bangladesh. It forced ten million people to flee to India, creating another relief operation. The combined natural and man-made disasters resulted in one of the biggest relief operations since World War II. The long-term perspective will reveal to us that disaster is an inter-action of combination of political, social, economic and environment factors. There is no wonder if disasters appear more frequently in developing world than developed ones.

11. It is difficult to predict precisely where and when a man-made disaster will occur, therefore, it is more difficult to prepare for one.

It is possible however, with varying degrees of accuracy to predict the occurrence of a natural disaster.

Policy Disasters[7]

12. Yet another category, including situations such as lack of rational policies to restrict the sale of hazardous and harmful drugs, free sale of tobacco and liquor, banned pesticides, and excessive displacement of people by development projects, consists of disasters caused due to negligence on the part of the policy-makers.

13. This classification is purely for logistic and explanatory purposes. For example, in 1996, the flood-accumulated water in the Western desert state of Rajastan became an ideal breeding ground for mosquitoes. This ignited vector proliferation, leading to a malaria epidemic outbreak. Amplified by a systemic failure, the epidemic look a heavy toll, far more than that of the flood disaster itself. The actual reason lay elsewhere than in just the quantum of rainfall, which had been undoubtedly relatively higher: it was the way in which civic structures that had come up (violating basic laws) in the past two decades amplified the flood.

14. Similarly in some drought-affected pockets in Odisha, acute food shortage malnutrition was to blame, despite a relatively good harvest. The reasons were linked to the people's interaction with the market and exploitative trade and business practices.

15. Similarly, the policy changes that weakened the public health system have been blamed for the re-emergence of many epidemics such as tuberculosis, which kills one Indian every minute.

Floods

16. A flood is defined as a body of water rising, swelling and overflowing land areas. Most river floods result from natural causes, such as excessive rainfall, melting snow, or ice jams. In general, floods are classified as either regular or flash floods. Regular floods can be predicted.

17. "India has always been visited by floods." This is a seasonal and endemic term of disaster, which causes great havoc and devastation each year. The primary cause of all floods in India is heavy and concentrated rainfall. June to September is the rainiest period of the

year. Rainfall also occurs from October to December in East Coast of Southern Peninsula due to North East Monsoons. Since preparatory and warning period is adequate, floods can be tackled satisfactorily.

Cyclones

18. A cyclone, is a violent windstorm, usually accompanied by much rain, thunder and lightening. Cyclones take form of very large revolving and moving form (200-300 miles per day), accompanied by lashing winds (80 to 100 miles per day), high tidal waves (10 to 20 feet). These are also known as hurricanes or typhoons. In the Bay of Bengal, these normally occur from December to March. The coastal areas and areas up to few hundred kilometres inland are more vulnerable to cyclone havoc particularly the coasts of Odisha, Andhra Pradesh and Tamil Nadu.

Earth Quakes

19. The three major types of earthquakes are volcanic, plutonic and tectonic, the attributes of these are covered below[8]:

(a) *Volcanic.* It is attributable to volcanic activity usually centred near the volcano. Damage usually is limited and local.

(b) *Plutonic.* These are deep focused quakes caused by explosion as deep as 435 miles within the interior of the earth. Though felt on the earth surface, little damage results except perhaps in a limited area directly above the explosion.

(c) *Tectonic.* These earthquakes are most common and most destructive of all quakes. They are caused by slippage along faults in the earth's crust. The grating or rubbing together the sides of a fault set up earthquake waves.

20. In most earthquakes the earth's crust cracks like porcelain. They generally occur on the so-called plate boundaries, where moving plates are pulled apart, slide past or converge. The earthquakes are usually preceded by foreshocks and followed by after shocks. Earth quakes strike without warning and there is no time for last minute preparation and therefore speedy emergency relief is of utmost importance. Although earthquakes may occur anywhere on the earth's surface, including bottom of the sea, approximately 65 per cent occur in certain seismic areas. The Latur and Koyna (Maharashtra) seismic

areas have experienced earthquakes, perhaps due to rifts that exist in this area.

Effects of Disaster

16. **General.** While each disaster has its own characteristics, it is possible to determine a common base of disaster effect. This is necessary to evolve common disaster relief / management operations to combat their effects[9].

17. **Effects**

(a) Extensive Deaths and Danger to Life.

(b) Destruction and Damage to Buildings.

(c) *Lack of Water, Food and Essential Requirements.* Need provision and distribution of survival requirements like water, food, fodder, blankets and so on.

(d) *Disruption of Communications.* This complicates assessment of damage and deployment of relief efforts.

(e) *Outbreak or Danger of Epidemics.* Preventive measures should include inoculation/ vaccination, water treatment and sanitation as part of disaster relief.

(f) *Threat to Crops, Vital Installations, Public Utilities or Fire Hazards.* Suitable damage control measures like crop spraying, reinforcements or demolition and fire services are required.

(g) *Panic and Disorder.* Effective public information measures and warden services are required.

Special Features of Disaster Management

18. Special features of disaster management are as follows:-[10]

(a) *Lack of Early warning and Information.* This results in delayed response due to lack of relief intelligence.

(b) *Inadequate Resources.* Mobilisation of resources in men and material from multiple sources is a critical planning and organisational problem.

(c) *Varying Requirements.* Each disaster situation requires separate consideration, planning and expertise to deal with its specialised problems.

Stages of Disaster Management

19. Comprehensive disaster management, which involves both assessment and response, can be seen to involve three chronological stages, although stages overlap. These phases are seldom readily separable but need to be determined as part of disaster management process.[11]

20. **Preparatory Stage.** This corresponds to the pre-disaster period and will include disaster prediction, warning and alert system, preventive measures, issue contingency plans. It will mainly involve government and specialised agencies.

21. **Emergency/Response Stage.** This stage commences after the disaster strikes and immediately before it including reaction to warnings and emergency relief activities.

22. **Rehabilitation and Reconstruction Stage.** Covers short and long term measures to restore essential services, communication and normal community life. Rehabilitation phase involves the following few weeks or months, while reconstruction may take long time, often years.

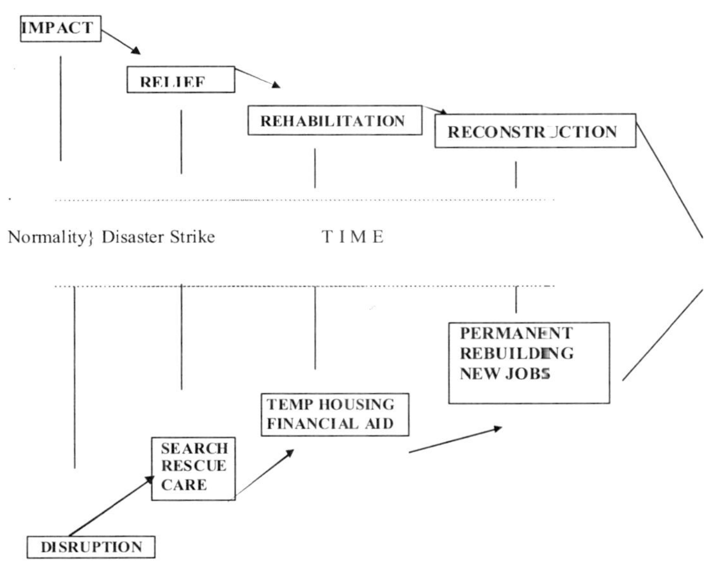

Figure Showing Progressive Restoration of Normalcy

Stages in the Progressive Restoration of Normality. The model given in figure gives out progressive restoration of normal situation in relation to time[12].

ROAD MAP TO IMPROVE DISASTER MANAGEMENT ORGANISATION IN INDIA

Introduction

1. For years disasters have been treated as singular events, and their management has ignored their implication on social and economic development of the society. However, over the past couple of years, there has been a slow but perceptible shift in the outlook of the government towards approach to disaster management. The new approach has its genesis in the conviction that overall development of the country cannot be sustained unless disaster mitigation is integrated into the development process. The new policy emanates from the belief that investments in mitigation are much more cost effective than expenditure on relief and rehabilitation.

2. India has usually been vulnerable to natural disasters on account of its unique geo-climatic conditions. Floods, droughts, cyclones, earthquakes and landslides have been recurring phenomena. About 60 per cent of the landmass is prone to earthquakes of various intensities; over 40 million hectares is prone to floods; about 8 per cent of the total area is prone to cyclones and 68 per cent of the area is susceptible to drought. In the decade 1990-2000, an average of about 4344 people lost their lives and about 30 million people were affected by disasters every year. The loss to private, community and public assets has been astronomical.

3. This brings us to the important question. Why have successive governments been unable to mitigate the impact of natural disasters in India? India today is one of the fastest developing economies of the world. To sustain this growth it is imperative that a detailed hazard and vulnerability assessment is done and we don't merely respond to calamities and reconstruction but focus on creating disaster reduction and mitigation techniques.

Recommended Measures – Organisational

4. **Disaster Management Framework.** The all party national committee setup under the chairmanship of the PM and the NDMC

needs to be institutionalised as permanent standing bodies. The former would help generate the necessary political will, consensus and support while the latter will evolve the appropriate strategy for the implementation of policies on disaster management. The NDMC has already come out with two valuable documents emphasising a structured, decentralised and systematic approach to the overall management of disasters. The process of disasater management upto the district and panchayat levels has already been initiated.

5. The primary responsibility of managing disasters lies with the state government, it is therefore, necessary to strengthen institutional mechanism at the state level. In the wake of recent disasters new structures and mechanisms have evolved in states of Gujarat, Odisha, Maharashtra and Uttranchal. States must develop systems tailor-made to suit their own environment and conditions, so as to deal with the hazard they are vulnerable to and include all aspect of disaster management.

6. Many state governments have disaster mitigation and management centres such as centre for disaster management and mitigation in Chennai. The creation of such centres will reinforce the disaster management apparatus of the country. The disaster mitigation and management centre should endeavour to take all such investigations and studies relevant to their region. Both central and state governmental should strengthen existing institutions and centres by capacity building, modernisation, staffing and funding.

7. The real action takes place at the district level, which is the cutting edge of administration. It is thus necessary to strengthen the setup and support system for the district magistrate who provides the overall leadership. Therefore it is recommended that the district relief committee that presently exists be reconstituted as district disaster management committee.

8. **Implementation Mechanisms.** No research mandate or conclusions are worth the effort unless these are realised to ground realities. With respect to disaster management it is all the more important, since it involves loss of lives, assets and property. The need is paramount for dedicated and accountable efforts which can oversee their implementation.

9. **Information and Technology.** Strategies of disaster management and reduction are very much based on information. Exercises that first identify the type of data to be gathered, then assimilate and generate it, and periodically update it are necessary. The role of technology is crucial. GIS and remote sensing are two technologies that have ample application in disaster management. Thus, the aspect of fusing technology in the present system needs attention and promotion. The gap between availability of technology in today's environment and its application for disaster management needs to be bridged.

Recommended Measures – Institutional

10. National centre for calamity management as suggested by eleventh finance commission and its structure needs to be set-up at the earliest. Building community leadership and a chain of trained community through participative approach will help harness local resources. A network of training institution led by a national level disaster management institute, rural development, IITs, IIMs etc will need to be forged and developed.

11. A national institute of disaster management needs to be established as a centre of excellence and knowledge including training. A full fledged emergency operation centre should also be established at the institute which would serve as alternative backup of the national Emergency Operations Centre during disasters.

12. All the state level ATI should have a full fledged department of disaster management responsible for establishing the alternate state EOC. A full fledged EOC with clear conceptualised roles and all necessary infrastructure and support should exist at the district level.

Recommended Measures – Infrastructure Support

13. It is recommended that the calamity relief fund provided by the tenth financial commission be earmarked for state level capacity building for disaster management and act as a buffer for handling disaster level L1 and state level L2 emergencies. State disaster management ministry at the centre should have full sway over decisions pertaining to this fund and its application on restoration of infrastructure. The CRF should be kept out of public fund and should be invested on approval of finance ministry.

Recommended Measures – Preparedness for Disasters

14. **Digitised Maps.** Availability of digitised maps is a step towards improvement of preparedness for disaster. The Survey of India could be the nodal agency for digitisation of maps for disaster relief operations. Some recommendations are:-

(a) Provisioning of GIS / digital maps of all states, districts and all urban centre with spatial and non-spatial data with appropriate scale.

(b) Survey of India maps to be suitably supplemented with information relating to specific disasters applicable to an area as well as for planning of developmental programmes.

(c) Production of topographic maps especially for hazard locations on a priority to serve as an essential input to production of building hazard maps.

(d) Seismic macro-zonation of all major cities and urban centre with priority assigned to the seven metros with detailed assessment of building and infrastructures for all cities in zone IV and V.

15. **Remote Sensing.** In general, remote sensing provide a data base which can be interpreted to aid production of hazard maps, which have immense value in any kind of activity related to disasters. For a quantitative base for disaster related operations the following activities should be build into our management systems:-

(a) Organise integrated, spatial and non-spatial data bases using GIS tools in a systematic manner. This would involve diverse information from a variety of sources, requires effective matching of similar entities and demands information consistency across data sets.

(b) Generation of spatial outputs supported by tables / charts to help in developmental planning and decision making.

16. **Information Data Base.** Robust and sound information data base is the backbone of any system and it facilitates any strategic planning, even disaster response with a privatisation of activities and optimisation of resources. It is therefore felt that access to such information is primary and following effort should be made as a part

of disaster knowledge network initiative to be spread all over the country:-

(a) A data base of all area / region giving the land use, demographic, socioeconomic data, infrastructure (like road, rail, network, hospital etc) maintained at national and local levels.

(b) Resource inventories of governmental and nongovernmental systems, personnel and equipment should be made and networked.

(c) Historical documentation of previous disasters should include location of disasters, history, cause, mitigation, details, finances etc available and accessible for future planning.

17. **Planning.** The most important component of preparedness is planning for all contingencies. The plans have to be linked with different support departments. Linking district plan to state plans and state plans to national plan, i.e. horizontal and vertical integration. Following measures are thus recommended in this regard:-

(a) There is a requirement of formulating a comprehensive disaster management plan at each level that should be linked to the national plan. These plans must be kept ready, practiced and rehearsed periodically.

(b) Each state to develop an integrated 'all hazard' disaster management plan on priority, which also should be practiced rehearsed and updated periodically.

(c) The district level plan to be integrated with state and national level plans, updated from time to time.

(d) Trigger mechanism should be used as a primary means of activation of disaster response.

(e) An 'all hazards approach' keeping in view the entire cycle of disaster management for all natural and man-made disasters need to be considered.

(f) Risk identification should be the basis of all planning.

(g) Infrastructure, maintenance and safety review should be built into the disaster management plans.

(h) Implementation and monitoring be integrated and worked out at all stages of planning process.

18. **Forecasting, Warning and Alert Systems.** Forecasting, warning and alert systems are an inseparable part of any disaster management organisation. These help in forewarning us about any impending disaster. However, previous studies have suggested that not much thought or attention has been devoted to this aspect. Therefore, there is a definite need to improve the warning and forecasting systems. Some of the measures in this regard are as under:-

(a) There is a need for earmarking / nominating specific agencies for forewarning and forecasting disaster, and these agencies should be made accountable.

(b) There is a need to network various agencies involved nationally/internationally for quick access to information from all networked sources.

(c) There is a requirement of modernising the computerised weather forecasting system of IMD by introducing very fine resolution numerical models for tropical cyclone production, thus requiring computing facilities at the IMD.

(d) Rainfall measurement method based on rain gauges is too coarse. Space based measurements have to be integrated with computed aridity anomaly based on field measurements.

(e) R & D on prediction and forecasting of landslides needs to be encouraged specially for early warning against those which are likely to be reactivated and in hazardous areas.

(f) Forecasting of drought and its impact on agriculture needs to be reviewed. Rigorous monitoring of drought conditions may be carried out at village level using network of automatic weather stations and satellite data.

(g) The observation system like the Doppler radars need to be upgraded to better systems and their areas of coverage increased.

(h) For detecting the tropical cyclone formation and movement there is a need to deploy ocean observance systems.

(j) There is a need to improve design of tide gauge to capture storm surges and augmentation of their network along east and west coast of India.

(k) There is an inescapable need to improve the seismic monitoring systems, by interlinking various monitors and networking it through V Sat systems to facilitate dissemination of seismic related activity in real time.

(l) The high frequency micro wave images have great utility as a warning and forecasting system specially when placed in polar orbits on orbiting polar satellites. The analysis of the data transmitted by them should be done in real time.

19. **Structural Measures.** These are the measures entailing improvement of shelters, roads etc which go a long way in reducing the disasters. Some of them are as under:-

(a) Construction of storage facilities at a suitable scale for food, fodder and essential relief material.

(b) Improvement of road network in terms of road capacity to take sustained traffic during any disaster.

(c) Retrofitting of buildings, building foundations and structures as a component of disaster management should be adopted as a policy of the Government of India as well as the State Government.

20. **Human Resource Development.** Following measures are required to be adopted with regards to human resource development:-

(a) There is a dire need for trained professional in all fields of disaster related activities be it construction, rescue or medical assistance.

(b) The number of trained people must be adequate along with the training of trainers. This will assist in improving disaster awareness.

(c) There is a requirement for updating, rehearsals, mock drills and simulations, to keep the plans realistically equipped to address all possible contingencies.

21. **Police and Para Military Force.** Police and Paramilitary forces like the CRPF etc play a vital role in managing disasters. Some of the measures recommended to improve their functioning are as under:-

(a) There is a requirement of making separate financial provisions for their training and equipping of these forces.

(b) All activities of the police and paramilitary organisation need to be coordinated for optimum results.

(c) Training of these organisations must be carried out in consonance with the local disaster management schemes, with clear cut jobs demarcated for these organisations. Resources like air transport, medical supplies etc needs to be dedicated to these services.

22. **Civil Defence and Home Guards.** There is a requirement of synergising the efforts of civil defence and home guards in the overall disaster management network. A comprehensive role for these organisations must be formalised in a harmonised structure for disaster management. Following steps need to be taken in this regard:-

(a) The state disaster, management act, should include civil defence as one of the components of disaster management.

(b) Some of the departments which are required to be co-opted into the disaster management process are Department of Science and Technology, Ministry of Family Welfare and Ministry for Environment and Forests.

(c) There is a need for a multidisciplinary unity, which would come into motion for activating and following up various functions and responsibilities, entrusted to DGCD under the union war book during war and to manage disasters.

23. **Youth Movement.** Disaster management should form a part of curriculum for NCC, boy scouts, Girls guides and NSS. They should be incorporated at the local level for support during any disaster. If harnessed properly they can become a force multiplier.

Recommended Measures for Quick Response

24. Quick response to any disaster reduces the number of casualties drastically. Response mechanises are to be worked out in detail for different situations. A number of factors govem quick response to a situation viz the interagency coordination, early warning systems in place, networking/ coordination SOPs, checklists, manuals, etc. The concept of trigger mechanism has been incorporated in the HPC report as a quick response mechanism. The trigger mechanism has been envisaged as a preparedness plan whereby the receipt of signal of an impending disaster would simultaneously energise and activate the mechanism for response and mitigation without loss of crucial time.

Some of the after issues pertaining to the aspect of quick response are discussed in succeeding paragraphs.

25. **Early Warning.** The early warning systems like the Doppler radars, seismographs etc have to be in place, functional at all times, to initiate proper actions to mitigate loss of life and property. These systems should be based on parameters developed for the trigger mechanism and give an indication of the level or magnitude of mobilisation required by the responders.

26. **Networking/Coordination.** Networking of various services and agencies involved in disaster management would certainly improve the response.

27. **SOPs, Formats, Checklists and Manuals**

(a) There is a need for prescribing SOPs, formats and field manuals for various agencies involved in disaster management to ensure uniformly of procedure thus ensuring quick response.

(b) Experienced officers should be deputed in limited geographical area for overall control. Incident command system must be utilised at the site of disaster.

(c) A 'Source book on District Disaster Management' has been finalised by Lal Bahadur Shastri National Academy of Administration, Mussoorie could be used as a basis of developing various manuals.

28. **State of the Art Control Rooms/Emergency Operation Centres**

(a) There is a requirement of setting up an Emergency Operation Centre (EOC) at each level up to at least the level of variable districts. These EOCs will be the new centres for conducting and coordinating all disaster related activities, including interagency coordination.

(b) These EOCs will be state-of-the-art with all modern facilities for networking and functioning in an international environment. The communication will be on UHF, VHF, low band, HF and Amateur radio frequencies. There will be a satellite link right up to taluka level with facilities of audio-video streaming, video conferencing and complete computer support at district, state and national levels.

(c) An emergency operation centre being the hub of all activities should comprise of certain essential components viz EOC room, EOC analysis room, Emergency Information Centre (EIC), Communication, reference library, Functional area work cells, Armed forces etc.

(d) The EOC room would be connected on LAN and would have digitised maps, servers, emergency response plans etc.

(e) Armed forces should be a part of the EOC to use their expertise in handling disasters and their command, control and communication facilities.

(f) All the EOCs should be interlinked with each other.

29. **Rapid Response Teams.** One of major lessons learnt during the past disasters in India was the absence / inadequacy of relief and rescue teams. These need to be constituted since these are the actions tools in case of any disaster. Following merit attention in this regard:-

(a) There is a requirement of developing rescue teams at the state level under an appropriate authority for deployment in case of a disaster. The team of strength 200 to 300 personnel should be trained suiting peculiar disaster related problems of the state.

(b) Search and Rescue teams, Disaster Medical Assistance Teams, Disaster Mortuary Assistance Teams, Specialised Emergency Operation Teams and medical assistance teams to be instituted at the state and district levels.

(c) The small search and rescue teams could be formed from interdisciplinary cadres, by reorienting the fire services and civil defence stratums in all metros, state capitals and valuable urban centres.

(d) Setting specialised Emergency Operations Teams to NBC disasters viz Nuclear Emergency Teams, Chemical Emergency Teams etc. The medical examination and post mortem teams would be established under the aegis of police authorities.

(e) An equipment cache can be maintained for various teams for each type of disaster, Teams and the geographical location.

30. **Delivery of Relief.** It has been learnt that there is no shortage of relief material. The problem area is the despatch of this relief material

to the correct person at the correct time and place. This presently is a grey area. There is an urgent requirement for an organisational setup at various levels to cope with this problem. Such a model can be formulated on the lines of SUMA, as discussed earlier. The involvement of community plays an important role in this. When addressing the relief requirement of disaster victims, focus should be placed on the quality and minimum standards of relief. The State and District authorities of vulnerable states should prepare socio-cultural needs in relief supplies. The rights of the victims to appropriate relief and dignified treatment should be ensured.

Recommended Measures – Strategic Aspects

31. **International Cooperation.** The United Nations and its specialised agencies very often play a key role in disaster relief. The primary actors in coordinating United Nations assistance in Natural disaster relief operations are the office of the United Nations Disaster Relief Coordinator (UNDRO) in Geneva and the United Nations Development Programme (UNDP). The main responsibilities and areas of activity are to establish and maintain cooperation with all organisations, to mobilise, direct and coordinate all relief activities and to assist the government of a disaster stricken country. International cooperation in science and technology of disasters is being pursued in India by the Departments of Science and Technology. International cooperation efforts have not been synergised to the extent desired. Some of the aspects which merit consideration are as under:-

(a) Voluntary contribution in terms of human resources sharing and financial support from government, international organisations, UN agencies and other sources need added care.

(b) Bilateral and multilateral programmes in the framework of mutually agreed protocols should be accorded priority.

(c) There is requirement of defining responsibilities for assisting and receiving organisations in the areas of humanitarian relief and response operations.

(d) International assistance programmes should not be limited to the calamity area, but should also have a component to build nation wide resilience.

(e) There is a requirement to prepare a protocol and detailed SOP for timely receipt of International Humanitarian response and assistance.

(f) There is a requirement for setting up a committee for coordination of international cooperation.

32. **Review of Disaster Mitigation Strategy.** Following measures need to be taken with regards to disaster mitigation strategy:-

(a) Development of multifaceted research and development infrastructures.

(b) Improve public awareness and human resource development.

(c) Creation of financial infrastructure for disaster prevention and mitigation.

(d) Safety of important installations like bridges, dams, nuclear power plants etc.

(e) Conducting technical audits, to discern any shift from regular practices and to detect anomalies.

33. **Creation of Information Network.** There is a requirement of creating an intelligent, integrated and comprehensive data base as a subset of disaster knowledge network. The information network should be a network of networks. It should serve as an interactive platform. Efforts should be made to network information domains of international agencies. There is also a requirement to exploit Global Information network, by having requisite links.

34. **Role of Media.** The Press Council of India celebrates the annual press day on November 16 each year. The theme for the year 2000 was "Role of Media in Disaster Management – preparing people to cope with Disasters". The HPC thus recommended 3rd December every year to be celebrated as National Prayer Day to commemorate Bhopal Gas Tragedy. The role of electronic media has during recent times emerged as a major component of disaster management, as was demonstrated during the recent Tsunami. Indian society which is still unreachable by the electronic media can be addressed by the print media which can generate appropriate community awareness.

35. **Role of Armed Forces.** The Indian armed forces are not the most suited for disaster management but they are deployed due to their rich experience and organisational structure. However, their services

should be utilised as a last resort and be called upon to interfere and take on specific tasks only when the situation is beyond the capability of civil administration. The following points however need to be implemented:-

(a) The employment of armed forces should be restricted to a minimum duration and only if out of the hands of civil administration.

(b) A military coordinating officer should be a part of the disaster management team at all levels.

(c) There could be a case in point to raise special disaster management battalions on the lines of Ecological battalions. Border Roads Organisation, where available, should be suitably incorporated.

(d) The Army commands may have fully equipped nodal centres to coordinate all disaster related activity. The armed forces should have a dedicated component of personnel and equipment at the unit level.

(e) The potential of ex-servicemen should be exploited to form a nucleus team at lower levels.

36. **NGOs.** The role of NGOs is extremely important in down-sizing the impact of disasters. The main aspects of NGO cooperation are donation, skill, grant, application and offering services. NGOs should be involved in civil defence and other organisations for disaster management by supplementing and not supplanting these services. NGOs are better equipped to handle accident relief rather than actual real time rescue. They can be used for ambulance services, medical services, rehabilitation activities like arrangement of food, shelter and clothing etc. NGOs should be co-opted down to Taluka levels and provided with training to handle modern communication equipment and other technology intensive gadgets.

37. **Corporate Sector.** There is a need to identify the infrastructures, equipment, expertise and other resources of large private and public sector units and its incorporation into the local, state and national disaster management plans. The corporate sector can help create markets for the produce of our cottage and village industries to generate gainful rural employment by extending this facility through their own marketing networks.

Recommended Measures – Training

38. The LBSNAA, the state ATIs and the NCDM are emerging as part of nation wide structure for disaster management. All training of all organisations should have a component of disaster management. The training facilities already existing need to be modernised and upgraded.

39. There is a requirement of organising workshops at suitable locations to discuss and evolve the necessary actions and planning for various types of disasters. The R & D and educational institutions may be directed to conduct the studies addressing the problems faced by hazardous industry and specific department. The disaster management personnel should be trained in use of emergency communication facilities. A consolidated and comprehensive training syllabus should be formulated by all agencies to suit their specific requirement in particular and inter agency operation in general.

However there are certain threats that plague the system

H-4. In the aftermath of the Tsunami, major changes are already in the pipeline. Quite recently, the Disaster management bill has been passed by the parliament. How it unfolds on ground is yet to be seen. But let me tell, how I feel this organisation needs to be structured:

(a) At the apex we have the NDMA with the PM as the chairman. As recently, Gen NC Vij an Ex COAS has been appointed the Dy Chairman. An executive committee, comprising of secretaries from all relevant ministries should in conjunction with the NDMA. During emergencies a crisis management group should also become operational.

(b) To ensure adequate integration of the armed forces a DEFENCE CRISIS MANAGEMENT GROUP should be set up. And of course, most importantly a we need a state-of-the-art national emergency operations centre. This should have facilities like communications, conferencing and media briefing rooms and adequate emergency Support Function work stations.

BIBLIOGRAPHY

Books

1. S Narayan. Anthropology of Disaster Management.
2. Brown Barbara J. Disaster Preparedness and the UN.
3. E L Quarentelli. Disaster Theory and Research.
4. Ingrid Eckerman. The Bhopal Saga-Causes and Consequences of Worlds Largest Industrial Disaster.
5. B Narayan. Disaster Management.
6. Brigadier (Dr) HK Kar. Silent Warfare. Managing Nuclear, Chemical and Biological Disasters.
7. Randolph Kent. Anatomy of Disaster Relief – International Network in Action.
8. Fredrick C Curry. Disaster and Development.

Articles

9. Shama Vinod K. "India Disaster Management Profile."
10. Rao Someshwar B. "Shortcomings of Existing Disaster Management Mechanism and Remedial Measures at State and District Levels in Tackling Disaster Situations."

Papers and Publications

11. Australia, Counter Disaster Handbook.
12. US Disaster Management Manual.
13. Army Training Command. 1996. Policy Approach and Role of Various Organisations for Disaster Management in India.
14. HPC Report on Disaster Management.
15. Paper on Incident Command System.

Newspapers and Magazine Articles

16. India Today. November 7, 2005.

Internet Sites

17. Govt of India home page on disaster management
18. www.rothstein.com Emergency management. Information on Crisis Management.

How to Manage a Crisis

19. www.info.com. Disaster management.

20. www.crisisresponsejournal.com.

21. www.Commerce-Database.com

22. www.SourceTool.com

23. Management. Management - Great Resources, Facts and Solutions providers. www.download-hub.com.

24. Disaster Management. Disaster Recovery Systems and Disaster Prevention Products. BlueClaw-DB.com

25. IT Disaster Management. Disaster Management and Recovery. Guide to IT Disaster Recovery. Recovery-Disaster.info.

26. News results for Disaster management - View today's top stories.

27. Emergency disaster centre in Mumbai soon - Business Standard - 29 Dec 2005.

28. www.ndmindia.nic.in National Disaster Management in India.

29. www.wcdm.org WCDM - 16th World Conference on Disaster Management, June 18-21. A conference sponsored by the Canadian Centre for Emergency Preparedness focusing on the changing face of disaster management, July 10-13, 2005, Toronto.

30. Information and services relating to the four pillars of all-hazards disaster management: preparedness, response, recovery and mitigation. www.disasterhelp.gov.

31. University of Wisconsin Disaster Management Centre. The Disaster Management Centre at the University of Wisconsin has served the learning needs of disaster/emergency management professionals in the developing ... dmc.engr.wisc.edu/ .1 Jan 2006.

32. www.ukresilience.info.

33. www.cosla.gov.uk.

34. www.crowdsafe.com.

35. www.defra.gov.uk

References

Adams, Lavonne M. "Mental Health Needs 01 Disaster Volunteers: A· Plea for Awareness." Perspectives in' Psychiatric Care 43.1 (Feb 2007): 52-54.

After Hurricane Rita:- Chaos on the Coast and on the Hill. "The Economist 377-8446 (1 Oct 2005). and Rita." Louisiana Cultural Vistas 16.3 (Fall 2005: 36 and 38.

Allen, Don. "Acadian Ambulance and Air Med Play Huge Rules in Hurricane Rescues and Evacuations, (Terrible Storms 012005)." Acadiana Profile 25.2 (Oct 2005): 36-38.

Angers, Trent. "Louisiana Gulf Coast Slammed by Two Major Hurricanes in Less than a Month (Terrible Storms 012005)." Acadiana Profile 25:2 (Oct. 2005): 16-24.

Audin, Curt. "Carbon Monoxide Poisoning Following a Natural Disaster: A Report on Hurricane Rita. Journal of Emergency Nursing: JEN 32 (2006): 409-411.

Ault, Susanne. "Rita Rumbles Retailers." Video Business 25.40 (3 Oct 2005): 8.

Balsamo, Gary; Martha Littlefield-Chabaud, and Terry Conger. "Hurricane Response in Louisiana: The Animal Perspective." Louisiana Morbidity Report 16:6 (Nov/Dec 2005): 6-8.

Bark, Beetles. Problem in Hurricane Zones. "Forest and People" 56.3 (2006): 7, 29. Available: Serials Collection.

Barry, Don. "The Road Back: Battered Parish, Officials Bear the Brunt of Neighbours' Anguish." The New York Times 155.53626 (30 June 2006): A12.

Boullion, Michelle T. Workplace implications for hurricane affected Gulf Coast region industrial companies. phD-dissertation, Louisiana State University, 2007.

Bradley, Vertna, ed. Hurricane Rita: Reflections of a Generation Witnessing Disaster. New York: iUniverse, 2006. 381p.

Breitenbeck, Gary, Johnny Saichuk, Howard Cormier and Sonny Viator, "Salt Damage to Agricultural Fields in South Louisiana." Louisiana Agriculture Magazine 50.3 (Summer 2007): 12-16.

Bush, George W. "Remarks Following a Tour of Recovery Efforts in the Areas Damaged by Hurricanes Katrina and Rita in New Orleans, Louisiana." Weekly Compilation of Presidential Documents 42.10 (13 Mar. 2006): 414-415.

Cameron, Parish. "The Long Road Back." Lagniappe. 24.1 (Jan 5, 2006) (series of articles).

Carpenter, Robert. "Telling the Unde ground Tell of Katrina and Rita." Underground Construction 61.9 (Sep 2006): 4.

Carpenter, S. Kay, et al. "Urban Evacuations and Rural America: Lessons Learned from Hurricane Rita." Public Health Reports 121 (2006): 775-779.

Chang, Joseph. "Storm to Intensify Tightness..." Chemical Market Reporter 268.11 (3 Oct 2005): 4.

Chauvin, Mindy. "Rita." Louisiana English Journal 10 (2006): 52.

Chisholm, Elizabeth Irene. Impact of hurricanes and flooding on buried urban infrastructure networks. MS Thesis, Louisiana Tech University, 2007. 195 leaves.

Chua, Alton 1. K. "A Tale of Two Hurricanes: Comparing Katrina and Rita through a Knowledge Management Perspective." Journal of the American Society for Information Science and Technology 58 (2007): 1518-1528.

Chuang, George T. "Houston, We've Got a Problem." Health Affairs 25 (2006): 488-489.

Compbell, Nell. "A Reckoning with Rita." Louisiana Cultural Vistas 17:1 (2006): 24-29.

Cormier, Eric. "Rebounding from Rita." Louisiana Cultural Vistas 17.2 (2006):

Cummings, Kristin et al. "Health Effects of Exposure to Water-Damaged New Orleans Homes Six Months After Hurricanes Katrina and Rita." American Journal of Public Health. 98 (2008): 869-875.

Daley, WR. "Public Health Response to Hurricanes Katrina and Rita — United States; 2005." MMWR: Morbidity and Mortality Weekly Report 55.9 (10 Mar. 2006): 229-231.

Frey, William H. and Audrey Singer. "Katrina and Rita Impacts on Gulf Coast Population: First Census Findings." The Brookings Institution Special Analysis in Metropolitan Policy, 2006, 22p.

Gates, Jamie. Surviving Rita: -Hope amid Ruin in Southwest Louisiana. Lake Charles LA: American Press, 2006, 175p.

Health Consultation: Mallard Bay Landing Bulk Plant Post Hurricane Soil Sampling Evaluation, Cameron Parish Louisiana. Baton Rouge: Louisiana Department of Health and Hospitals, 2006, 19p.

Hebert, Barbara B. and Mary B. Ballard. "Children and Trauma: A Post-Katrina and Rita Response." Professional School Counselling 11 (2007): 140-144.

Hennessy, Jefferson. "Hurricane Rita's Unwelcome Visit to Southwest Louisiana (Terrible storms of 2005)." Acadiana Profile 25.3 (Dec 2005): 30-31, 33.

Hill, John. "Recognizing Cameron's Plight." Lagniappe. 24.19 (Oct 5, 2006): 12-14.

Houze, Robert J. et al. "Hurricane Intensity and Eyewall Replacement." Science 315.5816 (2 Mar 2007).- 1235-1239.

Houze, Robert J.et al. "The Hurricane Rainband and Intensity Change Experiment: Observations and, Modeling of Hurricanes Katrina, Ophelia, and Rita." Bulletin of the American Meteorological Society 87(2007): 1503-1521.

Howard, Jennifer. "Stories fro", the Storm." Chronicle ofHigher Education 54.3 (14 Sep 2007): -AiO-Ail.

Hurricane Rita Rapid Response Wind Water Line Report. Task Order 446. Gaithersburg MD URS Group, 2006.41p. Available (Internet): Hurricane Rita Recovery Plan: City of Lake Charles LRA Initiatives. Lake Charles LA: City of Lake Charles, 2007.18p.

"Hurricane Rita Strikes Texas and Louisiana Coasts." Facts on File 65.338i (29 Sep-2005): 663-666.

Hurricane, Rita: "Little Damage, Much Disruption." Chemical Week 167.32 (28 Sep 2005): 8.

Hurricanes Katrina and Rita: "Lessons Learned by Doctors and Hospitals." Fire Engineering 159.9 (Sep 2006): 44-46.

Iles Curt ed. Hearts Across the Water: Stories of Hope from Hurricanes Katrina, Rita d the Tsunami. Dry Creek LA: Creekbank Stories,2005.218p.

Integrated Ecosystem Restoration and Hurricane Protection: Louisiana's Comprehensive Master Plan for a Sustainable Coast. Baton Rouge: Louisiana Coastal Protection and Restoration Authority, 2007. 113p.

Jasper, Pal, and Carl Lindahl. "The Houston Survivor Project: An Introduction." Callaloo 29 (2006): 1504-1505.

Javetski, John. "Preparation Keyed Entergy's Responses to Katrina, Rita." Power 150.4 (May 2006): 35-38.

Johnson, Richard D. II "Post Hurricane Black Turpentine Beetle Damage." MS thesis, McNeese State U; 2007. 39 leaves Knabb, Richard D., Daniel P. Brown, and Jamie R. Rhome. Tropical Cyclone Report: Hurricane Rita, 18-26 September 2005 Miami FL: NOAA National Hurricane Centre. 2006. 33p.

Kaiser, J. "Scientific Community. Hurricane Rita Spares Major Research Institutions." Science 309.5744 (30Sep 2005): 2143.

Kolin, Philip C. and Susan Swarthwout, eds. Hurricane Blues: Poems about Katrina and Rita. Cape Girardeau MO: Southeast Missouri State U Press, 2006, 181p.

Notes

1. Australian Counter Disaster Handbook, p. 1.
2. Prasad Hari - Crisis Management Trishul.
3. Brown Barbara J. - Disaster Preparedness and United Nations. p. 3.
4. *Ibid.*
5. Brown op cit., p. 5.
6. Brown op cit., p. 6.
7. Parasu Raman S and Unnikrishnan PV, Disaster Response in India: p. 4. An over view. India Disasters Report towards a policy initiative.

8. Bose BL Tragic Tremors, Statesman. 02 November 93.
9. DSSC Handout- Disaster Relief, p. 7.
10. DSSC Op. cit. p. 8.
11. Keith and Smith. Environmental Hazards, p. 79.
12. Keith and Smith. Op cit, p. 79.

Case Studies: E-governance

"To my mind, technology is an enabler and good governance essentially is a management project. I believe, in the years to come, Gujarat will emerge stronger as a state simply because of the empowerment of the masses that is happening all along."[1]

Technology led Strategy

E-government: the realities of using IT to transform the public sector Abstract: This paper examines how electronic government is being used in the delivery and improvement of public services in the UK, and the actual and potential problems inherent in this. Although there have been examples of very creative use of electronic government in the public sector, there have also been numerous spectacular failures. This paper highlights a number of problematic issues surrounding its use. These include the fact that government's two central aims, namely high quality customer service and value-for-money, could potentially be in conflict; and the lack of evidence to support the claim that the use of technology in service delivery results in less bureaucracy and increased quality. Clearly these tensions and issues need to be much more fully explored so that a "government for people" can be created. The paper concludes by posing the question: Can e-government produce truly innovative, responsive public services, or merely exacerbate electronically, existing shortcomings?

A Case Study of Karnataka, Kerala and Odisha : Strategies in Good Governance

The managerial orientation that is making way into the domain of public administration with thrust on economy, efficiency and effectiveness, is also emphasising the pursuance of governance for development by governments. This is a global phenomenon, our approach to development is now acquiring a new holistic orientation, integrating economic aspects, political elements and social processes. The human dimension to development based on accountability, responsiveness, decentralisation and empowerment is gaining importance. It is being increasingly realised that governance for development has to orient towards building and strengthening human capacities and capabilities and creating a conducive environment that fosters individual dignity and equality and achieving sustainable human development. This calls for unfolding various issues of concern in governance and devising suitable strategies for human governance. Good Governance Kautilya in his treatise Arthasastra elaborated the traits of the king of a good governance state as "in the happiness of his subjects lies his happiness, in their welfare his welfare, whatever pleases himself, he does not consider as good, but whatever pleases his subjects he considers as good" (Sharma, L.N. and Sushmita Sharma, 1998). Plato is credited with developing the concept of the philosopher king as the ideal ruler Aristotle was perhaps the first political theorist to deal with the term "governance", when he classified political organisations by indicating the manner in which they were ruled by a kind of numerical court of rule by one (dictatorship), a few (autocracy), or many (democracy) (Sinclair, 1962). Kautilya mentions the following few imperatives of good governance for a king (Sharmasastry, R.1929):

1. Merge his individuality with his duties.
2. Guide administration.
3. Avoid extremes without missing the goal.
4. Lead a disciplined life with a code of conduct.
5. Pay fixed salaries and allowances.
6. Maintain law and order.
7. Stress on lekhaks (writers).
8. Carry out preventive/punitive measures against corrupt officials.
9. Replace bad administrators by good ones.[2]
10. Emulate administrative qualities.

The World Bank in its Document

Governance and Development 1992 defined governance as the manner in which power is exercised in the management of a country's economic and social resources for development. The bank came to realise that "good governance is central to creating and sustaining an environment which fosters strong and equitable development and it is an essential complement to sound economic policies. It has defined good governance as the one epitomised by predictable, open, and enlightened policy making, a bureaucracy imbued with a professional ethos acting in furtherance" of the public good, the rule of law, transparent process and a strong civil society participating in public affairs. Poor governance (on the other hand) is characterised by arbitrary policy making, unaccountable bureaucracies, unenforced or unjust legal, a civil society unengaged in public life and widespread corruption. It identified the following three distinctive aspects of good governance.

1. The form of the political regions, military or civil, parliamentary or presidential, authoritative or democratic.
2. The process by which authority is exercised in the management of a country's economic and social resources for development.
3. The capacity of governments to design, formulate and implement policies and to discharge government functions. The characteristics of good governance laid down by UNDP are as follows:

1. Participation, 2. Rule of Law, 3. Transparency, 4. Responsiveness, 5. Consensus Orientation, 6. Equity, 7. Effectiveness and Efficiency, 8. Accountability and 9. Strategic Vision.

E-Governance

In the fast changing scenario, e-governance has become not only necessary but essential in a setup where people are the biggest stakeholders.

In this direction, the Union Ministry of Information Technology has already made a number of initiatives, including the setting up of a centre for e-governance at Massachusetts Institute of Technology (MIT) which will function as a forum for government officials, legislators, industry, and various other key players to come together, discuss learn and explore issues of shared importance. Some of the objectives indicative of a road map for e-governance are as follows:

1. Develop a system for the seamless transfer of information between offices dealing with proper administration, both at the Centre as well as the States.
2. Set-up and /or facilitate specific communication networks for the government sector.
3. Assist Central and State governments in identification and implementation of suitable hardware and software packages for e-governance.
4. Establishing links worldwide, among the institutions engaged in similar activities so as to optimize and for benefits by builders/sustaining platforms for interchange of ideas and experiences.
5. Develop special pilot projects or paperless government on like through an electric intelligent government concept by extensive use of electronic forms and data entry interface through the use of the web and internet technology.
6. Build convergence into connected services delivery programmes related to citizen devices.
7. Develòp commercial and governmental systems for issues and managing signatures/electronic signatures and smart cards.
8. Identify measures for suitable protection of data during filling up, transmission and alterations by using a combination of security measures.
9. Establish Industry Consultative Committees (ICC), Citizen Consultative Committees (CCC), Ministries Consultative Committees (MCC) to provide a forum to various users, implementation groups and organisations to contribute towards the 25 per cent goal and beyond. The e-government solution strongly supports digitisation of government administration by using network technology and security technology to meet the needs of both the people providing services and those receiving them. As the internet spreads throughout the society, and in public as well as private sectors, operations such as e-applications and e-procurement become common place. Internet access is thus prerequisite to the e-government

solution. Strategies for Reaching out to people Undeniably, in order to reach people and with a view to making them partners of the systems and processes of governance, greater emphasis needs to be laid on school education, especially computer education. The biggest challenge for this is making personal computers (PCS) available at an affordable cost. The Hardware Vision 2005 Plan envisages PC penetration to 26 per 1000 people by 2005 from the present 6 per 1000. According to a Confederation of Indian Industry (CII) paper, the best way of achieving this would be to go local in terms of local needs, local problems, local solutions and local contents while making PCs affordable.[3] Next to government and business establishments, schools would be the biggest consumers of PCs. The CII estimated that 18 million PCs would be needed at the rate of 20 sets in each of nine lakh schools in the country. To be affordable, the price needs to be brought down to below ₹ 15,000 per computer. The Massachusetts Institute of Technology (MIT) and the Government of India have agreed to collaborate on a one year project to create the Media Laboratory Asia, which is conceived as an independent, non-profit organisation. MIT plans to develop the technology to bring the benefits of the most sophisticated emerging technologies to the daily problems of India's poorest and least educated people. The Media Lab-Asia in collaboration with IIT, Mumbai has also undertaken an agro explorer programme so that farmers can benefit by various relevant information. The Ministry of Information Technology is very sensitive to the problem of language barrier and has therefore introduced a scheme of languages and IT localisation. Once the scheme becomes operational, it will go a long way in reaching out to and empowering the masses. This is an important strategy for the country's development. Strategies of Karnataka: The IT initiative of Karnataka aims to provide direct citizen interface, improve human resources and connectivity and improve the efficiency of government officials. IT has been applied in the following areas. Secretariat Local Area Network (LAN). This Programme envisages computerisation of all secretariat departments. It enables citizens to know the status of their file and the number of days they took to be cleared at various stages. It is a significant step in delivering good governance to the masses.

Khajane

This ₹ 45 crores project is in an advanced stage of implementation. The system keeps accounts for all payments of the state, which totals to approximately ₹ 24,000 crores a year. Besides government payments, the system makes payments to six lakh employees, three lakh pensioners, thirteen lakh aged, widowed and handicapped pensioners. The accounts, available, real time, are stored in data centres in Bangalore and a disaster centre in Dharwad. The STP is the network partner. The major benefit of the project is the instantaneous reconciliation of government accounts. In addition the system displays the money spent on all government schemes in every village. This enhances transparency and improves quality. Bhoomi and Nondani Bhoomi is the state's computerised land records project. It aims to cover 60 lakh farmers in 175 taluks. Operational in 12 sub-registration offices in Bengaluru, it accounts for about 40 per cent of the total revenue. This computerised registration is operating in 48 taluks of the state. Yava.com This programme envisages 225 training centres all over the state run by prestigious firms like Aptech, NIIT, SSI etc. The fees in the centre are already reduced. The government gives subsidy of ₹ 1500 for a three month course. A maximum subsidy of ₹ 4500 is offered for a six month course. The programme aims to train over 1,00,000 rural youths in a year. Over 100 centres are operational at present.

E-Lottery

The government has floated a tender to setup 10,000 terminals all over the state. Apart from running the electronic lottery the kiosks could be used to disseminate other public information.

Mukhya Vahini

This is the Chief Ministers decision support system. Presently it tracks the CMS instructions, the projects sanctioned under the Global Investor meet, the constituency management system, summarised data on major projects in health, housing, and other social sector schemes. Many modules are already in use. Common Entrance Test Karnataka has numerous institutions of higher education and attracts students from other Indian states and countries. Every year the state conducts the common entrance test. Over 1,50,000 students take the exams and around 50 per cent are from outside the state. The entire admission process is absolutely transparent. The fact that students from outside the state participate in large number shows their confidence in the local administration. Before computerisation, the process attracted many questions from elected representatives and a lot of litigation. Now the system is so transparent that it has rid itself of both.

Other Initiatives

The Commercial Tax Department tracks goods using check post entries. Information about movement of goods is automatically put in the dealers assessment file. In terms of tax collection per GDP, the state is one of the best in India. The Insurance Department uses computers to track all the government vehicle insurance details. Police salary bills are computerised. The irrigation department has a major project on e-tendering and e-procurement. Silk trading exchange in Karnataka has been computerised since 1985.

Friends Project of Kerala

Friends is an extraordinarily successful project in Kerala where an IT enabled, single window, front end interface called Friends (Fast, Reliable, Instant, Efficient, Network for Disbursement of Services) was set up for availing a range of popular public services like payment of taxes and utility charges and renewal of licenses without waiting for back-end computerisation or systems integration in the government. In the span of 3 years, this project has expanded to serve 13 million people in 12 of 14 districts in Kerala.[4]

Project Application

Usually, a citizen in Kerala has to interact with at least eight to ten government departments/agencies for accessing routine services. Traditional payment systems necessiate visiting each of these government offices and waiting in tedious queue. Some transactions take as long as a day to be completed. Often staff are rude and some times bribes are demanded through touts and intermediaries. The poor public perception of the government arises from these unpleasant experiences. Each Friends centre receives almost 1000 visitors every day and users are delighted with the service levels. The average waiting time is ten minutes. Unlike most government offices, the ambience here is pleasant and the service is courteous and corruption free. The project, likely to receive ISO certification soon. It has been a success largely because of its focus on training and motivates the employees manning these centres.

The Philosophy

The philosophy of Friends is to treat the citizen, who is paying for the services, as a valued customer. The underlying concept is simple to provide an integrated electronic interface whereby citizens can remit taxes, pay bills, access commonly required government services and obtain the latest information on government programmes. It was decided to focus on front-end computerisation, rather than wait the completion of back end computerisation of these departments to make these services immediately available. The pilot project was launched in Thiruvanthapuram in June. On the basis of its success, the project was extended to other districts.

An Innovative Approach

At Friends, 20 computerised counterwork from 9 A.M. to 7 P.M. on all days of the week, in an any service any counter mode. A computerised queue management system eliminates queues and customers receive a token and await their run in a pleasant setting. The services offered are free. Payments can be made in cash or by demand draft. A help desk is on hand for any required assistance. The centerworks on the principle of 'collect and remit' and 'receive and forward' by interacting with the concerned departments/agencies. Eventually, the computers at the centre will be linked with the servers of the departments on a real time basis, once the back-end computerisation is completed. Friends Computers are equipped to handle more than 1000 kinds of bills or documents. The software is robust enough to handle these requirements and new modules can be incorporated when new department / service are added. The indicative list of services offered boyfriends counters are water and power utility payments, bill payments, property tax, professional tax, traders license fee, building tax, land tax, revenue recovery, fee for new ration card, one time vehicle tax, motor vehicle tax etc. A notable feature of the project is that its personnel have been drawn from the participating departments, and no new jobs have been created. There are 50 staff members in each centre, and 500 people have thus been inducted. An innovative feature of the project is the employment opportunity it provides to poor women from self help group, who manage the help desks and provide supplementary services.

Dramatic Impact on People

Friends project has been the change in citizens perception about the government. Moreover, visitors have been impressed by the courteous and corruption free atmosphere. Friends has also demonstrated that ordinary government functionaries and poor women can deliver high quality services in an atmosphere of excellence. The demonstration value of this project is inestimable. An unforeseen, but key outcome is that Friends has succeeded in providing positive feedback on the benefits of inducting IT in all the participating departments.

Odisha Gramsat Pilot Project

The Grams at Pilot project initiated by the Government of Orissa is a significant step in good governance. It addresses issues of transparency, accountability, responsiveness, reduction of corruption, training and skills development, peoples participation, project planning and monitoring, disaster warning etc. It also provides live communication between the state capital, districts and blocks.

Infrastructure and Functioning

The Gramsat Pilot Project is a satellite-based digital communication network. The segment is supported by INSAT-3B in extended C-band. The ground segment of the network consists of a hub centre at Bhubaneswar, VSATnodes at the district and block headquarters and DRS (Direct Reception System) nodes at gram panchayats. The hub centre at Bhubaneswar will consist of a digital earth station providing satellite up link. The Vsat hub will have electronics with a network manager and a series of server computers holding data base and software. There will be proxy server acting to the internet. The centre will also have a transmission studio to serve at the teaching and for interactive training and at the transmission end for broadcasting. At each of these 314 blocks and 30 district headquarters, there will be Vsat hard ware consisting of Vsat electronics with access router. The Gramsat network proposes to provide this connectivity to 314 blocks and 30 district headquarters, the network is capable of supporting more

Vsat nodes. It is also proposed to provide direct reception system (DRS) to 800 gram panchayats in 8 KBK districts. Application and Utility: The project proposes to create a master data base which will include spatial data on land information such as land use, land form, groundwater, geology, soils, water body, village and forest boundaries, rail/road network, river and drainage network, canal network, telecommunications and power distribution network and rainfall etc. It shall be applied for interactive training for skill development, technology transfer and dissemination of information. The development information can rebroadcast to people, field functionaries at the grass root level. Spatial and non-spatial geographic data base information can be accessed especial relating to natural resources, environment and infrastructure development. Management information system for e-governance can be achieved. Disaster warning, relief and rescue operations and reconstruction can be monitored through this project.

Computerisation/E-governance Initiative of Panchayati Raj Department

Panchayat Samities have emerged as powerful institutions for implementing schemes relating to poverty alleviation programme on Social Security Primary Education, Co-operatives, Welfare of SC/ST, Natural Disaster and MP/MLA LAD fund etc. Computerisation of 314 Blocks and 30 District Rural Development Agencies has been completed to monitor fund flow and project transparency. Steps have been taken to make the system more transparent for both project management as well as financial management by using "Rural Soft" and "Priasoft" Software. PAMIS is being developed to maintain daily cashbook. A total of 344 computer operators have been engaged in Block and District Rural Development Agencies. This will help the citizens to access the data regarding financial and physical details of projects at the Block level easily. Further the Panchayati Raj Department have already implemented one software named BETAN, for drawing salaries of all the employees of Blocks and D.R.D.As.

CASE STUDY: GUJARAT

e-Governance in Gujarat

Gujarat has taken a series of groundbreaking steps that mark out Gujarat as a role model of e-governance in India.

Vision

- An e-Governed Environment Transparent, accountable and efficient governance, seamlessly integrated government machinery, networked key functions like police, judiciary, transport, etc. Web interface for every government department, Board and corporation.
- Abundant Infrastructure, Enterprise Multipliers Extensive critical infrastructure and a sound e-commerce foundation, plentiful opportunities in IT enabled services.
- Digitally Empowered social Fabric Higher standard of living, complete computer literacy and e-education Networked and digitally accessed Libraries; Tele-medicines enabled Multiplied revenue generation and large disposable income.

Guided by a multidimensional vision of transforming Gujarat into an e-governed state, the government has implemented solutions through systematic requirements analysis, pilot tests and performance benchmarking. Scalability and Sustainability issues too have been considered prior to replicating the success stories on a larger canvas.

Be it G2C (Government to Citizens) or G2G (Government to Government) mode of transactions, the government of Gujarat has ensured that the bigger picture the overall socio-economic development of the state by empowering the common man is never out of sight.

Change Management

Gujarat is the only state to have initiated a massive training programme to reorient over 5,00,000 state government employees as Karma Yogis. The Karma Yogi Maha Abhiyaan, an initiative unique to Gujarat is all about sensitising the government officials towards their responsibilities. Over and above technology training, this comprehensive programme imparts skills such as self motivation, communication, emphatic listening, cost consciousness and team work. The result is a professional team of citizen friendly government officials who have evolved from ordinary workforce into proactive workforce.

GSWAN – the backbone of e-Governance applications

The Gujarat State Wide Area Network is one of the biggest IP (Internet Protocol) based network in the Asia Pacific and connects over

12,000 nodes of more than 2300 government offices in 25 districts and 225 talukas with the state headquarters in a closed user group.

The GSWAN essentially is the backbone of all e-Governance activities in Gujarat and this massive network enables a seamless video, voice and data connectivity down to the last mile.

BISAG – Application of Space Technology and Geo-informatics for Development.

BISAG – Bhaskaracharya Institute of Space Application and Geo-informatics is a state level nodal agency to facilitate the use of spatial and geo-spatial technologies for the planning and developmental activities pertaining to Agriculture, Land and Water Resource Management, Wasteland/Watershed Development, Forestry, Disaster Management and Education.

Equipped with a rich satellite data archive, a multi-disciplinary team, a state-of-the-art Remote Sensing, GIS and Image Processing Laboratory, SATCOM facility and an Academy of Geo-informatics for carrying out research and training - BISAG has been instrumental in helping developmental planning, natural resources audit and supporting decision-making processes across departments.

BISAG has developed very useful softwares like PRAGATI, Image Processing Software and SDIS - An Satellite imagery archival and retrieval software. Gujarat State has received National Award in the Best Product Category for "PRAGATI" software at Elitex-2005 organised by Department of Information and Technology, Government of India.

SICN – state-of-the-art connectivity

The Sachivalaya Integrated Communication Network (SICN) enables excellent connectivity between the various government offices. The electronic telephone system with over 7000 connections handles around 1,25,000 internal calls and a further 70,000 calls outside the network each day. The system has resulted in tremendous savings for the government on internal calls and also provides enhanced facilities such as voice mailbox, conference calling, CCTV and disaster communication. A state-of-the-art Server Farm integrated with the network has been commissioned with web servers, DNS servers, mail servers and database servers to enable the government departments to host and manage their websites locally.

IWDMS – Streamlining Documentation for knowledge-led governance

Being a repository of information, the Secretariat plays a crucial role in the governance of the state. Decision-making and policy — Formulation processes within the Secretariat involve receipt, dispatch and maintenance of a huge volume of correspondence. For improvised governance, it is hence critical to have an efficient document control and monitoring mechanism in place. Integrated Workflow and Document Management System (IWDMS) is a perfect fit solution which addresses these concerns and aims to standardise and streamline document management by leveraging the established networks in the Secretariat (Departmental LANs and GSWAN).

Digital Signature Certificates – For a secure digital world

Gujarat is the first state in the country to set up a Public Key Infrastructure for Digital Signature, which facilitates authentication and validation of digital documents. The GNFC promoted (n)Code Solutions has been awarded the commercial Certifying Authority License from the Controller of Certifying Authorities, Ministry of Information Technology for the issuance and management of Digital Signature Certificates under the Indian cyber laws. The PKI Project of GNFC has also won the e-Gov Project (Technology) award at CSI 2005. Disaster Management – The most humane applications of Information Technology.

SDRN - State Disaster Resource Network - is one of the key projects initiated by the state under the Disaster Risk Management Programme. It is a comprehensive database of disaster management related inventory which is so critical for an organised response in case of a disaster. With complete information on the disaster prone zones, vulnerable elements, demographic data of villages, socio-economic profile, search and rescue equipment availability, emergency contact numbers etc. already keyed into the system, this becomes an excellent decision-making tool for the government machinery to respond quickly to emergency situations, mitigate such disasters and minimise the damage.

Citizen Convenience Centres – Setting standards in One-Day Governance

The citizen's charter is a set of almost 72 events/occasions wherein a citizen comes in contact with a municipal corporation, a mamlatdar's office or a collectors office. Whether it was for payment of taxes and utility bills or for registration of birth or death, a visit to the government offices used to be a harrowing process for the citizens. Long queues at every counter of the ancient and dilapidated work places and apathetic employees behind these counters were accepted facts of life. All this has changed now. The once dusty, gloomy and highly bureaucratic offices have evolved into Centres of Excellence. These Citizen Convenience Centres now provide impeccable services at mind boggling speed. All types of certificates, applications, affidavits and licenses e.g., Issue of an Income certificate which used to take 25 days earlier, now gets done in a day. Successful implementation and functioning of City Civic Centres in Ahmedabad and Vadodara has led to the replication of this model in five other municipal corporations.

e-Nagarpalikas – One-Day Governance for Everyone

The exemplary success of the One-Day Governance model in cities and bigger towns has captured the imagination of government, citizens and regulatory bodies across the state. 121 Nagarpalikas have already started offering the benefits of One-Day Governance to the local citizens. And by the end of 2006, all 141 City Civic Bodies will evolve into e-Nagarpalikas. Certificates, Licenses, Street Light complaints, Garbage removal requests, Water tap applications – all these are now just a click away, and citizens in smaller towns too are experiencing a 'never before' convenience and transparency.

Gyan Ganga – The river of knowledge

Gyan Ganga is one of the most ambitious initiatives of the Government of Gujarat to ensure wireless internet connectivity to all 18,000 villages. At the heart of the Gyan Ganga is corDECT - a technology based on Wireless in Local Loop (WLL) - specially developed by IIT-Madras. Rural citizens can now access a host of online services such as e-mail, Internet browsing, land records, rural job opportunities, status of various government projects etc. and even consult specialists through video conferencing for their agricultural, veterinary and healthcare queries.Today, over 400 kiosks are already operational in several talukas and 1000 villages will be networked by the end of 2006. Over the next few years, Gyan Ganga will reach all villages and e-Governance services available through e-Gram would be integrated on this network.

e-Gram – e-Governance at the Panchayat Level

The basic objective of e-Gram is total computerisation of the Gram Panchayats. This e-Governance application entails computerisation at the village level itself for instant processing of birth and death registration and issuance of certificates such as agriculture, caste, income and electricity. The computerisation also includes tax collection and issuance of certain forms.

Encouraged by the successful implementation of a pilot project in the Valukad village of Bhavnagar, the government has set a target of implementing this e-Gram concept across all villages of Gujarat. By now 8835 Village Panchayats have been covered with e-Gram facility. Efforts have been continued and it has been planned to equip all 13753 Village Panchayats to have e-Gram facility by 31st March 2007. Panchayat Department has planned to roll out e-Gram services in all villages of Gujarat State. Government aims to make these centres self-sustainable and therefore it has been decided to provide Technical and Training Support to these e-Gram Computer Centres.

e-Dhara – Land Records Online

The objectives of initiative-Dhara are to ensure an efficient, accurate and transparent delivery mechanism, facilitate conflict resolution in ownership, provision of electronic records of rights to land owners at nominal rates and empowerment of land owners through timely and accurate information. This user friendly system with a local language interface benefits citizens as well as the administration. The land owners can get printed copies of their land-holding documents with ease and tampering with revenue records is minimised. From an administration perspective, the data retrieval is now simpler and detailed reports of land use, crops taken, source of water, type of electrical equipment fitted, trees etc. can be instantly generated. As a part of the e-Dhara project, 98 lakh 7x12 forms and 54 lakh 8A forms have already been computerised and available online at the taluka offices. A pilot has also been successfully undertaken to provide land records from village itself in Lodhika Taluka of Rajkot District and guidelines have been issued for its replication in all other villages.

Talim Rojgar

This dynamic portal site is a virtual employment exchange that handles a database of over 11 Lakh job seekers from all over the state. Data related to all the jobseekers registered in the 36 employment exchanges of Gujarat is registered on this site, making it one of the biggest and most comprehensive database of jobseekers. Prospective employers can make use of this database free of cost. Talim Rojgar has already facilitated employment to thousands of youth and this site not only brings unemployed people within easy reach of the prospective employers, it also offers career tips, vocational guidance, and useful information on self-employment opportunities and training schemes.

SWAGAT – An epitome of transparency

SWAGAT - State Wide Attention on Grievances by Application of Technology, is a unique online grievance redressal system to put the common man in direct touch with the highest office in administration. The fourth Thursday of every month is a SWAGAT day and citizens can walk in any district 'Jan Sampark' office and register their complaints. All complaints are registered and sent to the relevant departments for redressal. These departments have to be ready with their responses by 3 pm the same day. The DDO, Collector or the SP concerned have to remain present for the video conferencing meeting and the CM personally addresses these issues and recommends appropriate steps to resolve them. With the CM himself keeping a vigilant eye on the pending issues, there has been a marked change in grievance redressal and in just three years, over 25,000 grievances have been effectively resolved. Little wonder that Manchester University has recognised this application as a model case of e-Transparency.

SWIFT - State Wide Information on Financial Transactions

SWIFT facilitates Finance Department and other Government Departments for monitoring the financial transactions done by the department itself and their sub-offices at respective District Treasuries and Pay and Account Offices (PAOs).

Financial transactions and its monitoring is a vital part of every Government Department. The departments are mainly collecting the inputs from the lower level offices and deriving the expenditure incurred and its funds availability. The majority of these transactions are done through treasuries and PAOs and all the treasuries and PAOs have computerised their operations and connected to GSWAN. This has provided the opportunity to disseminate the information to each office and its head office simultaneously. Initially it started with the online status and voucher information for each bill. Now the data from all treasuries and PAO is compiled at state data centre on daily basis and consolidated statements are generated at each level.

CCIS - Comprehensive Case Information System at High Court of Gujarat

CCIS is developed to take care of a case from the stage of filing to its disposal and centralised counters are setup for filing and issue of processes like notices, writs etc. Several statistical reports for monitoring purpose are generated on daily/monthly/yearly basis. Public centric applications like availability of case status at the query counter and on the internet, advocate wise cause list, simple copy of the order/ judgment instantly, certified copies of the judgment / orders, list of registered matters of an advocate over a period of time, advocate diary (passbook facility for the advocates for getting the copy of cause list / orders / filing list etc.) are operational. Court Case Monitoring System (CCMS), a web based application has also been developed for facilitating Government Departments for monitoring the proceedings of their cases in various Courts.

IDS - Integrated Disease Surveillance System (IDS)

NIC has developed IDS for Department of Health and World Health Organisation (WHO). For 16 identified diseases, data of new cases and deaths are collected weekly at Remote Units, Corporation Hospitals and Medical Colleges (Hospitals attached to it). Data on weekly basis is entered at the district level and transferred to Central server at Gandhinagar for detail analysis including District-wise details of new cases and deaths. Comparison of syndromes and laboratory results can also be obtained. Concerned authority can monitor the status of remote units who have not reported data in last four weeks.

e-PRIMA (Panchayati Raj Institutes – Maintenance of Accounts)

e-Prima is primarily designed considering recommendations of Eleventh Finance Commission for monitoring the utilisatoin of local bodies grant for the development of Gram Panchayat, Taluka Panchayat and District Panchayat by using Information Technology (IT). Local fund officials will monitor financial data and progress of funds, income, expenditure, sources of revenue. This system captures data of opening and closing balance of PRIs, works carried out in PRIs under particular schemes, income and expenditure, closing balance, financial progress of funds received from CFC, State Government, own funds etc. Trainings have also been conducted for District, Taluka Panchayat staff, Talatis, Sarpanch, etc. about use of the system.

HMIS – Health Management Information System

The Hospital Management Information System (HMIS) has been envisaged to not only help the administrators to have better monitoring and control of the functioning of hospitals across the state using decision support indicators but also assist the doctors and medical staff to improve health services with readily reference patient data, work flow enabled less-paper process and parameterised alarms and triggers while patient treatment cycle. The HMIS monitors pre-defined health indicators and the embedded exception reporting enables decision-making by the hospital management and state level administrators for policy and strategic decisions.

Government's Futuristic Plan for IT Savvy Manpower

Government is contemplating CCC and CCC Plus courses for government employees. The content of these courses will address the change in the requirements for training government employees in today's context. Moreover, DOEACC "O" level certification State Government is considering proposal for making compulsory for the new entrants in the government. Thus, government is ensuring that it has IT Savvy Manpower in the long run. .

Industry-Institute Linkages – College to Career Programme

Government of Gujarat in collaboration with IBM had conducted a project INVITE – Initiative to Nurture a Vibrant Information Technology Ecosystem in 2005, which concluded in March-2006. Under this programme, more than 1800 Engineering and MCA students of about 31 colleges from 9 Universities have participated and they have developed a Prototype solution for local E-Governance needs at various levels. Under this project, technical seminars and workshops have been conducted in major cities across the state to benefit local IT Professionals and college teachers.

The Final Analysis

Happiness and prosperity of the citizens is the only legitimate objective of any good government. And the Government of Gujarat is on the right track. Whether it is ration cards or old age pensions; smart card licenses or gram panchayat computerisation; city civic centres or land records digitisation Gujarat is a state where technology has synchronised with civic needs.

- Red Tapism is being eliminated.
- Transactions are now absolutely transparent.
- Government offices are getting into a 'less paper' environment.
- File processing is now faster and efficient.
- Government employees have evolved into proactive Karma-yogis.

Be it the urban citizens in cities or the rural populace in remote villages the distance is dead and Good Governance is just a click away...The One-Day Governance concept is already operational in all the 225 talukas and citizens are reaping the real benefits of IT. Earlier, the minimum number of tables through which each application moved was 65. Now the number of tables through which each application in the citizens charter moves ranges from 5 to 30. And that too, electronically. This transformation has not happened overnight. It called for an overhaul and re-engineering of existing processes.

End Note

E-governance is good governance and every government is supposed to provide good governance to its citizens. Citizens want excellence in governance, high quality of governmental services delivered on time and minimum costs. They want governance to citizen centric. The focus must change from procedure-orientation, to service-orientation from supply driven to demand-driven governance. Govern-ments should try to give up ruling attitude and should endeavour serving attitude towards its owners, the citizens. Originality is good, we all pose to be original, but lack the originality to do something original. In that case, comparative governance studies and following the best and well done can benefit the governments. Effective use of Information Technology (IT) is increasingly becoming synonymous with good governance. It is all about connectivity. Connectivity brings proximity, which improves the delivery of services by the government. Truly information is power and the informed are powerful. Citizen should have access to information related to various policies, procedures, development schemes, government order and official pronouncements on matters concerning their life and work.

References

1. Bekkers, V.J.J.M. Governance in Modern Society (Eds) Oscar van Heffen et al, Kluer Academic Publishers, 2000.
2. Bhattacharya, M. New Horizons of Public Administration, Jawahar Publishers, 1998.
3. Minocha, O.P., Good Governance, New Public Management Perspective, The Indian Journal of Public Administration, July-Sept., New Delhi, 1998.
4. Mukhopadhyaay, A. Reinventing Government for Good Governance, The Indian Journal of Public Administration IIPA, July-Sept., 1998.
5. Government of India, An Agenda for Effective and Responsive Administration, Ministry of Personnel, Public Grievances and Pensions, New Delhi, November 1996.
6. Minocha, O.P., Good Governance, Concept and Operational Issues, Management in Government, Oct.-Dec. 1997.
7. E. Vayunandan, Dolly Mathew, (Eds) Good Governance Initiatives in India Prentice Hall of India, New Delhi, 2003.

Kulamani Padhi is the Asst. Registrar, Dairy Cooperatives, Directorate of Animal Husbandry and Veterinary Services, Odisha, Cuttack-1.

Bibliography

Internet Sites

1. www.dft.gov.uk

2. www.asa.uk.net
3. www.animaldisasters.com
4. www.audit-commission.gov.uk/comsafe
5. www.uneptie.org/pc/apell/disasters/lists/technological.html
6. www.basics.freeserve.co.uk/basics/home.htm
7. www.bbc.co.uk/connectinginacrisis/index.shtml
8. www.benfieldhrc.org
9. www.bl.uk/services/npo/npo.html
10. www.bacp.co.uk
11. www.britishcivildefence.org
12. www.redcross.org.uk
13. www.bsi-global.com
14. www.btp.police.uk
15. www.bea-fr.org/anglaise
16. www.cabinetoffice.gov.uk
17. www.coi.gov.uk
18. www.cieh.org
19. www.cacfoa.org.uk Papers and Publications
20. Australia, Counter Disaster Handbook.
21. US Disaster Management Manual.

Books

22. Fredrick, C Curry. Disaster and Development.
23. E L Quarentelli. Disaster Theory and Research.
24. Randolph Kent. Anatomy of Disaster Relief – International Network in Action.
25. Brown Barbara, J. Disaster Preparedness and the UN.

References

- (ed.). The Nation Builders: A Sesquicentennial History of the Corps of Topographical Engineers, 1838-1863. Washington, DC: US Army Corps of Engineers, 1988.
- Exploration and Empire. New York: Alfred A. Knopf: 1966.
- Bache, Richard Meade. Life of General George Gordon Meade.

Philadelphia: Henry T. Coates and Co., 1.898.

- Bancroft, Hubert Howe. A History of California. 7 vols. San Francisco: A.L. Bancroft and Co., 1884-1890. History of Mexico. 6 vols. San Francisco: AL Bancroft and Co., 1883-1888.
- Bashford, Herbert and Wagner, Harr, A Man Unafraid: The Story of John Charles Fremont. San Francisco: Harr Wagner Publishing Co., 1927.
- Bauer, K. Jack. The Mexican War, 1846-1848. New York: Macmillan Co., 1974.
- Bigelow, John. Memoir of the Life and Public Service of John Charles Fremont. New York: Derby and Jackson, 1856.
- Billington, Ray A. The Far Western Frontier, 1830-1860. New York: Harper and Row, 1950.
- Brooks, Nathan C. A Complete History of the Mexican War. Chicago: Rio Grande Press, 1965.
- Burr, Edward. "Historical Sketch of the Corps of Engineers, US Army." Occasional Papers of the Engineer School. No. 71. Washington, DC: Government Printing Office, 1939.
- Carleton, James Henry. Battle of Buena Vista. New York: Harper and Brothers, 1848.
- Clarke, Dwight L. Stephen Watts Kearny, Soldier of the West. Norman: University of Oklahoma Press, 1961.
- Cleaves, Freeman. Meade of Gettysburg. Norman: University of Oklahoma Press, 1960.
- Cowdrey, Albert E. A City for the Nation: The Army Engineers and the Building of Washington, D.C., 1790-1967. Washington, DC: US Army Corps of Engineers, Government Printing Office, 1979.
- Crump, Irving. Our Army Engineers. New York: Dodd Mead and Co., 1954.
- Cutts, James Madison. The Conquest of California and New Mexico. Philadelphia: Cary and Hart, 1847.
- De Voto, Bernard. The Year of Decision, 1846. Boston: Houghton Mifflin Co., 1943.
- Dellenbaugh, Frederick S. Fremont and '49. New York: Knickerbocker Press, 1914.
- Dufour, Charles L. The Maxican War; A Compact History, 1846-1848. New York: Hawthorn Books, 1968.
- Dyer, Brainerd. Zachary Taylor. Baton Rouge: Louisiana State University Press, 1946.
- Eisenhower, John S.D. So Far From God: The U. S. War with Mexico, 1846-1848. New York: Random House, 1989.
- Eyer, Alice. The Famous Fremonts and Their America. n.p.: Fine Arts Press, 1948.

- Freeman, Douglas Southall. Robert E. Lee, Q Biography. 4 vols. New York: Charles Scribner's Sons, 1933.
- Frost, J. The Mexican War and Its Warriors. New Haven, CT: H. Mansfield, 1849.
- Fry, Joseph Reese. A Life of General Zachary Taylor. Philadelphia: Grigg, Elliot and Co., 1847.
- General Taylor and His Staff Philadelphia: Grigg, Elliot and Co., 1848.
- Goetzmann, William H. Army Exploration in the American West, 1803-1863. New Haven, CT: Yale University Press, 1959.
- Goodwin, Cardinal. John Charles Fremont: An Explanation of His Career. Stanford, CA: Stanford University Press, 1930.
- Govan, Gilbert, and Livingood, James W. A Different Valor: The Story of General Joseph E. Johnston. C.S.A. New York: Bobbs-Merrill Co., 1956.
- Grivas, Theodore. Military Governments in California, 1846-1850. Glendale, CA: Arthur H. Clark Co., 1963.
- Haferkorn, Henry E. The War with Mexico, 1846-1848: A Select Bibliography. New York: Argonaut Press, 1965..
- Henry, Robert Selph. The Story of the Mexican War. New York and Indianapolis: Bobbs-Merrill Co., 1950.
- Hill, Forest G. Roads, Rails and Waterways: The Army Engineers and Early Transportation. Norman: University of Oklahoma Press, 1957.
- Hine, Robert V Edward Kern and American Expansion. New Haven, CT: Yale University Press, 1962.
- History and Traditions of the Corps of Engineers. Engineer School Special Text, ST 25-1. Fort Belvoir, VA: Engineer School, 1953.
- Howard, Oliver Otis. Great Commanders, General Taylor. New York: D. Appleton and Co., 1897.
- Hughes, Robert M. Great Commanders, General Johnston. New York D. Appleton and Co., 1897.
- Huston, James A. The Sinews of War: Army Logistics, 1775-1953. Army Historical Series. Office of the Chief of Military History. Washington, DC: Government Printing Office, 1966.
- Jackson, W. Turrentine. Wagon Roads West: A Study of Federal Road Surveys and Construction in the Trans-Mississippi West, 1846-1869. New Haven, CT: Yale University Press, 1965.
- Jenkins, John S. History of the War Between the United States and Mexico. Auburn: Derby and Miller, 1850.
- Johannsen, Robert W. To the Halls of the Montezumas: The Mexican War in the American Imagination. New York and Oxford Oxford Univ. Press, 1985.
- Johnson, Bradley T: (ed.). A Memoir of the Life and Public Service of Joseph

E. Johnston. Baltimore: R.H. Woodward and Co., 1891.

- Lavender, David. Climax at Buena Vista: The American Campaigns in Northeastem Mexico, 184647. Philadelphia: J.B. Lippincott Co., 1966.
- Lewis, Lloyd. Captain Sam Grant Boston: Little, Brown and Co., 1950.
- Mansfield, Edward D. The Mexican War. New York: A. S. Barnes and Co., 1850.
- Marti, Werner H. Messenger of Destiny: The California Adventures, 1846-1847, of Archibald H Gillespie, US Marine Corps. San Francisco: John Howell Books, 1960.
- Matloff, Maurice (ed.). American Military History. Washington, DC: Office of the Chief of Military History, 1969, rev. 1973.
- Moore, Jamie W. The Fortifications Board 1816-1828 And the Definition of National Security. The Citadel: Monograph Series: Number XVI. Charleston: The Citadel, Jan 1981.
- Nevin, David. The Mexican War. The Old West Series. Alexandria, VA: Time-Life Books, 1978.
- Nevins, Allan. Fremont, Pathmarker of the West. New York: Longmans, Green and co., 1955.
- Nichols, Edward J. Zach Taylor's Little Army. New York: Doubleday, 1963.
- Occasional Papers of the Engineer School No. 37. Washington, DC: Press of the Engineer School, 1910.
- Pennypacker, Isaac R. Great Commanders, General Meade. New York: D. Appleton and Co., 1901.
- Ripley, R. S. ·War With Mexico. 2 vols. New York: Harper, 1849.
- Rives, George L. The United States and Mexico, 1821-48. New York: Charles Scribner's Sons, 1913.
- Royce, Josiah. California from the Conquest in 1846 to the Second Vigilance Committee in San Francisco. Boston and New York: Houghton Mifflin and Co., 1914.
- Sabin, Edwin L. Kit Carson Days, 1809-1868. 2 vols. n.p.: Press of the Pioneers, Inc., 1935.
- Schubert, Frank N. Vanguard of Expansion: Army Engineers in the Trans Mississippi West, 1819-1879. Washington, DC: US ·Army Corps of Engineers, Government Printing Office, 1980.
- Singletary, Otis. The Mexican War. Chicago: University of Chicago Press, 1960.
- Smith, Justin H. The War with Mexico. 2 vols. New York: Macmillan Co., 1919.
- Steele, Matthew F. American Campaigns. 2 vols. Washington, DC: US Infantry Association, 1935.

- Stewart, 'George R John Phoenix, Esq. The Veritable Squibob, A Life of Captain George H Derby,' USA. New York: Da Capa Press, 1969.
- Taylor and His 'Generals, a Biography...Together with a Sketch of the Life of Major General Winfield Scott, Hartford, CT: Silas Andrews and Son, 1848.
- Upham, Charles W. Life, Explorations and Public Service of John Charles Fremont. Boston: Ticknor and Fields, 1856.
- Wallace, Edward S. The Great Reconnaissance: Soldiers, Artists and the Scientists on the Frontier, 1848-1861. Boston: Little, Brown and Co., 1955.
- Weigley, Russell F. History of the United States Army. New York: Macmillan Co., 1967.
- Wheat, Carl I. Mapping the Trans-Mississippi West, 1540-1861. 5 vols. San Francisco: The Institute of Historical Cartography, 1957-1963.
- Wilcox, Cadmus. History of the Mexican War. Washington, DC: Church News Publishing Co., 1892.
- Wood, Richard G. Stephen Harriman Long, 1784-1864, Army Engineer, Explorer, Inventor. Glendale, CA: Arthur H. Clark Co., 1966.
- Youngblood, G.A. "History of Engineer Troops in the United States Army, 1775-1901."

Global View in Indian Context

"Natural resources and inanimate energy are increasingly regarded as affected with a public interest." — **Stuart Chase**

General

1. As discussed earlier, because of actual and potential consequences of disaster, the concept of international disaster relief system is changing from mere relief to the victims after disaster to cover entire gamut of issues involved from prevention to rehabilitation. The major actors in the International Relief System can be grouped into four general categories[1]:

(a) The Governments.

(b) International Organisations.

(c) Voluntary Agencies.

(d) Media.

Role of Government

2. The government inevitably bears the prime responsibility for the administration of relief operation. Usually the responsibility for execution of relief programmes is transferred to the appropriate ministry. However, the methods used by governments to administer disaster relief vary greatly from one government to another.

Role of International Agencies

3. At international level, relief assistance may be provided in the following manner:-

(a) Bilateral inter-governmental contributions This is processed through diplomatic channels.

(b) Voluntary Agencies such as Red Cross and contribution from charitable organisation such as OXFAM.

(c) Aid through United Nations Disaster Relief Organisation (UNDRO) and other United Nations Organisation.

Role of UNO[2]

4. There are two broad sets of circumstances in which relief assistance is provided by the United Nations viz. man-made disaster situation and emergencies arising from natural disasters. When a refugee situation occurs as a result of some man-made disaster (for example, civil disturbances, war, revolution), the office of United Nations High Commissioner for Refugees (UNHCR) is usually involved in relief operation and for natural disaster it is the office of the United Nations Disaster Relief Organisation (UNDRO) that takes the necessary actions.

5. **United Nations Disaster Relief Organisation (UNDRO)**. The primary actors in co-ordinating United Nations assistance in natural disaster relief operations are the office of the UNDRO in Geneva, and the United Nations Development Programme (UNDP) Resident Representative in the disaster stricken country. The UNDRO was established at Geneva on 01 March 1972 as a focal point of the UN system for disaster relief. Its main functions are to co-ordinate aid from various sources, promote better disaster preparedness and undertake "clearing house" functions between donors and disaster stricken country. It aims at achieving this co-ordination without restricting or duplicating work of existing organisation of UN.

6. **Representation**. The resident representative of UNDP functions on behalf of UNDRO in each country. He is responsible for drawing together as team personnel of other UN agencies to work with representatives of potential donor governments, international voluntary agencies and the Red Cross. This team works in close association with officials of government disaster relief authority and may if required; serve as the local co-ordinator of all external relief assistance at the request of the host government. If necessity arises, UNDRO sends experts to the disaster-affected country to assist the UNDP Resident Representative and the government in assessment and local co-ordination[3].

7. **Communication Set-up**. UNDRO's co-ordination centre in Geneva provides a facility for rapid communication with over

90 potential disaster relief donors, the league of Red Cross Societies (LORCS), and with any telex subscriber anywhere in the world. Information disseminated goes not only to donors but also to the many other governments and agencies with a "Need to Know" basis.

8. **International Agencies**. The various international agencies involved in disaster relief directly or indirectly are listed at Appendix A. Of these UN systems The United Nations Children's Fund (UNICEF), The Food and Agriculture Organisation, World Food Programme (WFP) of FAO and the World Health Organisation (WHO) are nearly always active in disaster relief operations. Most of these organisations have memoranda of understanding with UNDRO, specifying their operational responsibilities in relief activities in relation to that of UNDRO.

9. **Methodology for Assistance**. When the government of a disaster-stricken country makes a request for relief assistance from UNDRO, this requirement is regarded as an appeal to the UN system in general. If the requirements for relief assistance are made directly to UNICEF, WHO, or FAO; UNDRO is still consulted and advised of the action taken. UNDRO also informs the agencies involved, actions taken so far, that would modify or satisfy the request made to the agencies concerned. It co-ordinates each agency's response with other relief donors and informs the disaster stricken government through

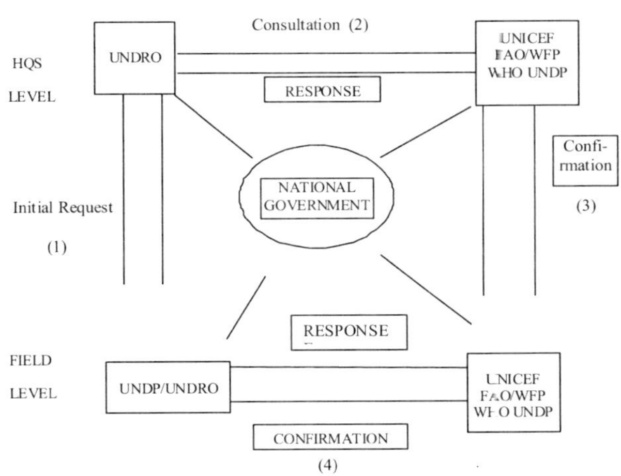

UNDP field office. UNDP Resident Representative, co-ordinates relief activities at the field level. To summarise, the UN disaster relief system is characterised by two types of the focal points- one at headquarters and another is the field. Figure 2 illustrates the channels through which messages are transmitted. This is simplified version of the procedure that is followed.[4]

The Role of Voluntary Agencies

10. Voluntary agencies, because of their greater organisational flexibility and tendencies to work more closely with "grass roots" level, provide welfare and relief services according to specific needs of the people. It acts as intermediary between the people and the government. They play two major roles:-

(a) Alerts the public and provides an individual response to concern generated by the media.

(b) Filling gaps in long-term development programmes or alternative relief distribution system.

11. **Red Cross**. Today the Red Cross is the principle non-governmental network for mobilising and distributing international assistance in times of disaster. It was founded by Mr J Dunant in 1863 who had witnessed the horrors of the battle of Solteinne in 1859. It has three basic organisational elements[5]:-

(a) *The International Committee of the Red Cross (ICRC).* Independent, Geneva based body, mainly concerned with victims of armed conflict.

(b) *The National Societies.* Found at present in 125 countries. They conduct programmes and activities directed towards the particular needs of their own countries. In some Muslim countries, they operate as Red Crescent Society and in Iran as the Red Lion and Sun Society.

(c) *The League of Red Cross Societies (LORCS).* LORCS is the federation if the 125 national societies with secretariat in Geneva. It acts as the international spokesman of the national societies, co-ordinates their relief activities.

Other Organisations

12. The other main voluntary organisations include Catholic Relief

Service, Leitheran world federation, OXFAM, the world council of churches. The OXFAM was founded in 1942 and which now maintains disaster relief programmes in over thirty countries.

The Role of the Media

13. The media plays an important role in disaster management. Often the first news of a major natural disaster event comes from media. Large-scale damage and loss of life is always a news event and the attendant publicity moves the national and international community to respond generously with offers of assistance to the disaster stricken area. Media also gives out the real needs of the victims, badly administered relief operations. It provides useful publicity to achievements made by the various agencies during disaster relief and later during rehabilitation and reconstruction. Benefits of media disaster coverage cannot be overemphasised. However, there could be negative reporting if media persons are not handled properly. There is a differing demand by media on government for news and information. Good public relations with media means more support for the relief operations. An honest exchange of information and sincere efforts on both sides i.e. Government as well as media will benefit disaster victims and relief operations.

Problem Areas

14. The problems faced in connection with international disaster relief co-ordination can be grouped into two general categories viz.: operational Co-ordination and Policy Co-ordination.

15. **Operational Co-ordination**. The specification and diversification of relief activities by various agencies and donors create major problem of co-ordination at operational level. Most difficult problems of disaster relief co-ordination accrue with voluntary agencies. These agencies are far from a homogenous group; they have major philosophical and religious differences, differences in their operations and budgets. Differences create problems of working together; similarities create problems for relief co-ordination. Voluntary agencies compete each other for funding/money raising and recognition, which is seldom conducive to relief co-ordination.

16. **Policy Co-ordination.** Problem of policy co-ordination arises as number of agencies involved, the relationship between different

relief donors and between donors and recipients regarding jurisdiction and authority. These difficulties can also arise as a result of political problems within a disaster stricken country. Many governments do not want their own population to realise the mismanaging of disaster. If disaster is likely to hurt tourism industry, less information on disaster will be divulged. There is also a common acknowledgement problem, as government hesitates to acknowledge such situations.

DISASTER MANAGEMENT IN SOME FOREIGN COUNTRIES

General

17. This part has been included to give general idea about the disaster management in some countries. Programmes and organisations differ widely in terms of emphasis, financial support, public interest and involvement. The organisations of Australia, USA and Iran have been covered.

Australia

18. The Australian government established the Natural Disasters Organisation (NDO) in July 1974, replacing existing civil defence organisation.[6] The philosophy of this organisation is that within a community three basic objectives need to be achieved before the effects of disaster can hope to be mitigated effectively. These objectives are: -

(a) An alert and informed community.

(b) An active and involved Local/State government.

(c) A local/state level counter disaster plan, supported by local organisation.

19. The headquarters of the NDO is in Canberra and functions under auspices of the Department of Defence and Director General is two star General. The NDO through its National Emergency Operations Centre (NEOC) provides a focal point for the co-ordination of national effort in times of disaster and ensures that states receive physical support from national resources. In addition, it conducts number of limited financial support programmes and training support for states.

20. **Manning and Communication.** The NDO only has a small permanent staff to run the NEOC. They can handle one-off requests and small-scale operations. Supplementary staff is produced by the

Department of Defence from its panel of trained persons in NEOC procedures and volunteers, civil officials who are similarly trained. It has communications with emergency centres in each Australian state and has an emergency radio system, which enables it to talk to every military installation, ship and aircraft in the country.

21. **Disaster Service Liaison Officer (DSLOs).** NDO by itself does not own any resources for assisting states, but relies on other central government departments to provide requested support. DSLOs are nominated from each department, which is capable of providing assistance. These officers are Nod's point of contact to the respective departments and all requests are processed through DSLOs.

22. **Australian Counter Disaster College (ACDC).** The college conducts Counter Disaster studies, briefings, planning, management and leadership courses for officials, administrators and volunteers alike.

23. **State Emergency Services (SES).** Responsibility for day-to-day running of operations rest with various state authorities. Each state has a State Emergency Service (SES); it comprises headquarters, a number of district/regional headquarters or staffs and units of volunteers who support the efforts of statutory authorities. Such unit is under local controller who is an appointed officer from state government. The DG NDO, heads of SES and director of ACDC meet yearly to discuss matters of mutual interest and to facilitate co-operation amongst various agencies.

USA

24. The disaster relief system is a part of the National Organisation of Civil Defence. The Office of Emergency Preparedness (OEP) is the Central agency for national operations and is part of Executive Offices of US President. It works closely with Defence and State Civil Preparedness Agencies. Under State Civil Preparedness Agencies, there are number of Local Civil Preparedness Agencies. Through these agencies, i.e. State and Local, Defence Civil Preparedness Agency ensures development of disasters preparedness and execution. It is also responsible for giving early warning of impending disasters through a National Resources Evaluation Centre. At State levels, State Adjutant General and his staff prepare plans for military support of civil defence and disaster relief operations. He is also commander of the National Guard, which is State's Integral Military Force. The force is under

overall control of State Governor. Its Organisation is similar to that of army units (infantry).

25. The National Guards, Reserves, regular military force and volunteers NGOs like Red Cross work in conjunction with each other to create effective disaster relief force. If magnitude of disaster requires extensive reconstruction programme the governor and the President may declare the area "Major Disaster Area", thereby making citizens and cities eligible for federal interest free loans, subsidies and grants.

26. **Decision Information Distributing System.** It has been developed to give early warning of predictable disaster. It combines federal, state and local systems with Regional offices and State centre. Radio and Television networks as well as military communications are also available to this system whenever required.[7]

Iran

27. After experiencing devastating earthquakes in 1962 and 1968 Iran has evolved an efficient relief network which integrates the armed forces, civil government and an Iranian version of the Red Cross known as Sher-e-Khoshed. The planning and co-ordination of relief is done at the highest level by the Deputy Prime Minister who is also the Deputy Chief of the Joint Staff- a serving Lt General. He thus combines the authorities to issue orders to civil authority and the military commanders with regard to relief work. This is his sole function.

28. Iran is divided into three military districts, each normally having an army corps and parallel civil administration and unit of Sher-e-Khoshed. This triangular organisation percolates right down to district and village level. Even in the remote areas the armed forces are represented by persons of the Army Revolutionary Corps comprising of the Literacy Corps, Health Corps and Construction Corps.

29. This vast network backed by elaborate communications, facilitates relief assessment and operations. The reserve stocks of the Armed Forces are automatically made available to meet relief requirements. Regular monthly conferences are held at corps level to review contingency plans. Many hundreds of helicopters are on call and kept at a high state of readiness in a potential disaster situation. In the event of disaster, the resources of the civilian government,

Sher-e-Khoshed, Police, Navy, Air Force come under relevant military district commander.[8]

The Global Perspective in Indian Scenario

Introduction

1. The end of the twentieth and the start of the twenty-first centuries have been marked by a significant number of major crises linked to natural disasters, such as floods, hurricanes and earthquakes as also technological disasters. Man has made tremendous technological progress in his existence on earth but he is still virtually helpless against vagaries of nature. Natural disasters such as flood, cyclones and earthquakes ravage man's domain at will and cause much loss to life and property. In addition to natural disasters, man has contrived to add to his miseries by waging wars and creating other man-made disasters. This subject has assumed major relevance in the present day context and is an essential element of state policy. This part of research will cover disaster management under aegis of the United Nations and disaster management systems and agencies prevalent in advanced nations of the world to include US, Europe and Australia.

United Nations in Disaster Management

2. The United Nations is the main international organ for co-ordination and mobilisation of assistance in the event of any disaster anywhere in the world. This aspect is looked after by two main agencies which are the focal point coordinators and advisors in the event of a disaster. These are the United Nations Department of Humanitarian Affairs agency of the United Nations (UN) and the Office for Co-ordination of Humanitarian Affairs (OCHA).

3. United Nations Department of Humanitarian Affairs agency of the United Nations (UN) Secretariat was originally established in 1972 to coordinate international relief activities to countries struck by natural or other disasters. It is headed by a disaster relief coordinator who reports directly to the UN Secretary-General and works closely with the United Nations Development Programme (UNDP).

4. Responding to requests from stricken states for disaster assistance, OCHA not only directs UN assistance but also mobilises aid from non-governmental organisations such as the International

Red Cross. OCHA also functions as an information coordination centre. Since the 1980s, OCHA has emphasised disaster preparedness and prevention and the execution of UNDP-assisted projects.

Disaster Management Programme (DMP)

5. As the lead agency within the United Nations system for coordinating activities in the field of human settlements, UN-HABITAT activities contribute to the overall objective of the United Nations system to reduce poverty and promote sustainable development within the context of a rapidly urbanising world. Within the broader context of sustainable human settlements development, UN-HABITAT focuses much of its work on the two key themes of the Habitat Agenda – adequate shelter for all and urban governance and promotes concepts of inclusion, participation and sustainability in the human settlements context. These overarching issues are also reflected in the work of the DMP to support sustainable, people-centred solutions in disaster management.

6. The DMP operates under the Disaster, Post-Conflict and Safety Section, Urban Development Branch of UN-HABITAT. DMP was created to marshal the resources of UN-HABITAT and other international agencies to provide local government, civil society and the private sector with practical strategies for mitigating and recovering from conflicts and natural disasters in the context of human settlements.

7. Specific areas of attention include the following:-

(a) Protection and rehabilitation of housing, infrastructure and public facilities.

(b) Provision of technical and policy support to humanitarian agencies before and after crisis in the context of human settlements.

(c) Building partnerships and provision of complementary expertise in resettlement of displaced persons and refugees.

(d) Restoration of local social structures through settlement development.

(e) Rehabilitation of local government structures and empowerment of civil society.

(f) Land and settlements planning and management for disaster prevention.

Disaster Management Training Programme (DTMP)

8. DMTP is a learning platform addressing crises, emergencies and disasters for the UN Member States, the UN System and international and non-governmental organisations. The programme was launched by the United Nations Development Programme (UNDP) and the Office of the United Nations Disaster Relief Co-ordinator in co-operation with UN Agencies in 1990. DMTP has raised awareness of the need for a more effective crisis and disaster management to reduce risks and vulnerabilities.

9. DMTP's long-term development objective is to reduce incidence and impact of crisis and disaster occurrences in programme countries, elimination of risks and vulnerability to such events, promote effective national and regional strategies in crisis and disaster prevention, preparedness, mitigation, response and recovery, and encourage efficient coordination and collaboration at all phases of crisis and disaster management, between and among national and international partners.

10. The DMTP has also been successful in establishing synergies between development and humanitarian responses in crisis and disaster situations and in creating a culture of people and agencies that embrace crisis and disaster-management issues within the scope of their overall concern.

United Nations Disaster Management Team (UN DMT)

11. A UN Disaster Management Team (UN DMT) is formed in the event of a disaster. If the disaster clearly falls within the competence and man-date of a UN agency, then this organisation will normally take the lead. The UN DMT is convened and chaired by the UN Resident Co-ordinator (the UNDP Resident Representative) and should normally comprise a core group represented by the country level representatives of FAO, UNDP, UNICEF, WFP, WHO and UNHCR.

12. The primary purpose of the UN DMT is to ensure that a prompt, effective and concerted response by the UN system is made at country level in the event of a disaster. The team co-ordinates all disaster-related activities, technical advice and material assistance provided by UN agencies, as well as taking steps to avoid wasteful duplication or competition for resources by UN agencies.

13. **United Nations Development Programme (UNDP).** UNDP focuses primarily on the development-related aspects of disaster risks and occurrences, and on providing technical assistance to institution-building in relation to all aspects of disaster management. Its emphasis is on:-

(a) Incorporating long-term risk reduction and preparedness measures in normal development planning and programmes, including support for specific mitigation measures where required.

(b) Assisting in the planning and implementation of post-disaster rehabilitation and reconstruction, including the definition of new development strategies that incorporate risk reduction measures relevant to the affected area.

(c) Providing technical assistance to the authority managing major emergency assistance operations of extended duration (especially in relation to displaced persons and the possibilities for achieving durable solutions in such cases).

14. **UNDP in India.** UNDP has been supporting various initiatives of the Central and State Governments in India to strengthen the disaster management capacities. In the aftermath of Maharashtra earthquake in 1993, UNDP supported preparation of district disaster management plans as a part of the Maharashtra Emergency Earthquake Rehabilitation Programme of the State. Initiatives for the training of elected representatives of the Panchayats, especially women representatives, as well as creation of awareness among communities regarding earthquake resistant construction tech were also undertaken.

15. In 1996, UNDP initiated the National Capacity Building Project in Disaster Management to enhance the capabilities of the government for disaster management. The project aimed at strengthening the National Centre for Disaster Management (NCDM), training government functionaries and faculty of Disaster Management Cells in the State Institutes of Public Administration. The strategy was to develop NCDM as a resource centre to produce manuals and guidelines; formulate policy and disaster management strategy proposals.

16. UNDP supported initiatives in the aftermath of the three last major disasters - the Super Cyclone in Orissa (1999) and the devastating

earthquakes in Gujarat (2001) and Kashmir (2005) – demonstrated the effectiveness of development of approaches to disaster risk mitigation and vulnerability reduction in India. Integration of community-based disaster preparedness and mitigation plans into the development plans prepared by local governments, and strengthening of local capacities and institutions, have proved to be successful in mitigating the impact of subsequent disasters.

17. **United Nations Children Fund (UNICEF).** Within the mandate conferred to UNICEF by the General Assembly, UNICEF plays a special role in emergency relief in ensuring that the immediate and particular needs of children and mothers are met, with due regard for to the urgency of the needs and the resources available. This applies in all emergency situations, regardless of their cause - whether natural or human-made, and assistance is provided without discrimination. Where relief needs are able to be met by the government or other organisations, UNICEF concentrates its effort and resources on rehabilitation and long-term child survival and development objectives.

18. **World Food Programme (WFP).** In the event of an emergency WFP may, depending on the needs, do the following:-

(a) Provide advice and assistance to the government, other concerned agencies and local authorities in assessing possible requirements for emergency food aid and in planning and managing appropriate food aid interventions.

(b) Provide food aid to meet emergency food needs, subject to the availability of resources and the assessed need for international food aid.

(c) Help to mobilise and ensure co-ordination in the planning and delivery of food assistance from all sources, and any necessary logistics supply and other complementary inputs.

19. **World Health Organisation (WHO).** The World Health Organisation is the health arm of the UN. Within the areas of public health and medical care WHO:-

(a) Responds to requests from the competent national authorities in situations which are, or threaten to become, emergencies and for which the resources available nationally are insufficient.

(b) Offers emergency relief and health assistance, even in the absence of a request, if it is clear that such assistance would be beneficial and the situation would otherwise represent a threat to public health in the country or adjoining countries.

(c) Promotes disaster preparedness planning, management and, where possible, prevention.

Deployable UN Co-ordination Support Mechanisms

20. There are several co-ordination support mechanisms and specialised units that can be deployed to support and complement mechanisms and specialised assets already in country. They include the following:-

(a) *Field Coordination Units (FCU).* Field Coordination Units are used essentially in complex emergencies. Although their structure, size and precise activities vary, depending on the nature of the complex emergency, the primary role of FCUs is basically to support Resident/Humanitarian Coordinators and as the case may be, the UNDMTs, in carrying out their coordination responsibilities, and thus help ensure common programming among humanitarian actors in the field.

(b) *United Nations Assessment and Coordination (UNDAC).* The UNDAC System, managed by OCHA, is designed to assist the United Nations in meeting international needs for early and qualified information during the first phase of a sudden onset emergency and, when necessary, in the co-ordination of international relief ops at the site of the emergency. It also aims at strengthening national and regional disaster response capability in disaster prone countries.

(c) *Other International Entities.*

(i) *Donor Governments.* Donor Governments are typically involved in emergencies through their embassies or aid organisations.

(ii) *Non-Governmental Organisations.* International, as opposed to national, non-governmental organisations of widely differing size, character, purpose and funding can be present in large numbers in large-scale humanitarian emergencies. Most of the NGO aid, however, will be provided by some twenty or thirty large NGOs with institutional experience and resources for disaster and emergency response. Of these, some are mandated exclusively for the provision of humanitarian relief, while others normally have development oriented programs but will become involved in humanitarian relief operations when a crisis occurs.

Non Deployable UN Coordination Entities

21. **The Inter-Agency Standing Committee (IASC).** The IASC facilitates inter-agency decision-making in response to complex emergencies primarily by development and agreeing on system-wide humanitarian policies; allocating responsibilities among agencies in humanitarian programmes; advocating common humanitarian principles to parties outside the IASC; identifying areas where gaps in mandates or lack of operational capacity exist; and building consensus between humanitarian agencies on wide humanitarian issues.

22. **The Executive Committee on Humanitarian Affairs (ECHA).** The ECHA addresses matters relating to humanitarian situations in which political peacekeeping and security concerns predominate, and work to define principles, goals and institutional arranging for a coherent and effective UN response to a particular country in crisis.

23. **The Emergency Relief Coordinator (ERC).** The Emergency Relief Coordinator is also the Under-Secretary-General for Humanitarian Affairs in the UN Secretariat and is the Head of OCHA. As Emergency Relief Coordinator, he is responsible for coordination among the humanitarian community. As head of OCHA he is responsible for ensuring the coordination of humanitarian emergency response, policy development and policy coordination and advocacy of humanitarian issues. The UN setup for disaster management is as given on next page.

UN ORGANISATION FOR DISASTER MANAGEMENT

UN's Role in Some Recent Disasters

24. The UN has had a significant contribution to disaster management, the world over. It has rendered aid and expertise in all recent disasters, be it the Gujarat earthquake, the Odisha Super-cyclone, the tsunami or the recent earthquake in Pakistan. Two examples of the UN's involvement are briefly outlined in the succeeding paragraphs.

25. **Super Cyclone 1999.** In the aftermath of the Super Cyclone on 29 – 30 Oct 99, the Pilot Orissa Disaster Management Project was set up. The project model proceeded from the suggested framework of disaster management for the State of Orissa as recommended by a study commissioned by the United Nations Development Programme (UNDP) to the Yashawantrao Chavan Academy of Development Administration (YASHADA), Pune. The ODMP was implemented by the Orissa State Disaster Mitigation Authority (OSDMA) with technical assistance from UNDP. The total damage of the super-cyclone was assessed to be Rs 1800 crores. The monetary assistance from the UN amounted to US $ 18 million (Rs 81 crores) with approx US $ 210,000 (Rs 90 lakhs) being used for development of villages within a block. The UN mobilised Rs 2.2 crores worth of medicines and approximately Rs 275 crores of food and relief material. The Indian Government in comparison released Rs 300 crores from the PM's Relief Fund apart from mobilising about 4000 tonnes of relief material.

26. **Tsunami, 26 Dec 2004.** In response to the widespread destruction caused by the massive earthquake and resulting tsunami that hit large areas of Southeast Asia on 26 December 2004, the UN took the leading role in coordinating an unprecedented international relief effort involving a broad coalition of UN agencies, governments, and aid organisations. Coordination was carried from a new coordination centre in Indonesia. UN efforts included:-

(a) Emergency aid distribution within the first 48 hours of the disaster and continued relief operations by UN agencies such as United Nations Children's Fund (UNICEF), the World Health Organisation (WHO), and the United Nations Development Programme (UNDP), which all had existing operations on the ground in the nations impacted by the tsunami.

(b) Coordination of air and logistics operations for the trans-port of relief goods and personnel by the UN Joint Logistics Centre (UNJLC), using transport assets provided by the militaries of the US, Australia, India, Malaysia, and Singapore.

(c) Ground assessments of damage by UN 'country teams' and the UN Disaster Assessment and Coordination division (UNDAC).

Recommendations

27. There is a need to set up an apex agency for disaster management which will be responsible for coordination and providing leadership in such situations. This agency should be the focal point for coordinating all activities at the national level. The assistance from various foreign governments, international organisations, state governments and NGOs should be coordinated by this agency. This will ensure a streamlined, cohesive and synergistic approach to cover the disaster struck area more effectively.

28. A Disaster Management Team on the lines of the UNDMT can be set up in the country which will be the quick reaction element in the event of any disaster to provide relief in the initial stages of any disaster. As of today most other agencies are grouping together their resources and are unable to provide any immediate assistance. Assistance rendered during this crucial period will mitigate to a large extent the damage caused by the disaster.

29. The Disaster Management team should be in a state of preparedness at all times. It should monitor warnings and indications, keep an uptodate knowledge bank of resources available at various locations, potential dangers and update its systems, procedures and facilities accordingly.

Disaster Management in Australia

30. In order to be able to look up to some guiding light in our quest for optimising disaster management, it may be worthwhile to examine certain disaster management policies the world over. In order to get a holistic picture, we shall analyse the policies across the globe and thus study the systems of Australia, USA and Europe.

31. Australia, like India, is a country of vast geographical land mass with different facets of terrain. Tasmania is prone for bushfires, New South Wales and Queensland are prone to floods as well as draught, Northern territories face cyclones and Western Australia is prone to Tsunami. Earthquakes, floods, bush fires and tropical cyclones occur regularly across the Australian continent, causing more than $1.14 billion damage each year to homes, businesses and the nation's infrastructure, and serious disruption to communities.

32. **Natural Disasters in Australia** – An Though the history of disasters in Australia is centuries old, reliable info on the frequency of disasters in Australia extends only from 1967. Major disasters witnessed by Australia in near past are as follows:-

(a) *Cyclone.* While Cyclone Tracy (1974) is probably the most well known of the cyclones to hit Australia, earlier cyclones viz Mahina in March 1899 and Ada in January 1970 have also left their mark on the nation. On Christmas Eve 1974, Cyclone Tracy struck the city of Darwin in the Northern Territory leaving 25,000 of 43,000 residents homeless. A cyclone profile of Australia is as given below:-

(b) *Floods.* In January 1974, heavy rainfall in Brisbane and in many parts of south-eastern Queensland and northern NSW, flooded one-third of the city's centre and leaving many died and homeless. In another major flood in 1990; over one million square kms of Queensland and New South Wales were submerged.

(c) *Droughts.* Two major droughts in the last twenty years have resulted in huge financial losses, immeasurable personal hardship and massive environmental damage to large areas of central and eastern Australia in 1983-84, and in New South Wales and Queensland in 1991 and 1995. The effects of the drought laid the groundwork for the catastrophic 1983 'Ash Wednesday' bushfires across Victoria and South Australia.

(d) *Bushfires.* Destructive bushfires have dotted Australian history, including the recent 1993-94 NSW fires and the 1997 Victorian blazes. In the 1967 Tasmanian fires, 264,270 hectares were burnt.

33. **Analysis of Disasters.** Analysis of disasters between 1967 and 1999 shows that Australia encounters approximately eight disasters each year and the total loss per event is greater than $10 million. However, since 1980, the average number of disasters of such magnitude has been on the increase. The worst year was 1998, with 17 recorded events resulting in a loss of 10 million dollar. Total cost of natural disasters in the period 1967–99 shows the variable annual costs which average more than $1.14 billion per annum for events costing

more than $10 million each. However, the deaths from natural disasters have continued to fall throughout the period of European settlement. The death rate from all natural hazards combined has fallen from 10 per 1,00,000 people in 1875 to below 1 per 1,00,000.

34. **System of Disaster Management in Australia**

(a) Prime responsibility for the protection of life, property and the environment rests with the States and Territories. However, the role of Australian Central Government is to support States and Territories in developing their capacity for dealing with emergencies and disasters, and to provide physical assistance to requesting States or Territories when they cannot reasonably cope during an emergency. The Attorney General exercises Australian Government's responsibility for emer-gency management matters through Emergency Management Australia (EMA).

(b) The Australian Government also provides financial assistance to the States and to individuals to assist in the recovery from disasters. In particular, it facilitates education, training, research, public awareness, and info collection and dissemi-nation activities. It also provides specialised warning and monitoring services for met and geological hazards as appropriate.

(c) The Australian Government facilitates development of policy coordination and support programmes to ensure expansion of existing State and Territory emergency management capabilities to provide an effective civil defence organisation. Planning for the transition to a war footing needs to be undertaken during peacetime.

35. **Disaster Management Structure in Australia.** In the event that State Government or commercial resources are inadequate, inappropriate or unavailable, the State or Territory Governments may call upon the Australian Government for assistance. Each State and Territory has an authorised officer empowered to request assistance from the Australian Government. To assist the state in distress various agencies under Australian Government are given tasks for different contingencies. At all levels coordination committees are formed to

ensure synergized effort and rapid response. These committees and their role in Disaster Management are as under:-

(a) *Commonwealth Counter-Disaster Task Force (CCDTF).* The Commonwealth Counter-Disaster Task Force (CCDTF) is a senior inter department committee, chaired by the department of the Prime Minister and Cabinet, comprised of representatives of Australian Government Departments and agencies with a significant role to play in the provision of disaster relief or rehabilitation assistance. On the advice of the Director General EMA, the Chair may activate the CCDTF during the response and recovery phase of a disaster in support of EMA activities.

(b) *The Australian Emergency Management Committee.* The Australian Emergency Management Committee is Australia's peak consultative Emergency Management forum. It is chaired by the Secretary of the Attorney-General's Department and comprises chairpersons and executive officers of State Emergency Management committees and the President of the Australian Local Government Association. The Committee meets twice a year to provide advice and direction on the coordination and advancement of Australian Government and State interests in Emergency Management issues.

(c) *State/Territory Disaster Management Organisations.* Each State and Territory has established a committee of senior members of appropriate departments and agencies to consider Emergency Management matters. These organisations are responsible for ensuring that proper plans and arrangements are made at State or Territory and local government level to deal with emergencies and disasters.

(d) *Australian Emergency Management Organisation.* The Attorney General is responsible for Disaster and Emergency Management matters. The agency through which the Attorney General exercises this responsibility is Emergency Management Australia (EMA).

(e) *Emergency Management Liaison Officers.* The Australian Government agencies likely to become involved in emergency response have appointed Emergency Management Liaison

Officers (EMLOs) to assist with the provision of specified physical resources and specialist skills, available within their agencies, during the initial response and ongoing recovery phases of a disaster operation.

(f) *National Registration and Inquiry System.* To facilitate a rapid response to enquiries from Australia and overseas in relation to people effected by disaster in Australia, EMA sponsors a computer-based national disaster victim registration and inquiry system, called NRIS. The system uses info from the disaster-affected State or Territory and computer support from the Australian Government Department of Health and Aging to provide information, accessible from any inquiry centre in Australia.

36. **Procedures for Activation of National Response.** All requests for Australian Government assistance are made to the Director General, Emergency Management Australia (DGEMA). If DGEMA agrees to, Ministerial approval to commit Australian Government resources is sought from the Attorney General. Thereafter, DGEMA has access to, and can call upon, the total resources of the Australian Government to satisfy a State request. This request sequence is shown on diagram in the next page.

PATH OF REQUEST FOR ASSISTANCE

37. **Organisations Involved in Disaster Management.** During a natural disaster the community response is coordinated by the local Emergency Services organisations. At national level it is organised by EMA. Various government organisations which play important role in disaster management are as follows:-

(a) *Centrelink.* A major statutory authority established in 1977, Centrelink plays a key role in the whole of government's response to emergencies by supporting the recovery of individuals, families and communities through the delivery of income sp, and other assistance, to those affected by a disaster.

(b) *Department of Transport and Regional Services (DOTARS).* DOTARS administers the Natural Disaster Relief Arrangements, to alleviate the financial burden on States and Territories by providing partial reimbursement of State and Territory expenditure on a range of relief and recovery measures.

(c) *Australian Maritime Safety Authority (AMSA).* The Australian Maritime Safety Authority (AMSA) is the agency with a primary role in maritime safety, protection of the marine environment and maritime and aviation search and rescue. It coordinates maritime and aviation search and rescue operations in Australia's internationally agreed search and rescue region.

(d) *Department of Agriculture, Fisheries and Forestry.* Farm Help and the Rural Financial Counseling Service Programme are two programmes developed as part of the Australian Government's Agriculture Advancing Australia (AAA) package that may be of assistance to affected primary producers.

(e) *Bureau of Meteorology.* The Bureau of Meteorology provides weather, hydrological, climate and oceanographic forecasts and information. The Bureau is responsible for the issue of warnings to the Australian community of gales, storms and other weather conditions likely to endanger life or property including weather conditions likely to give rise to flood or bush fires; tsunami and extreme climate events.

(f) *Department of Defence.* Assistance includes, but is not limited to, transport and logistic support, evacuation, rescue, medical services, provision of emergency accommodation and supplies.

(g) *Family and Community Services (FaCS).* The FaCS support the recovery of individuals, families and communities.

(h) *Geosciences Australia.* It provides national geo-scientific research and information to assist government make informed decisions about resource use, Management of the environment, and the safety of the community. Its also maintains a network of seismographs throughout the continent as part of Australia's earthquake alert system, a 24 hour monitoring facility used to inform the Emergency Management community of seismic events. In addition, risk assessments are developed using an extensive network of spatial databases that include topographic maps, satellite imagery, critical infrastructure and post-disaster information.

38. **The New Approach.** The Council of Australian Government (COAG), was commissioned in June 2001 to identify the strengths and weaknesses of current arrangements for managing natural disasters. A High Level Group (HLG) of senior officials from Federal, State and Territory Governments and the Australian Local Government Association (ALGA) was established to undertake the review. It recommended a systematic national process of disaster risk assessments and a fundamental shift in focus towards cost-effective, evidence-based disaster mitigation. A key recommendation of the review is that all levels of government agree to a comprehensive five-year package of commitments to reform the way natural disasters are managed to achieve safer, more sustainable communities and regions in economic, social and environmental terms. The new Natural Disaster Mitigation Programme will provide funding for a range of natural disaster mitigation works, measures and related activities. These could include disaster research, risk assessments and mitigation strategies; structural works and disaster-resilient infrastructure; warning systems, community education campaigns and other preparedness measures.

39. **Lessons in the Indian Context**

(a) In India, there is a requirement to bring down the death toll by constituting various measures like providing early warning to and constructing shelters for the affected population.

(b) Standardise emergency management procedures and equipment and provide an effective civil defence organisation in our country to minimise loss of life and property due to natural disasters by gearing up our state and civil administration.

(c) Incase of a disaster, to facilitate a rapid response to enquiries within Australia and overseas in relation to the affected people, EMA has a computer based national disaster victim registration and enquiry system, called NRIS. We in India can also establish a similar type of system which can use the states database of the voters list for providing on line registration and enquiry system.

Disaster Management in the USA

40. Disasters such as forest and urban fires, floods, oil spills, accidents, earthquakes, hurricanes and tornadoes are frequently faced by the US. Study of disaster management techniques in US is relevant as it has developed an effective system of disaster management and mitigation. To achieve a coordinated national approach to the disaster management, a national response plan (NRP) exists which incorporates all the sections of the society and clearly demarcates tasks of each and every organisation in the eventuality of a disaster.

41. **Disasters in the US.** Some of the major disasters which have struck US in the past are as follows:-

(a) Nearly 8000 died due to tidal surge in Galveston, Texas in 1900.

(b) 500 died in an earthquake accompanied by fire in San Francisco in 1906.

(c) About 100 lives were lost in an avalanche in Wellington, Washington in 1910.

(d) Largest drought of the twenty-first century covering 50 million acres in South Central Plains from 1930 to 1940.

(e) 10 million gallons of oil spilled into water during the collision of the tanker Exxon Valdez with an undersea reef in Alaska in 1989.

(f) On 29 Aug 2005 Katrina struck Louisiana, New Orleans, Mississippi, Alabama and Florida with high wind speed of 175 mph resulting in damage of US $ 75 bn and loss of 1420 lives.

(g) On 21 sep 2005 with the high wind speed of 175 mph, Rita struck Bahamas, Florida and parts of Texas and Arkansas causing a damage of $ 9.4bn and resulting in the loss of 119 lives.

(h) On 19 Oct 2005, with high wind speed of 185 mph, Wilma struck Florida and Bahamas resulting in a loss of $ 20bn and 62 lives.

42. **Current Disaster Management Structure in the US**

(a) Though various agencies and institutions have existed for the disaster management, but it was only after 9/11 that a unified and coordinated approach to the disasters and disaster management took place. This took the form of National Response Plan (NRP). NRP is a concerted national effort to prevent major disasters, terrorist attacks, reduce American vulnerability to the emergencies, terrorism, minimise the damage and recover from attacks that occur. NRP works directly under the US president and is chaired by the secretary of the Homeland Security.

(b) The NRP incorporates best practices and procedures from various disaster management disciplines which are homeland security, emergency management, law enforcement, firefighting, hazardous materials response, public works, public health, emergency medical services and integrates them into a unified body. The NRP establishes mechanisms to:-

(i) Maximise the integration of disaster related prevention, preparedness, response and recovery activities.

(ii) Improve coordination and integration of Federal, State, local, tribal, regional, private-sector and nongovernmental organisation partners.

(iii) Maximise efficient utilisation of resources needed for effective disaster management and Critical Infrastructure/ Key Resources (CI/KR) protection and restoration.

(iv) Improve disaster management communications and increase situational awareness across jurisdictions and between the public and private sectors.

(v) Facilitate emergency mutual aid and Federal emergency support to State, local and tribal governments.

(vi) Facilitate Federal-to-Federal interaction and emergency support.

(vii) Provide a proactive and integrated Federal response to catastrophic events.

(viii) Address linkages to other Federal disaster management and emergency response plans developed for specific types of incidents or hazards.

43. **Roles and Responsibilities**

(a) *State and Local Governments.* Mutual aid agreements between the states provide mechanisms to mobilise and employ resources from neighbouring jurisdictions. When State resources and capabilities are overwhelmed, Governors may request Federal assistance under a Presidential disaster or emergency declaration.

(b) *Federal Government.* Various departments responsible are as follows:-

(i) *Department of Homeland Security (DHS).* This is responsible to prevent terrorist attacks within the United States; reduce the vulnerability of the United States to terrorism, natural disasters and other emergencies; and minimize the damage and assist in the recovery from terrorist attacks, natural disasters and other emergencies. DHS is also a focal point regarding natural and manmade crises and emergency planning.

(ii) *Department of Justice.* The Attorney General, being the chief law enforcement officer in the United States is responsible for criminal investigations of terrorist acts or terrorist threats by individuals or groups inside the United States. This includes actions to prevent, preempt and disrupt specific terrorist threats or actual incidents that are based upon specific intelligence or law enforcement information.

(iii) *Department of Defence (DOD).* The DOD has significant resources that may be available to support the Federal response to a disaster of National Significance. The Secretary of Defence authorises Defence Support of Civil Authorities (DSCA) for disasters as directed by the President or when consistent with military readiness operations and appropriate under the circumstances and the law.

(iv) *Department of State.* The Secretary of State is responsible for coordinating international prevention, preparedness, response and recovery activities relating to disasters and for the protection of US citizens and US interests overseas.

(v) *Other Federal Agencies.* During a disaster of National Significance, other Federal departments or agencies may play primary, coordinating and/or support roles based on their authorities and resources and the nature of the disaster.

(vi) *Emergency Support Function.* A grouping of government and certain private-sector capabilities into an Organisational structure to provide support, resources and services.

(vii) *Nongovernmental and Volunteer Organisations.* The NGOs collaborate with first responders, governments at all levels and other agencies and organisations providing relief services to sustain life, reduce physical and emotional distress and promote recovery of disaster victims when assistance is not available from other sources.

(viii) *Private Sector.* DHS and NRP, the primary support agencies coordinate with the private sector to effectively share information, form courses of action and incorporate available resources to prevent, prepare for, respond to and recover from disasters of National Significance.

(ix) *Citizen Involvement.* The US Citizen Corps brings various citizen groups together and focuses efforts of individuals through education, training and volunteer service to help make communities safer, stronger and better prepared to address the threats of terrorism, crime, public health issues and other disasters. Citizen Corps affiliated Programmes expand the resources and materials available to States and local communities through partnerships with programmes and organisations that offer resources for public education, outreach and training; represent volunteers interested in helping to make their communities safer; or offer volunteer service opportunities to support first responders, disaster relief activities and community safety efforts.

44. **Structure of NRP.** At the apex of NRP is the secretary of the Homeland Security who is directly responsible to the US President.

The responsibility starts right from the disaster command posts which are at field level performing on scene emergency management. The focal point of coordination at field level is that of an area command which is activated only when the complexity of the disaster management goes out of control. Supporting them in discharge of their duties is the multi agency coordination centre. Supervising in the discharge of duties and coordinating the overall effort is the regional response coordination centre. The response support teams provides on scene support to the disaster command post or to the area command. They deploy within 2 hrs of notification.

45. **Recommendations in the Indian Context.** Following are the recommendations which are applicable in the Indian context:-

(a) Nomination of central agency under the Prime Minister.

(b) Earmarking of various agencies and organisations in support of the central agency so nominated.

(c) Provision of disaster response support teams at district levels.

(d) Disaster management cell at state level to oversee the functioning of the response support teams.

(e) Develop national database system.

(f) Proactive approach to disaster management by creating system of early warning, responder agencies, educating masses, creating infrastructure and placing reserves for contingencies.

Disaster Management in Europe

46. **Europe as a Union.** Europe is fast transforming from one continent of many nations to one continent, one nation. While this new geopolitical setup clearly indicates that the Europe or 'European Union' with its 25 member states and approximately 460 million citizens can no longer afford to stay regionalised or nationalised in its approach towards handling disaster over its vast area of 3,892,685 Sq Km. Ms Ann-Louise Eksborg, Director General, Swedish Emergency Management Agency echoed this when she said, "Cross-border co-ordination is more important than ever. We can no longer rely on national solutions for handling disasters and vulnerabilities that are European, or global, in nature. In this intricate state of vulnerable inter-dependence, the protection of our critical infrastructure is only as strong as the weakest link. And we no longer have a choice."

47. **Natural Disasters in the Recent Past.**

(a) *Floods.* Floods comprised 43 per cent of all disaster events for the period 2000–2005. During this period, Europe suffered about 100 major damaging floods, causing some 1200 fatalities, the displacement of about half a million people and at least 25 billion euro in insured economic losses.

(b) *Storms.* Storms have been amongst the most costly types of disasters in Europe. Until the summer 2002 floods in central Europe, windstorm *Daria* in January 1990 and then storms *Lothar* and *Martin* in late December 1999 held the record for Europe's most expensive disasters, at nearly six billion euro and around 6.7 billion euro respectively. The three storms killed around 220 people in total.

(c) *Forest Fires.* Forest fires, mostly affect Mediterranean and Black Sea countries but occur throughout Europe, including as far North as Northern Norway. In the five Mediterranean member states of the European Union — France, Greece, Italy, Portugal and Spain — the area burnt in forest fires has varied between 2,00,000 and 6,00,000 hectares a year over the past 20 years.

(d) *Droughts.* In Europe, drought mostly affects the Mediterranean region. In Europe, droughts do not trigger famines and so do not kill people. However, human, environmental and economic impacts can be devastating, especially when droughts are associated with heat waves. A heat wave across much of Europe during August 2003, claimed possibly as many as 35,000 lives, with France alone recording almost 15,000 deaths.

(e) *Landslides.* Most of Western Europe suffers relatively few significant landslides. By contrast, the Mediterranean basin and the mountain regions of Central and Eastern Europe are particularly vulnerable to these events.

(f) *Avalanches.* The Alps, stretching in a crescent from Southern France up through Switzerland, Liechtenstein and Northern Italy Eastwards into Southern Germany, Austria and finally Slovenia, suffer more avalanches than any other region in the world. Alpine avalanches kill around 100 people a year (average for the past 30 years).

(g) *Earthquakes.* In Europe, earthquakes have killed far more people than any other extreme event and have caused extensive damage. Europe's major earthquake-prone areas are in the Mediterranean and Black Sea basins, along the active fault lines between the Eurasian and African plates. The most dramatic events in recent decades include the 1980 earthquake in southern Italy, which killed 4500 people and left more than a quarter of a million homeless; and the 1997 succession of earthquakes in Central Italy, which badly damaged, among other things, the Basilica of Saint Francis of Assisi and its natural environs. By far the most powerful and destructive of these was the Izmit earthquake in Turkey in August 1999, which killed an estimated 17,000 people and caused more than 15 billion euro in losses.

48. **Concept of Disaster Management in Europe**

(a) Disaster management in Europe has matured from an individual national effort to a combined initiative involving complex co-operations and initiatives. National, regional and local expertise lies at the heart of all of Europe's disaster response initiatives. This approach has allowed the European Union to develop some of the world's best disaster-response strategies.

(b) *Objectives.* Community cooperation in the field of disaster management has the following objectives:-

(i) Support and supplement efforts at national, regional and local levels to prevent disasters.

(ii) To contribute to public information so that European citizens are better able to protect themselves.

(iii) Establish a framework for effective and rapid cooperation between national civil protection services.

(iv) To enhance the coherence of actions undertaken at international level in the field of disaster management.

49. **Backdrop.** European Union's governments first formally agreed to coordinate their civil protection strategies at a ministerial meeting in Rome in 1985. Between 1985 and 1994, they approved a number of preliminary initiatives that laid the foundations for today's

extensive coordinated approach for dealing with and planning for managing major disasters. In 1997, the Council of the European Union took an important step forward by approving a major civil protection action programme, designed to support and supplement European Union Member States' civil protection efforts at national, regional and local levels, and further facilitate exchanges between Europe's disaster-response specialists.

50. **Structure of Projects.** A large Number of Projects funded jointly by the European Community and at least one Member State are being executed at various levels. The concept behind these projects is as follows:-

(a) Risk Evaluation, Prevention and Mitigation.

(b) Information to the Public.

(c) *Preparedness and Response.* These projects are designed to ensure that citizens benefit from the same high standard of disaster preparedness wherever they find themselves in the Union.

(d) *Analysis after the Disaster.* These projects are designed to ensure that the European Union civil protection experts learn as much as they can from past disasters, so that they can tackle future catastrophes more effectively.

(e) *Horizontal Actions.* Schemes underway so far include a study into the uses of new information technologies in disaster relief situations, role the non-governmental organisations (NGOs) can play when it comes to tackling catastrophes.

51. **Present Structure**

(a) *National Initiatives.* At the level of individual nations in Europe, it is the government run or sponsored agencies that co-ordinate the work to develop the preparedness of society to manage serious crises. To carry out this task, they have an established network of county administrative boards, central authorities and others that may be affected by or have knowledge of an emergency. Nations are also investing heavily in educating their citizens on responding in an organised manner during disaster situations by including 'Disaster Management' in the curriculum at schools and colleges.

(b) ***Regional Initiatives.*** Some of the initiatives and organisations operating are as mentioned below:-

(i) *Mechanism of Coordinated Disaster Relief.* In October 2001, European Union governments agreed to create a new 'mechanism' to facilitate their cooperation in civil protection assistance interventions. The mechanism sets out detailed strategies for dealing with all major emergencies, which may require urgent response action, ranging from peacetime disasters like earthquakes to terrorist threats or attacks. It focuses on facilitating cooperation between member states so that the authorities in a region hit by a disaster can call on an extensive community network of civil protection experts as quickly as possible. At the heart of the new mechanism is an improved 'European Union Civil Protection Monitoring and Information Center'(ECPMIC). This center is being operated by the European Commission in Brussels and, is on call 24 hours a day, 365 days a year. The centre is drawing on a network of expertise, is able to assemble a tailor-made disaster response team, and ensures its dispatch to the scene of a catastrophe anywhere in the world within 12 hours.

(ii) *The Permanent Network of National Correspondents (PNNC).* The PNNC is made up of high-level representatives from national civil protection administration and is the first coordinated civil protection network set up in the European Union. It serves as a forum for the exchange of information and discusses different civil protection initiatives. The commission is composed of representatives from the member states and chaired by the commission itself.

(iii) *The Vade-mecum — A Civil Protection Guidebook.* The European Commission has published and regularly updates a civil protection *Vade-mecum*, which gives a general of the measures taken by European Union Member States to deal with disasters. This is a detailed document, designed for responsible officials working in the field of civil protection at national, regional and local levels, volunteers and NGOs, and interested members of the public.

(iv) *The Open Partial Agreement of the Council of Europe (EUR-OPA Major Hazards Agreement).* The purpose of this agreement, which was adopted in March 1987 by the Council of Europe, is to promote closer cooperation among Member States on preventing and responding to natural and technological disasters.

(v) *The Central European Initiative (CEI).* This agreement on the forecasting, prevention and mitigation of natural and technological disasters was concluded in 1996 between Austria, Croatia, Hungary, Italy, Poland and Slovenia (the European Commission has observer status). It covers the exchange of scientific and technical information and relevant data on a regular basis, common research programmes and the training of experts.

(vi) *Committee on Earth Observation Satellites Disaster Information Server (CEOSDIS).* CEOSDID is one of six projects intended to develop the integrated global observing strategy. It provides an opportunity for space agencies and emergency management authorities with broad geographical responsibilities to harmonise their respective disaster management support activities and to begin addressing how they might work together to strengthen disaster management support through the expanded use of Earth observation (EO) satellite data.

(c) *International Cooperation.* The European Commission actively participates in a number of international cooperation agree-ments on civil protection and disaster relief. These take the form of activities either in the context of European Union policies or separate initiatives.

(i) *Activities in the Context of European Union Policies.* In the Mediterranean region, the Union is financing a Euro-Med pilot project in the field of civil protection through the MEDA programme. The broad objective is to contribute to political and security confidence-building in the Euro-Mediterranean area.

(ii) *Euro-Canadian Space Programme.* In Europe, European Space Agency (ESA) has created a European space programme with great depth and capability beyond the reach of individual member states, from launch to orbital facilities and to deep-space probes. It has 15 member states (including Canada, as a Cooperating State), a budget equivalent to Euro 5.7 billion and some 1700 employees.

(iii) *European Commission's Humanitarian Aid (ECHO).* ECHO was set up in 1992 to provide rapid and effective support to the victims of crises outside the European Union. Recognising the importance of pre-emptive measures, ECHO launched its disaster preparedness programme, DIPECHO, in 1996. ECHO's disaster preparedness programme (DIPECHO) targets, vulnerable communities living in the main disaster-prone regions of the world. Between 1996 and 2004, DIPECHO provided more than €78 million for 319 projects worldwide.

52. **Road Map for Future**

(a) *Increasing Community Cooperation.* It is the firm belief of all the member states that while being able to react swiftly and effectively when a catastrophe strikes is vital, it is better to stop such emergencies before happening wherever possible. To achieve this, closer links between the local, regional and national experts who form the backbone of Europe's disaster-response strategies will be necessary.

(b) *Remote Sensing.* By organising collected information in a geographic information system (GIS), European Union humanitarian organisations can more effectively analyse situations and coordinate relief efforts. GALILEO is one such initiative providing information concerning the positioning of users in many sectors such as transportation, social services, customs services, public works, search and rescue system. However, GALILEO can also be used in Disaster Monitoring and Prediction, Optimising Disaster Relief and Facilitating Humanitarian Aid Operations.

53. **Relevance to India and SE Asia.** There is a lot that India can learn and imbibe from the European model of Disaster Management while evolving its own. Some important aspects as relevant to India in particular and SE Asia in general are:-

(a) Establish a centralised command, control and communication grid across the nation down to district level.

(b) There is a definite need for greater regional initiatives in SE Asia with an aim to exploit each other's strengths and cover each others criticalities.

(c) India must introduce disaster management as a subject in curriculum at schools and colleges with an aim to create general awareness.

(d) Participation in international initiatives on the matter and establishing strategic partnerships to share knowledge and benefit from those who possess enhanced capabilities in terms of real time information and resource mobilisation.

(e) India, in its endeavour to establish itself as a credible world power needs to overcome its inward looking policy and take initiatives in establishing and providing for some of the regional initiatives in disaster management

Conclusion

54. The developed nations have learned the issue of Disaster Management and have constituted various organisations and agencies which are constructively working during peace time to standardise emergency management procedures and equipment. These organisations are also working towards development programme to ensure expansion of existing state and emergency management capabilities to provide an effective civil defence organisation. Hence, there is a need to develop a similar system in our country as also in the regional context to minimise loss of life and property due to natural disasters.

References

- Andrew Stewart Limited, 2006, Managed Retreat from Coastal Hazards: Options for Implementation, report for Environment Waikato.
- Auckland Regional Council, 1996, Tsunami and Storm surges in the Auckland Region.
- Auckland Regional Council, 1997, Auckland Engineering Lifelines Project, Stage 1 report.

- Auckland- Regional Council, 2000, Coastal Hazard Strategy and Coastal Erosion Management Manual, Auckland Regional Council, Technical Publication No. 130.
- Brodnax, R C, 1991, Cliff erosion in the Waitemata Harbour and Hauraki Fulf, Masters Thesis, University of Auckland.
- Brookes, H O and Benson, A P, 1999, Review of Report "Coastal Hazard Assessment for Papamoa Township, Tauranga District, Bay of Plenty, New Zealand", Unpublished report for Tauranga District Council.
- Bruun, P, 1988, The Bruun Rule of erosion by sea-level rise: A discussion on large scale two- and three-dimensional usages, Journal of Coastal Research, Vol. 4(4), 627-648.
- Defra, 2002, Soft Cliffs Manual for Managers, Defra Flood Management Division, London, UK.
- Environment Waikato, 1999a, Coastal Erosion Risk Mitigation Strategy For the Waikato Region, Environment Waikato Policy Series 1999/03, Doc # 480281.
- Environment Waikato, 1999b, Coastal Flooding Risk Mitigation Strategy, Environment Waikato Policy Series 1999/06, Doc # 4800895.
- Environment Waikato, 2002a, Coromandel Beaches: Coastal Hazards and Development Setback Recommendations.
- Gibb, J G, 1984, 'Coastal erosion', In: Speden I and Crozier M J (Eds), 1984, Natural Hazards in New Zealand, UNESCO, New Zealand, pp. 134-158.
- Gibb, J G, 1994, Standards and information requirements for assessing coastal hazard zones for New Zealand, report prepared for Department of Conservation.
- Glassey, P, 2002, Defining Coastal Hazard - A pilot project in the Auckland Region, Proposal for, Manukau City Council.
- Glassey, P, Gibb, J, Hoverd, J, Jongens, R, Alloway, B, Coombes, K, Benson, A, 2003, Establishing a methodology for coastal cliff hazard mapping: An East Coast Bays, Audc/and pilot study, In: Coasts and Ports 2003, Proceedings of 16th Australasian Coastal and 'Ocean Engineering Conference, Auckland.
- Healy and Dean, 2000, Methodology for delineation of CHZ and development setback tar open duned coasts, Handbook of Coastal Engineering, McGraw-Hill.
- Kay, R C, Eriksen, N J , Foster, G A , Giligren, Healy, T R , Sheffield, A T and Warrick, R A, 1994, Assessment of Coestst :Hazards and their Management for Selected Parts of the Coastal Zone Administered by the Tauranga District Council, A report to the Tauranga District Council and Environment Bay of Plenty.

- Ministry for the Environment, 2001, Planning for Climate Change Effects on Coastal Margins, report prepared by NIWA as part of the New Zealand Climate Change Programme.
- Moon, V G and de lange, W P, 2003, Estimating long-term cliff recession rates in soft Flysch Deposits, Waitemata Group, Auckland, New Zealand, Coasts and Ports Australasian Conference, Paper No. 93.
- Moon, V G and Healy, T, 1994, Mechanisms of Coastal Cliff Retreat and Hazard Zone Delineation in Soft Flysch Deposits, Journal of Coastal Research, 10: 3.
- New Zealand Climate Change Office, 2004a, Coastal Hazards and Climate Change: A guidance manual for local government in New Zealand, ME512, New Zealand. Climate Change Office, Ministry for the Environment, Wellington. National Institute for Coastal and Marine Management of the Netherlands et al, 2004, Living With Coastal Erosion in Europe: Sand and Space for Sustainability, Part VII - Guidance Document for Quick Hazard Assessment of Coastal Erosion and Associated Flooding, April 2004, National Institute for Coastal and Marine Management of the Netherlands (RIKZ).
- Patel, J, 1997, Engineering geology of coastal cliff stability along the northern. Manukau Harbour, Masters Thesis, University of Auckland.
- Reeve, D E, 1998, Coastal Flood Risk Assessment, Journal of Waterway, Port, Coastal and Ocean Engineering, Sept/Oct. pp. 219-228.
- SCOR Working Group 89, 1991, The response of beaches to sea-level changes: A review of predictive models, Journal of Coastal Research 7(3): 895-921.
- Tonkin and Taylor, 2002b,Coastal Hazard Analysis, Unpublished report for Whakatane District Council, Tonkin and Taylor Report Ref. 18731, Auckland, November 2002.
- Tonkin and Taylor, 2003, Regional Coastal Hazard Assessment, Unpublished report for Hawke's Bay Regional Council, Tonkin and Taylor Report Ref 20514, Auckland.
- Tonkin and Taylor, 2005, Regional Coastal Erosion Hazard Assessment (Draft), Unpublished report for Auckland Regional Council, Tonkin and Taylor Report 19891.100, September 2005.

Emergency Management

- Ministry of Civil Defence and Emergency Management, 2002, Working Together: Developing a CDEM Group Plan; Director's Guidelines for CDEM Groups, DGL 2/02, ISBN 0-478-25453-9.
- Ministry of Civil Defence and Emergency Management, 2004, Resilient New Zealand: A Aotearoa Manahau: National Civil Defence Emergency Management. Strategy 2003-2006, ISBN 0-478-25461-X.

- Ministry of Civil Defence and Emergency Management, 2005, Proposed National Civil Defence Emergency Management Plan (for consultation), August 2005; ISBN 0-478-25466-0. Ministry of Civil Defence and Emergency Management, 2006, The Guide to the National CDEM Plan (Draft Version, 16 February 2006).
- Taranaki Regional Council, 2004a, Civil Defence Emergency Management Group Plan for Taranaki, prepared by Taranaki Regional Council on behalf of the Taranaki CDEM Group.
- Taranaki Regional Council, 2004b, Taranaki Civil Defence Emergency Management Group: Hazard and Risk Analysis: Explanatory Notes.

Flooding

- Department of Infrastructure, 2002, Applying the Flood Provisions in Planning Schemes: A Guide for Coundls, VPP Practice Note, Victoria, Australia.
- Reeve, D E, 1998, Coastal Flood Risk Assessment, Journal of Waterway, Port, Coastal and Ocean Engineering, Sept/Oct. pp. 219-228.
- Wellington Regional Council, 2001, Hutt River Floodplain Management Plan: For the Hutt River and its Environment, Publication No. WRC/FPSA-G-Ol/32, ISBN: 0-909016-76-3, Flood Protection Group, Landcare Division, Wellington Regional Council.

Landslides/land subsidence

- Australian Geomechanics Society, 2000, Landslide risk management concepts and guidelines, Australian Geomechanics, March 35(1) 49-92.
- Australian Geomechanics Society, 2006, Guidelines for landslide susceptibility, hazard and risk mapping for land use planning, Draft B: March 2006.
- Brooks, S, Crozier, M J, Glade, T and Anderson, M G, 2004, Towards establishing climatic thresholds for slope instability: use of a pttvsicsttv-based combined soil hydrology-slope stability model, Pure and Applied Geophysics 161(4): 881-905.
- Casini, L, Bonnard, C H, Corominas, J, Jibson, R, and Monteero-Olarte, J, 2005, 'Landslide hazard and risk zoning for urban planning and development', In: Hungr O, Fell R, Couture R, and Eberthardt (Eds), Landslide risk management, Taylor and Francs, London: 199-235.
- Crozier, M J, 1993, Management issues arising from landslides and related activity, New Zealand Geog rapher 49 (1): 35-37.
- Glade, T, Anderson, M, 'and Crozier, M J, 2005, Landslide Hazard and Risk, Wiley, Chichester.
- Hancox, G T, Perrin, N 'O, Dellow G O, 1997, Earthquake-Induced Landsliding in New Zealand and 'Implications for MM Intensity and Seismic Hazard Assessment, IGNS (EQC funded project 95/196) - December 1997.

- Ministry of Civil Defence and Emergency Management, 2002, Earth Movements, Tephra 19.
- Wilson, H and Crozier, M, 2000, 'Quantitative hazard assessment: rainfall triggered landslides', In Bromhead, Dixon, and Ibsen (Eds), 2000, Landslides in Research Theory and Practice, Vol. 3, Thomas Telford: 1575-1581.

Meteorological Hazards

- Environment Waikato, 2002b, The Weather Bomb, Environment Waikato Technical Report 2002/10, 21 June 2002, prepared by Adam Munro for Environment Waikato, IS5N: 1172-4005, Dowment #: 760464.
- Ministry of Civil Defence,1997, Storms, Tephra 16 Ministry of Civil Defence and Emergency Management, 2003, Wet and Wild, Tephra 20.
- Ministry for the Environment, Climate Change Guidance Note.
- National Institute of Water and Atmospheric Research Ltd, 2002, Meteorological Hazards and the Potential Impacts of Climate Change in Wellington Region: A Scoping Study, NIWA Client Report WLG2002/19, WRC Pub. No. WRC/RP-T-02/16, Prepared for Wellington Regional Council.
- National Institute of Water and Atmospheric Research, 2004, Managing New Zealand's Climate: a Resource and a Hazard, NIWA Information series No. 54. ISSN 1174-264X.
- National Institute of Water and Atmospheric Research Ltd, 2005, Meteorological Hazards and the Potential Impacts of Climate Change in the Manawatu-Wanganui Region, NIWA Client Report: WlG200S-17, April 2005, NIWA Project: HRC05301, Prepared for Horizons Manawatu-Wanganui Regional Council.
- New Zealand Climate Change Office, 2004b, Climate Change Effects and Impact Assessment: A guidance manual for Local Government in New Zealand, MES13, New Zealand Climate Change Office, Ministry for the Environment, Wellington.
- NZIER, 2002, The Waikato Weather Bomb: Understanding the impact, March 2004, A report commissioned by the New Zealand Climate Change Office (Ministry for the Environment) in conjunction with Environment Waikato and the Ministry of Civil Defence and Emergency Management.
- Tomlinson, 1980, The frequency of high intensity rainfalls in New Zealand, Water and Soil Technical Publication 19, National Water and Soil Conservation Organisation.

Seismic Hazards

- Department of Building and Housing, 2005, Earthquake-Prone Building Provisions of the Building Act 2004: Policy Guidance for Territorial Authorities, Department of Building and Housing.

- Dowrick, O J and Cousins, W J, 2002, Historical Incidence of Modified Mercalli Intensity in New Zealand and Comparison with Hazard Models, Bulletin of the New Zealand Society for Earthquake Engineering.
- Dowrick, D J and Rhoades, O A, 1999, Attenuation of Modified Mercalli Intensity in New Zealand Earthquakes.
- Dowrick, D J, Rhoades, O A and Davenport, PN, 2001, Damage Ratios for Domestic Property in the Magnitude 7.2 1968 Inangahua, New Zealand, Earthquake, Bulletin of the New Zealand Society for Earthquake Engineering, 34(3): 191-213.
- Environment Waikato, 1997a, Earthquake Risk Mitigation Plan, Environment Waikato Policy Series 1997/12, Doc # 487363.
- Hancox, G T, Perrin, N D, Dellow, G O, 1997, Earthquake-Induced Landsliding in New Zealand and Implications for MM Intensity and Seismic Hazard Assessment, IGNS (EQC funded project 95/196) - December 1997.
- Hastings District Council, 2004, District Plan Monitoring: Earthquake Hazard, Section 12.3 - Natural Hazard Review, Hastings District Plan, Report by Nia Belcher, Environmental Planning, Hastings District Council, April 2004.
- Horizons Manawatu-Wanganui Regional Council, 1999, Hazard Analysis Manual Volume 2, Horizons Manawatu-Wanganui Regional Council, ISBN: 1877221-45-7, Ministry of Civn·Defence,1998, Earthquakes, Tephra 17(1).
- Ministry for the Environment, 2004, Planning for Development of Land on or Close to Active Faults: A guideline to assist resource management planners in New Zealand, Report prepared for the Ministry for the Environment by Janine Kerr, Simon Nathan, Russ Van Dissen, Peter Webb, David Brunsdon and Andrew King, Ministry for Environment, December 2004, Ref. ME565, ISBN: 0-478-18901.
- Wellington Regional Council, 1993, Seismic Hazard Map Series, Wellington Regional Council Publication WRC/PP-T-93/74.

Tsunami

- Auckland Regional Council, 1996, Tsunami and Storm Surges in the Auckland Region.
- Bell, R G, 2005, 'Lessons from Boxing Day tsunami: implications for disaster reduction and detection/warning systems' In: Collen, J (Ed), Abstracts of papers presented at the STAR Session 2005, held in conjunction with the SOPAC 34th Annual Session, Apia, samoa, 23-30 September 2005, pp. 1113. SOPAC Miscellaneous Report No. 603. SOPAC Secretariat, Suva, Fiji.
- Berryman, K (Compiler), 2005, Review of Tsunami Hazard and Risk in New Zealand, Institute of Geological and Nuclear Sciences client report CR2005104, Lower Hutt.

- Chick, L M, Healy, T and de Lange, W P, 2001, Tsunami Hazard in the Firth of Thames, Hauraki Gulf, NZ, Journal of Coastal Research, special issue 34.
- de Lange, W P and Hull, A G, 1994, Tsunami Hazard-for the Auckland Region, Auckland Regional Council.
- de Lange, W P and Bell, R G, 1998, 'Tsunami risk from the southern flank: Balleny Islands earthquake; Water & Atmosphere 6(3): 13-15.
- Environment Waikato, 2004, Tsunami Hazard for the Bay of Plenty and Eastern Coromandel Peninsula: Stage 1, Environment Waikato Technical Report TR04/33, ISSN: 1172-4005.
- Gisborne District Council, 2005, Gisborne District: Emergency Services Tsunami Contingency Plan, Gisbome District Council.
- Goring, D G and Bell, R G, 1998, 'Canterbury shelf waves and the PNG tsunami', Water and Atmosphere 6(3): 15-16.
- Institute of Geological and Nuclear Sciences Ltd, 2005, Review of New Zealand's preparedness tsunami hazard, comparison to risk and recommendations for treatment, compiled by Terry Webb, Client Report 2005/162, Prepared for Ministry of Civil Defence and Emergency Management, December 2005.
- Ministry of Civil Defence, 1999, Tsunami, Tephra 17(2).
- National Tsunami Hazard Mitigation Program, 2001, Designing for Tsunamis, NOAA, USGS, FEMA, NSF, Alaska, California, Hawaii, Oregon, and Washington, (http://www.pmel.noaa.gov/tsunami-hazard/).
- Tonkin and Taylor Ltd, 2002a, Options for Managing Risks from Tsunami in the Wellington Region, report for Wellington Regional Council, WRC Publication No. WRC/RP-T-02/17.
- Walters, R A, 2002, Long wave resonance on the New Zealand coast, NIWA Technical Report 109.32.

Volcanic hazards

- Department of Conservation. 1999, Environmental and risk assessment for mitigation of the hazard from Ruapehu Crater Lake - Assessment of environmental effects.
- Environment Waikato, 1999, Volcanic Risk Mitigation Plan, Environment Waikato Policy Series 1999/10, ISSN: 1174-7234.
- Hancox, G T, Nairn, I A, Otway, P M, Webby, M G, Perrin, N D, and Keys, J R, 1997, Stability assessment of Mt Ruapehu Crater Rim following the 1995-1996 eruptions, IGNS Client Report 43606.
- Ministry of Civil Defence, 1995, Volcanic hazards in New Zealand, Tephra 14(2) Ministry of Civil Defence and Emergency Management, 2004, Living with Volcanoes, Tephra 21.

- National Institute of Water and Atmospheric Research, 1998, Potential effects of lahar from Mt.· Ruapehu on the Tongariro River and Lake Taupo, NIWA Report, DOC 80219.
- Tephra,1995, Volcanic hazards in New Zealand, Tephra October 1995 issue.
- Tonkin and Taylor Ltd, 1998, Lower Tongariro Natural Hazard Management Plan, Auckland.

End Note

1. Brown op. cit. pp. 14-32.
2. ARTRAC Policy Approach and Role of Various Organisations for Disaster Management in India, p. 10.
3. Brown op. cit. pp. 14-31.
4. Brown op. cit. p. 27
5. Brown op. cit. pp. 14-31.
6. Australian Counter Disaster Handbook, pp.15-30.
7. Pandey Mohan.- Disaster Relief Trishul, Vol. iii, No. 2, 1992.
8. Pandey Mohan. Op. cit.

Preparedness and Mitigation in Restoration of E-Governance

The safety of the people shall be the highest law. – **Cicero**

NATIONAL POLICY ON DISASTER MANAGEMENT

General

1. The national approach to management of disasters has evolved over a period of time. Currently, the primary responsibility of providing relief in the wake of natural disasters has been recognised to be that of the **State governments.**[1] The Centre's role has been restricted to one of providing resources to the States for this purpose and acting in a supportive manner in relation to economic activities and infrastructure mobilisation.

2. Even though the States are primarily responsible for relief activities, the Central Government associates itself with measures aimed at alleviating the suffering of the people on account of these calamities. Towards this end, the Central Government with its resources including finances does provide the need help and assistance to buttress relief efforts in the wake of major calamities.[2] The dimensions of the **responses by the Central Government** are determined in accordance with the existing policy of financing the relief expenditure and keeping in views the factors like:-

(a) The **gravity** of the calamity.

(b) The **scale** of the relief operation necessary.

(c) The requirement of Central assistance for augmenting the **financial resources** at the disposal of the State government.

Disaster Management Planning[3]

3. The disaster management plan for the country has four essential components. These are:-

(a) Application of scientific inputs to forecasting and relief programmes.

(b) Timeless and dynamism of management of relief delivery.

(c) People's participation in relief delivery and monitoring.

(d) Contribution to resilience of societies and areas for improvement in quality of life.

4. Despite the recognition of the need to build up society's capabilities to meet the challenges of disasters, the **thrust** of **relief** effort has, for a variety of reasons, concentrated on the **alleviation and restoration** aspects. On the occurrence of disasters, the need for continued vigil, preparedness and conscious effort to reduce the occurrence and impact of disasters has often been neglected. **In a country, which boasts of planned developmental effort, perspective action still remains an ideal.**

5. **Type of Response**. The Central response can be:-

(a) Policy response.

(b) Administrative response.

6. **Policy Response**. The Prime Minister, Cabinet Committees and the concerned Minister of the nodal ministry (Agriculture Ministry in case of Natural Disaster) would be responsible for providing the policy response to natural calamity.

The objectives of policy response would be:-

(a) To empathise with the sufferings of the people affected by natural calamity.

(b) To sub-serve long-term and short-term policy objectives of the government.

7. **Administrative Response**. The response of the Administration to a situation arising out of a natural calamity can be on account of:-

(a) A follow-up of a policy objective of the government.

(b) The need for an assessment of the situation and for a central response.

(c) States requests for Central assistance.

(d) The need for information as a governance objective.

8. **Central Response**. Central Government's response at the policy level, to a natural calamity would lead to Central initiative in the form of:-

(a) Visits of the calamity affected areas by dignitaries like President, Prime Minister etc.

(b) Activating the administrative machinery for assisting in relief measures.

(c) Setting up machinery for implementing, reviewing and monitoring of relief measures.

9. **The administrative response** at the Central Government level would broadly be related to:-

(a) Operational requirement.

(b) Provision of Central assistance as per existing policy.

10. **The operational aspects** of the administrative response could, further, be classified into:-

(a) Primary relief functions.

(b) Secondary relief functions.

Primary Relief Functions[4]

11. The primary relief functions of the Central Government would relate to:-

(a) Forecasting and operation of warning systems.

(b) Maintenance of uninterrupted communication.

(c) Wide publicity to warnings of impending calamity, disaster preparedness and relief measures through TV, AIR and Newspapers.

(d) Transport with particular reference to evacuation and movement of essential commodities and petroleum products.

(e) Ensuring availability of essential commodities at reasonable prices particularly the commodities through the Public Distribution System.

(f) Ensuring availability of medicines, vaccine and drugs.

(g) Preservation and restoration of physical communication links.

(h) Investments in infrastructure.

(j) Mobilisation of financial resources.

Secondary Relief Functions[5]

12. The secondary functions of the Central Government, which supplement the States relief efforts, would relate to: -

(a) Flood/inflow forecasts from the Central Water Commission.

(b) Relief, rehabilitation and restoration through military aid to authorities.

(c) Contingency plan for crop and cattle preservation, nutrition and health measures.

(d) Technical and technological inputs for provision of drinking water.

(e) Technical assistance in the water budgeting and water management for various uses.

(f) Coordination of the activities of the State agencies and voluntary agencies.

COORDINATION AND CONTROL[6]

National Level

13. For effective implementation of relief measures in the wake of a disaster, the cabinet has set up a **National Crisis Management Committee (NCMC).** The concerned Secretary shall provide all necessary information and seek directions of the Cabinet Committee in all maters concerning relief and step for effective implementation of its directions. In the absence of such a Cabinet Committee all matters relating to relief shall be reported to the Cabinet Secretary.

14. The **National Crisis Management Committee (NCMC)** has been consisted in the Cabinet Secretariat. The composition of the Committee is as under:-

(a) Cabinet Secretary - Chairman.

(b) Secretary to Prime Minister - Member.

(c) Secretary (MHA) - Member.

(d) Secretary (MOD)	-	Member.
(e) Director (IB)	-	Member.
(f) Secretary (R&AW)	-	Member.
(g) Secretary (Agriculture & Cooperation)	-	Co-opted Member.
(h) An officer of Cabinet	-	Convenor

15. **Central Committee**. A central committee is also constituted in time of crises. The composition if this committee is also follows:-

(a) Special Secretary (ISP) MHA.

(b) Special Dir IB.

(c) OSD (R and AW).

(d) JS (P), MHA.

(e) JS (IS-I), MHA.

(f) JS (R and AW).

(g) IG (Ops), BSF HQ.

(h) Additional DGMO (A), Army HQ.

(i) IG (Ops) CRPF.

(j) Joint Dir, IB.

(k) DS (CPO), MHA.

(l) Dir (IS-I), MHA.

(m) Dir (G), MOD.

(n) Dir (R and AW).

(o) Dir MO6, Army HQ.

(p) Additional DIG (Ops), CRPF.

16. In addition, nodal Ministries for various disasters have been designated.

These are:-

(a) Natural Disasters	-	Agricultural and Cooperation.
(b) Chemical Disaster	-	Environment and Forest.
(c) Nuclear Disaster	-	Department of Atomic Energy.
(d) Biological Disaster	-	Health.
(e) Civil Strife	-	Home.

18. The resident Commissioners of the States affected by major natural calamity may be co-opted on the CMG during the period.

Contingency Action Plan

19. The nodal agency in the Government of India for natural calamities relief, is the Department of Agriculture & Cooperation, (DAC), where an Additional Secretary is designated as the Central Relief Commissioner. A National Contingency Action Plan (CAP) has been notified by DAC. It facilitates the launching of relief operations without delay. This is updated every year. CAP identifies the initiative required to be taken by various Central Ministries/Departments in the wake of natural calamities, sets down the procedure and determines the focal points in the administrative machinery.

FINANCIAL ASPECTS[7]

Procedure for Extending Financial Assistance to States

20. The present scheme of financing the relief expenditure arising out of natural calamities has come into force with effect from 1st April 1990, consequent upon the acceptance of the recommendations of the National Finance Commission. Under this scheme, a Calamity Relief Fund (CRF) is constituted for each State. Seventy-five per cent of this amount is to be contributed by the Central Government in four quarterly installments and the balance 25 per cent is to be provided by the State Governments from its own resources. Following the constitution of the CRF. It is the responsibility of the State Government to meet all expenditure arising out of the natural calamities.

Arrangement for Financing Relief

21. As per the Scheme for financing relief expenditure, which was based on the recommendations of VII and VIII Finance Commissions and was in force till 31st March 1990, every State had margin money at its disposal for meeting the emergent expenditure in the wake of natural calamities. Both Central and State Government (SG) shared this margin money equally. The SGs were required to incur the expenditure on relief operations from the State share of the release of the Central share of margin money in the first instance. They would request for the release of the Central share of margin money keeping in view of the severity of the situation after sending full details of the

expenditure incurred on relief operations. In case the magnitude of the calamity warranted incurring of expenditure beyond the total margin money for a particular State, the SG concerned would submit a memorandum seeking Central assistance for natural calamities. On receipt of the memorandum from a SG, a multidisciplinary Central Team was constituted to make an on the spot assessment of the damage and assistance required for relief operations. The Report of the Central team was then placed before the High Level Committee on Relief (HLCR) for determination of ceilings of expenditure The recommendation of the HLCR formed the basis for a decision of the Ministry of Finance on the quantum of central assistance.

Ninth Finance Commission's Recommendations

22. On the recommendation of the IX Finance Commission, the scheme for financing relief expenditure has been revised. As per this scheme, each State has a corpus of funds called Calamity Relief Fund (CRF), administrated by the State Government. The size of the corpus is determined having regard to the vulnerability of the State to different natural calamities and the magnitude of expenditure normally incurred by the State on relief operations. The corpus is built by the annual contributions of the Union Government and the SGs concerned in the ratio of 3:1. At present, the aggregate annual accretion in the States CRF amounts to Rs 804.00 crores. The SGs are free to draw upon this corpus for providing relief in the event of any natural calamity. In the event of a major disaster warranting intervention at the national level, a provision exists for the Union Government to supplement the financial resources need for relief operations.

WARNING SYSTEMS[8]

23. The crucial warning systems are:-

(a) **Indian Meteorological Department (IMD)**. For drought, rainfall, cyclone, crop position.

(b) **The Department of Space (DOS)**. Satellite monitoring of drought and floods.

(c) **Ministry of Water Resources**. Floods in river systems.

24. **IMD**. The IMD monitors the rainfall situation through a network of 4000 rain gauge stations spread over the country. It is also linked to the World Meteorological Organisation (WMO). Before the

onset of the monsoon, long range forecast is made for the monsoon season as a whole to facilitate agro-economic planning. A weekly rainfall analysis is available with 35 meteorological sub-divisions, which cover 127 agro-climatic regions. Rainfall monitoring also gives early monitoring of about drought. The National Remote Sensing Agency, through satellite technology, reports on the status of crops based on the moisture vegetative index, which is used for planning for drought management. A crop weather watch group meets once a week during monsoons to assess the behaviour of rainfall, crop situation and water level in reservoirs. However, the challenge before the IMD now is to make predictions four to five days in advance.

25. **Cyclone Warning**. The IMD has an observation network to detect cyclones through 10 cyclone detection radars on the coasts. The range of these radars is 400 km. Simultaneously the INSAT-1B satellite monitors cyclonic movements. In addition, ships and commercial radars are also used for cyclonic warnings. About 260 ships of the merchant fleet have meteorological observation systems.

26. **Flood Forecast**. The Central Water Commission in the Ministry of Water Resources has a flood forecast system with 157 flood forecasting centres covering 62 interstate river basins. In collaboration with IMD, they monitor rainfall and water levels in reservoirs. India has now developed radar, which gives accurate estimate of rainfall up to 200 km around the radar site.[9]

28. **Seismic Observatories**. There are 35 observatories to monitor seismic disturbances.

State Level Mechanism

29. In view of their autonomous jurisdiction, the States have evolved their own relief machinery. At State level the **Relief Commissioner or Revenue Secretary,** is the nodal agency for direction of relief effort. In most State, a State level committee, chaired by the Chief Minister, acts as a policy formulating forum and monitoring body. At the **district** level, the District Collector or the **Deputy Commissioner** is the 'focal points' for all relief effort. The existence of a body of non-official personnel, comprising people representative in legislatures, panchayats and NGOs, to advise, it is more common to see such organisation operating during the period immediately

following the occurrence of discharged by the personnel of various functional departments under the control of the Deputy Commissioner.

30. On the above model, some States have evolved efficient disaster management plans with the requisite infrastructure and organisational support. These as in the case of Maharashtra, include an **Emergency Operations Centre** in the State Secretariat, which is linked to the district by an efficient wireless and satellite based communication network. This is backed by a computerised **District Management Information System, community disaster preparedness programmes** training. The **District Control Rooms** would be the nodal facility for directing all operations on disaster

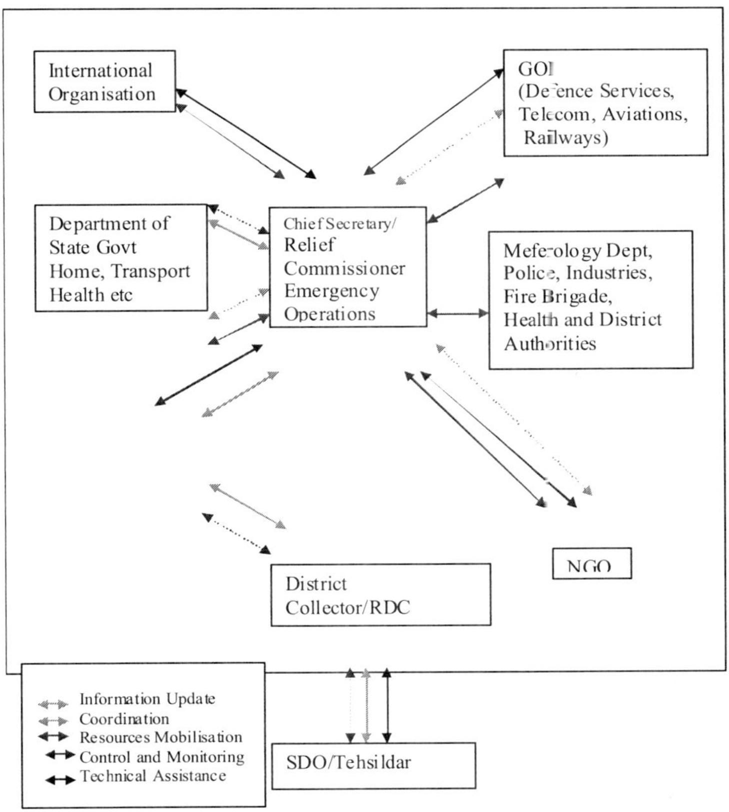

emergency situation, and hence are required to be supported by disaster management information and communications to function efficiently. **Information** is essential not only for **risk analysis** and **vulnerability assessment** but also for organising the response. Figure on the next page shows the model.

MODEL SHOWING DISASTER RELIEF CYCLE AT STATE LEVEL

ROLE OF ARMED FORCES[10]

31. The **primary role** of the Armed Forces is to preserve national interest by safeguarding the territorial integrity of the nation against external threats, as well as the nation's strategic interest in the region. Its **secondary role** is to assist civil authorities in handling internal threats, maintenance of essential **service,** as also to assist the Central Government or States during natural and other calamities. In organisational and infrastructural terms, the Armed Forces provide a speedy and efficient response in dealing with a disaster situation which is beyond the resources of civil administration. They are also capable of providing emergency health operations and relief measures, particularly in search, rescue and evacuation, shelter for victims and damage assessment. Consequently, the government often fallen back on the Armed Force during emergencies. As a result, efficient disaster management mechanism incorporated in the Armed Forces at each level when **contingency plans** are formulated and specify the assistance likely to be required in the disaster prone areas. This facilitates a more efficient response by the Armed Forces when called upon and provides interface mechanism in an emergency, thereby ensuring synergy and effective response. The Army's presence in under-developed areas along our borders helps it contribute to the relief endeavours where the governments' relief mechanism and sources are weakest.

32. Armed Forces may be called upon provide the following types of assistance:-

(a) Providing **infrastructure for command and control** organisation for providing relief is an important function. This is would involve provision of communications and making available technical specialist manpower.

(b) Provision of **medical** care at the incident site and evacuation of Casualties.

(c) Logistic support for **transportation of relief material**.

(d) Setting up and running of **relief camps**.

(e) Construction and repair of **roads** and **bridges** to enable to relief term/material to reach effected areas.

(f) Repair, maintenance and running of **essential services** especially in the initial stage of disaster relief.

(g) Assist in **evacuation** of people to safe place before and after the Disaster.

(h) Stage management and handling of **international relief,** if requested by the civil administration.

ROLE OF POLICE AND HOME GUARDS IN RESCUE AND RELIEF OPERATION[11]

33. The **Police** have always played a very useful and effective role in various situations of natural disasters or calamities for preservation of human life (and also cattle) and protection of property. The salient features of police assistance are as under:-

(a) Before and during relief/rescue operations the police can effectively assist the local administration by disseminating information as well as warning, as and when necessary, through is spread out telecom system. All Police Stations and most of the police outpost in the State are equipped with wireless communication.

(b) Being a fairly spread-out organisation, responsible of enforcement of the law of the land, the Police can become an effective instrument for persuasion for evacuation in emergencies.

(c) Due to blockade of other means of transport of road as well as rail, the police help can reach interior areas in no time, faster than any other service organisation and carry relief to the affected masses.

(d) With their good knowledge of local people and resources the Police officers at the local level can provide guidance to other people for effective execution of tasks.

(e) The Police can provide traffic control and direction for evacuation apart from providing protection to evacuated people and villages. They can cordon off areas and control the miscreants as a means of providing protection.

(f) By their vigilant eye on the grim situation, the police can render invaluable assistance to people and administration even in the distribution of food, medicine, food grains, clothes etc. and maintain law and order during these operations.

(g) As on organisation given the task of collection and administration of information, the police can be of help of administration during such operations.

34. However, the police being a law and order-maintaining agency has its limitations in providing all kinds of relief in the event of natural disasters. There are specialised agencies such as the PWD, Health Department, Public Health Engineering, Irrigation, Housing, Food and Civil Supplies, Home Guards etc, who have the responsibility to provide the technical service on such occasions.

Home Guards

35. Home Guards are a force of volunteers constituted under the legislation enacted by the State Government. The Home Guards apart from assisting the local administration in performance of various police duties have also been assigned the role of the helping the State and society during emergences relating to natural disaster.

36. Home Guards Compendium of Instructions spells out their role as:-

(a) Serve as auxiliary to the police and assist in maintaining internal security.

(b) Assist the community in any kind of emergency such as air raid, a fire, a flood, epidemic etc.

(c) Organise functional units to provide essential services such as motor transport, pioneer and engineer groups, fire brigade, nursing and first aid, operation of water and power supply installation etc.

(d) Promote communal harmony and give assistance to the administration in protecting the weaker section of the society.

(e) Participation in socio-economic and welfare activities such as adult education, health and hygiene, developmental schemes and such other tasks as are deemed useful.

37. The Home Guards are a very important adjunct to police and the revenue administration to carry out rescue and relief work during an emergency, after natural calamity has struck as:-

(a) Help in the evacuation of the affected people and cattle to safer areas, with the help of boats and other improvised material.

(b) To rescue people trapped under the debries of collapsed houses, by employing various techniques of 'Rescue'.

(c) To rescue during people with the help of life buoys, life jackets, or other improvised floating aids.

(d) To render first aid to the injured, including artificial respiration etc.

(e) To help police in the maintenance of law and order during these operations.

Role of Voluntary/Non Governmental Organisation (NGOs)[12]

38. The role of voluntary organisations, both local and international is help people to overcome problem posted by natural disasters by providing welfare and relief services according to the specific needs of the people. It also works as the ears and eyes of the people and also acts as an intermediary between the people and the government to avoid duplication, to impress proper distributions of scarce resources, and to organise vigilance group for prevention of misuse of resources. Some of the activities, which are taken by such organisations are given in Paragraph 39 below.

39. **Activities of NGOs**. During various stage of disaster management based on identified type and their capabilities, the NGOs can be useful for:-

Stage	Activity
Pre-Disaster	: Awareness and information campaigns
	: Training of local volunteers
	: Advocacy and planning

During Disaster	:	Immediate rescue and first aid including psychological aid
	:	Supply of food, water medicines and other immediate need materials
	:	Ensuring sanitation and hygiene
	:	Damage assessment
Post Disaster	:	Technical and material aid in reconstruction
	:	Assistance in seeking financial aid monitoring

41. There is a need to co-ordinate the relief work of both Government and Non-governmental agencies to avoid duplication of effort and wastage of scarce resources. The Centre, State and District level Relief Committees should be formed, headed by a responsible persons (PM/CM/DC's) for securing and co-ordinating voluntary effort for relief. These Committees should include representatives of local international voluntary agencies to avoid on relief operations.

DISASTER MANAGEMENT IN INDIA: NEED AND RECOMMENDED INTEGRATED APPROACH

GENERAL

1. In the last three chapters the general terms, disaster management organisations at home, some foreign countries and the role and tasks being carried out by international organisations such as UN have been discussed. It has clearly emerged that India needs to improve its performance in this aspect. In light of the forgoing, in this chapter the policy, an approach, and organisational integration will be discussed.

CURRENT CONCERNS[13]

General

2. The provision of relief in the wake of natural calamities has largely been left to the initiatives and polices of State Governments. Development programmes, which got to meet the capabilities of areas and population to meet natural disasters over the years, have been left to the general exercise of planning. Therefore, measures to reduce the impact of natural disasters have not received the focus, they deserve

particularly in view of the fact that 85 per cent of the country is prone to one disaster or another. If the concern and effort, required for tackling specific problems, are to be taken care of in a general exercise of planning, then the urgency of action get subsumed by macro considerations, strategy of and sectoral priorities. The consequence is in adequate attention to the particular problem area, without which the vulnerable areas never get out of the pathetic cycle of disasters and rehabilitation. It is therefore necessary that some of the issues relating to natural disasters management would have to receive specific attention at the national and sub-national levels. Broadly, in the context of IDNDR, it will be appropriate to highlight these concerns in natural disaster management with a view to creating an opportunity for translating them into specific action points.

3. The current concerns are broadly related to:-

(a) Disaster relief execution capability.

(b) Disaster preparedness.

(c) Sustainability of disaster mitigation efforts.

(d) Development thrusts.

Disaster Relief Execution Capability

4. Documentation of impact and relief activities in the country would have to be considerably improved to provide the insight into the hazard, vulnerability, and requirement of machinery for relief. An inventory of experience would go a long way in ensuring in terms of crises the adoption of time-tested methods for minimising the adverse impact of disasters. The system of placing senior officers in charge of relief operations in the wake of natural calamities, presently in vague in many States is a significant effort in this direction. However, for the smooth execution of relief programmes, knowledge and skills should be available at varying levels of implementation. In the long-term, specific human resources development programmes would have to be continuously implemented to ensure appropriate initiatives at different levels of the relief machinery, the availability of experienced personnel would speed up the relief effort at any point of time. Presently the State Government machinery depends on current personnel for most of the relief effort, whether they have the necessary skills or not. It would, therefore, be necessary to introduce the system of maintenance

of reserves of experienced personnel in different spheres such as logistics, health, rescue and relief.

5. The building-up of a database encompassing hazards, vulnerability and resource endowment is the crying need of the hour. Such database would have to be updated continuously at the local level and State level.

Preparedness Aspects

6. The Government of India has asked the States to formulate **contingency plans at the district and State levels for dealing** with different types of disasters. Such contingency action plan could clearly delineate the responsibilities of different organisations and agencies and also identify the triggering mechanism for various agencies. The continuous updating of the contingency plan in the context of earlier experience would have to be ensured through an annual exercise. Reassessment of the Contingency plans for an area could be made more effective by the association for personnel who dealt with earlier disasters in that area.

7. As earlier pointed out, scientific and technological inputs in disaster management are largely in the realm of early warning and forecasting and contingency measures. Scientific and technology in-put in the preparedness exercise would go a long way in ensuring that appropriate relief effort is addressed. The medical community is associated, in the wake of sudden disasters, with the relief and emergency medical aid operations. **The promotion of public awareness** about the precautionary measures and preparedness would go a long way in helping the community in the face of isolation. The **building up of appropriate capabilities within the community** would have to be a task, which could be entrusted to non-governmental action and the scientific and technological community in an area.

Sustainability Aspect

8. **Public awareness and non-government participation** in disaster mitigation efforts are **crucial** for disaster preparedness to meet natural disasters. Apart from the association of medical personnel in relief effort, there are other groups of persons, who help could also be mobilised in a planned manner for dealing with emergency operations in time of disasters. For example, the Amateur Radio Operators an

association, rendered signal servicing in providing effective communication on a real time basis in the recent cyclone and earthquakes witnessed by the country. One of the **major difficulties** encountered in ensuring effectiveness of non-governmental action is the problem of **coordination and direction**. In the case of sudden disasters during the initial phases, intervention by non-governmental bodies has always tended to **duplicate effort or result in misappropriation of resources**. It is therefore necessary to establish a proper system of assignment of areas and coordination and make this widely known to non-governmental bodies and the public at large, with a view to ensuring that intervention by NGO reinforces each other's effort and the State effort. This would help in ensuring that rehabilitation effort. Are much faster and proceed without wastage.

Development Thrusts

9. Substantial resources are currently spent on alleviating in alleviating the impact of natural disasters and in the process of alleviation; community assets and infrastructure get reinforced. The **disaster mitigation effort** could improve capabilities of disaster prone area to avail of development opportunities. Many of the development programmes improve the resilience of areas and population to vagaries of nature. Nevertheless, **long-term disaster mitigation can be brought about** only by **identifying, at the micro level, critical factors contributing to disaster occurrence** and effecting community ability to pull through a crisis and devising specific programmes to remove such factors. For achieving this, vulnerable analysis and a micro level plan to remove such vulnerability would have to become a concise attempt. The allocation of resources, in this context becomes a major instrument for ensuring the adoption of a proper strategy. The basic parameters for regulating resources allocation would, therefore have to carefully evolved, and should meet with acceptance at political and community levels.

10. **Multi Disciplinary Cell**. At the State and national levels, disaster management comes to the centre stage in time of crises and as a crisis reduces there is no machinery to take care of the needs of perspective planning and formulation on the initiatives for long-term disaster reduction. Thanks to the preoccupations of the planning bodies, **disaster management concerns do not figure high in the priority**

list. There is, therefore, a **need for a multi-disciplinary cell at the State level** to **appraise the occurrence of disasters and the relief effort** and continuously work on programmes and initiative to be focused on, from time to time. A decadal programme, envisaged by the UN General Assembly, could be meaningfully put into operation only through a concise attempt at appraisal, formation and implementation of relief programmes.

Other Concerns

11. **Unity of Control of Operations**. Presently relief is managed by adhoc organisations and agencies with little or no training in their respective fields, and with no or very little accountability. Relief/ Disaster management is a specified job and should be organised accordingly. Command and control of the entire relief should vest with one authority

12. **Theatre Reserves of Resources**. Time lag between occurrence of disaster and relief provide is unacceptably long. Cases for this include the immediately non-availability of manpower, equipment and essential supplies. While manpower and equipment could be made available from a dedicated organisation, the minimum essential quantity of essential perishable supplies of food and medicines must be held centrally as reserves on the lines of "War Wastage Reserves" of the Army for particular period, and rotated periodically to ensure its serviceability.

13. **Publicity**. Lack of publicity of occurrence and effects of a disaster results in lack of sympathy and assistance from neighbouring states. States must overcome the inhabitation of such exposures so as to involve the entire nation/country to mitigate such disasters.

14. **Communication**. Inadequate communications have always posed a hindrance in the timely intimation of such impending disasters as also in the rendering of timely assistance to these areas. Spread out and intensive network of secure Satellite/Microwave communication centres and helipads/landing strips are imperative to provide timely assistance.

15. **Long Term Planning**. Long-term development effort should be such nature that these build the capacity to successfully cope with the disaster. The development programme should organised on area basis. Proper planning should be done based on socio-economic and

technical survey of the areas. Training of the voluntary workers should be an integral part of the implementation of the action programme. All efforts should be made to organise the beneficiaries into groups to monitor implementation of the programmes. There should be no duplication of efforts between the government and the voluntary agencies. The effort should be coordinated and basis on the under standing and the appreciation of each other's roles.

16. **Emphasis on Creation of Assets to Benefit Max Population**. The benefit of programme (relief as well as development work) should reach the poor. Efforts should be made to ensure that the creation of assists should, as far as possible, help the max number of needy public Committees with representatives of disaster affected people should be set up wherever programmes are initiated and the responsibility of the monitoring should be assigned to such committees.

APPROACH TO DISASTER MANAGEMENT

General

17. In view of the foregoing it clearly emerges that as far as the requirement of resources and organisations is concerned, there is no dearth, what is needed is a method to put this all together in an efficient and effective manner. Therefore, disaster management needs to be seen as a national imperative and duty rather than just providing succour to the victims. In a country where 85 per cent of its area is prone to one type of a disaster or other it is necessary that effective and feasible measures be adopted to reduce the impact of such calamities. The succeeding discussion suggests one comprehensive approach and organisation required for the same.

18. **Principles of Effective Counter Disaster Arrangements**. Effective counter disaster arrangement would be governed by the following principles:-

(a) **Primacy of Civil Administration**. Disaster management is the primary responsiblity of the civil administration both at the centre and State levels. All other organisations are subsequent to this principle.

(b) **Organisation**. To be effective, counter-disaster arrangements must be supported by the organisation structure in which they should operate.

(c) **Command and Control**. Prior to the disaster arrangements the responsibility of the overall control of the situation and for command of each organisation and element involved, will need to be clearly specified in the disaster plan and communicated to all concerned agencies.

(d) **Coordination and Support**. Resource management and co-ordination is essential for its optimal and speedy application.

(e) **Information Management**. Effective management of information is essential for dealing with disaster. Communication network between organisation and agencies is essential to ensure that preparedness, measures and responses are properly coordinated.

(f) **Timely Activation.** Timely activation of plan is vital to disaster management. Authority must be delegated to the designated controller to ensure implementation of plans and avoid bottlenecked.

COMPREHENSIVE EMERGENCY MANAGEMENT[14]

Definition and Applicability

19. **Comprehensive Emergency Management (CEM) concept** consists of three interrelated components: -

(a) **All types of hazards**: The commonalities among all types of technical and natural disaster suggest strongly that many of the same management strategies can apply to all such emergencies.

(b) **An emergency management partnership.** The burden of emergency management, and the resources for it, require a close working partnership among all levels of government (country, state, district and local) and the private sector (business and industry, voluntary organisation and the general public); the society at large and affected segment of society in particular.

(c) **An emergency lifecycle:** Disasters do not just appear one day, rather they exist throughout time and have a lifecycle of occurrence, which must be matched by a series of management phase that include strategies to mitigate hazards, prepare for and responds to emergencies, and recover from their effect.

20. "Emergency" is an event, which threatens to, or actually does, inflict damage to property of people. Large disaster can range from hurricanes and floods, to explosions and toxic chemical releases.

21. "Management" is the coordination of an organised effort to attain specific goals or objectives. In emergency management, Management means an organised effort to mitigate against, prepare for respond to add recover from an emergency.

22. "Comprehensive" is the word, which clarifies "emergency" by including all forms of natural and technological events, which threaten or adversely affect lives and property. Comprehensive gives more definition to the word management. Management means bringing together the proper mix of resources from the central, state, and local governments, from business and industry, and from the public.

23. Comprehensive adds a new factor to the meaning EMERGENCY MANAGEMENT PHASES. Phases come from the idea that disasters have a lifecycle, Figure l. Disasters don't just suddenly appear. A hazard exists but it takes some event and accident to turn it into a disaster. For example, a river always flows through a town and propane gas trucks pass through the streets. A large amount of rain, or a breaking dam can produce a flood. Equipment failure or human error, similarly, can turn a routine gas delivery into a disaster. As a result, one of the basic principles of CEM is something useful both before and after hazard occur. CEM suggests that there are four phases of emergency management, which must work together to protect a community.

24. The four phases of CEM are MITIGATION, PREPAREDNESS RESPONSE and RECOVERY. The four-phases are visualised as having a circular relationship to each other. Each phase results from the pervious one and establishes the requirements of the next one. The activities in one phase may overlap those in the previous.

(a) Mitigation refers to activities, which actually eliminate or reduce the chance of occurrence or the effect of the disaster.

(b) Preparedness is planning how to respond in case emergency or disaster occurs and working to increase resources available respond effectively.

(c) Response activities occur during the immediately following disaster. They are designed to provide emergency assistance to victims of the events and reduce the likelihood of secondary damage.

(d) Recovery is the final phase of the emergency management cycle. Recovery continues until all systems return to normal, or near normal. Short-term recovery returns vital life support systems to minimum operating standards. Long-term recovery from a disaster may goon four years until the entire disaster area is completely re-developed either as it was in the past or for entry new purposes that are less disaster-prone.

COMMENDED ORGANISATION FOR DISASTER MANAGEMENT IN INDIA

National Policy

25. An integrated, broad spectrum is called for, with a shift in emphasis from post relief action to mitigation, pre-disaster planning and preparedness. The objectives should include:-

(a) Swift response to disasters.

(b) Minimisation of losses through disasters preventive and preparedness measures.

(c) Reduced vulnerability through concerted action and transfer of technology especially to designs and housing sectors.

(d) Building of community capability.

(e) Provide insurance cover.

National Disaster Organisation

26. The recommended organisation is given at Appendix B. It is suggested that NDO should be established under Cabinet Secretariat for better co-ordination lies on an effective management. Essentially, it should have the capability to intervene rapidly and effectively in any form of disaster, large or small.

27. **Responsibilities**. As enumerated below:-

(a) To enhance disaster management capability.

(b) Develop disaster management plan.

(c) Co-ordinate aid from various agencies from national to international organisation.

(d) Establish and operate National Emergency Operations Centre.

(e) Training of personnel.

(f) Workout and implement damage assessment procedure.

28. **Design of Organisation**. The NDO should be located at Delhi, director be appointed as its head. Presently CMG along with cabinet secretary co-ordinates resources required during emergency. However, need for specialist agency to oversee and muster all resources during disaster relief, subsequently to monitor rehabilitation and reconstruction cannot be over emphasised. The director of NDO could be appointed from Defence, Home or Agriculture Department or any person having expertise in this field.

29. **Structure**. The NDO will be suitably manned with trained staff, however only small nucleus staff will be maintained. The departments, which are likely to be involved, will post and maintain liaison officers with their staff for co-ordination and application of resources during emergency. These officers will be point of contact between NDO and their department. They will assist in preparation of disaster plans and its implementation.

Basic Components

30. **Command, Control and Co-ordination**.

(a) Command relates to organisation and operates vertically within it. The control relates to situation and functions horizontally across organisation.

(b) Co-ordination relates primarily to resources. It is concerned with the systematic acquisition and application of resources. Co-ordination is also between states, voluntary organisation and international agencies.

(c) NDO should be suitably empowered through legislative approval to carry out above roles.

31. **Facilities**. Facilities must be able to house the command and control structure and may include operations room, communication centres, equipment stores, etc.

32. **Communication**. Duplicate communication network serving all levels of control must be available. It should have facility to hook on Army/Air Force/Naval communication network.

33. **Equipment**. A full range of equipment must support each operational activity. These should either be held in a decentralised manner by states or by different departments. It may include vehicles, trailers, communication equipment, and specialist equipment for particular disaster situations, stores and supplies.

34. **Trained Man Power**. Adequately trained manpower within each state should be available to perform all required functions as dictated by disaster situation.

Functional Component

35. **Warning System**. It must be built-in in the system.

36. **Information Gathering/Processing System**. Information is the lifeblood of any operation, the NDO should have assured capability for acquiring information; which must flow along certain functional channels. Essentially, it must be linked to cyclone forecasting station, Remote Sensing Satellites, Flood/Rain monitoring radars and seismic laboratories. Data Network must be established at all levels of control.

37. **Liaison**. As explained earlier, to improve co-ordination liaison is necessary and must be maintained by the NDO.

National Institute of Disaster Management (NIDM)

38. The setting up of such institute has been approved since sixth five-year plan; however, it has not been implemented. It will be a functional part of NDO. The institute will conduct counter disaster studies, courses for various categories of personnel from top bureaucrats, leaders and personnel actually involved in relief/ rehabilitation operations.[15]

State Level Organisation

39. At state level, a director/assistance director of disaster management must be appointed. He will be responsible for:-

(a) Prepare disaster contingency plans for the state.

(b) Training of community and volunteers to tackle disaster situation.

(c) Maintain and control disaster management unit as required by the state.

(d) Co-ordinate with armed forces.

(e) Co-ordinate disaster relief operations.

40. **State Disaster Management Unit**. It will be worthwhile to maintain minimum of battalion to company size force depending upon the size of the state and threat from disasters. A vast manpower of ex-servicemen could be enlisted in this force. Rajasthan is actively contemplating this concept so as to make their counter-disaster operations effective. Such task force could be used for different tasks such as guarding of forest resources or development of wasteland/ social forestry. Ecological TA battalion located at Dehra Dun and Bikaner have been performing exceedingly well in aforestation and conservation of forest.

41. **District Level**. A class one gazetted officer of the rank of Deputy Collector under Deputy Commissioner of the district should be appointed for disaster management, who will carry out following functions:-

(a) Prepare district contingency plan.

(b) Recruitment of volunteers.

(c) Training of personnel at Panchayat level.

(d) Liaison with other government departments including armed forces.

(e) Maintenance of equipment, if required.

(f) Open a control centre during disaster.

42. **Panchayat/Municipality Level**. It is at this level that implementation of preventive and preparedness measures such as land use planning, design and construction, self-help by community and even alerting and creating well organised volunteer force will be effective. Therefore, responsibility of such actions should be entrusted to chief executive officer of Municipal towns or village development officer with equal accountability to elected members of panchayat. The personnel at this level should be trained, equipped and motivated for such eventualities.

Role of Armed Forces

43. The role of armed forces during disasters will continue as hither to fore. They should also get persons trained for disaster management and be aware of disaster plans at appropriate levels. It is suggested that a section in military operations branch be dedicated to disaster relief operations. A liaison officer with requisite staff from all three services should to be posted to the NDO.

Financial Implications

44. Finances will be required by centre for creating infrastructure for the NDO and NIDM at New Delhi. As far as other aspects are concerned, it is just integration of various resources already available in the country. Therefore, not much finances will be required. Similar expenditure will be incurred at state level, as they will have to maintain a force for disaster management. The cardinal principle is that integrated approach and application of resources in a coordinated manner will save much of expenditure. In overall analysis, investment in this system will save finances, which are released as emergency measures without due care and consideration. The money for NDO could be financed from CRF and NCRF.

Conclusion

45. Disasters, manmade or natural are on increase. There is also increased awareness of this problem and of the need for a co-ordinated approach to the disaster management at national/international level. India, a nation aspiring to play major role in international arena cannot afford to put up poor performance in handling of disasters. Notwithstanding this, for welfare of its own people, India needs to give priority for disaster management in its planning and policies. The points that merit attention can be summarised as under:-

(a) Need for a single coordinator/Director at each level with adequate resources and authority to control all relief agencies. Therefore, the need to create organisation for this purpose as recommended.

(b) Integration and co-ordination of functions of various organisations/government departments involved in this process.

(c) Warning systems must be integrated and updated. Need for creating data network in future.

(d) Continuous studies, evaluation, review of disaster management process by NDO.

(e) Need to educate community to play its part in disaster management.

References

- Andrew Stewart Limited, 2006, Managed Retreat from Coastal Hazards: Options for Implementation, report for Environment Waikato.
- AS/NZS, 2004a, Australian/New Zealand Standard: Risk Management, HBAS/NZS 4360:2004.
- AS/NZS, 2004b, Australian/New Zealand Standard: Risk Management Handbook, companion to AS/NZS 4360:2004, HB 436:2004.
- Auckland Regional Council, 1996, Tsunami and Storm Surges in the Auckland Region.
- Auckland Regional Council, 1997, Auckland Engineering Lifelines Project, Stage 1 report.
- Auckland Regional Council, 1999, Auckland Regional Policy Statement, Auckland Regional Council.
- Auckland Regional Council, 2000, Coastal Hazard Strategy and Coastal Erosion Management Manual, Auckland Regional Council, Technical Publication No. 130.
- Australian Geomechanics Society, 2000, Landslide risk management concepts and guidelines, Australian Geomechanics, March 35(1) 49-92.
- Australian Geomechanics Society, 2006, Guidelines for landslide susceptibility, hazard and risk mapping for land use planning, Draft B: March 2006.
- Bell R G, 2005, 'Lessons from Boxing Day tsunami: implications for disaster reduction and detection/warning systems' In: Collen, J (Ed), Abstracts of papers presented at the STAR Session 2005, held in conjunction with the SOPAC 34th Annual Session, Apia, Samoa, 23-30 September 2005, pp. 11-13. SOPAC Miscellaneous Report No. 603. SOPAC Secretariat, Suva, Fiji.
- Berryman K (Compiler), 2005, Review of Tsunami Hazard and Risk in New Zealand, Institute of Geological and Nuclear Sciences client report CR2005-104, Lower Hutt.
- Blakey R J and Mosley, M P, 1984, 'River and streambank erosion and sedimentation', In: Speden I and Crozier M J (Eds), 1984, Natural Hazards in New Zealand, UNESCO, New Zealand, pp. 159-205.

- Brodnax R C, 1991, Cliff erosion in the Waitemata Harbour and Hauraki Gulf, Masters Thesis, University of Auckland.
- Brookes H D and Benson A P, 1999, Review of Report "Coastal Hazard Assessment for Papamoa Township, Tauranga District, Bay of Plenty, New Zealand", Unpublished report for Tauranga District Council.
- Brooks S, Crozier M J, Glade, T and Anderson, M G, 2004, Towards establishing climatic thresholds for slope instability: use of a physically-based combined soil hydrology-slope stability model, Pure and Applied Geophysics 161(4): 881-905.
- Bruun P, 1988, The Bruun Rule of erosion by sea-level rise: A discussion on large scale two- and three-dimensional usages, Journal of Coastal Research, Vol. 4(4), 627-648.
- Carterton District Council, 2000, Carterton District Plan, Carterton District Council.
- Casini L, Bonnard C H, Corominas J, Jibson R, and Monteero-Olarte, J, 2005, 'Landslide hazard and risk zoning for urban planning and development', In: Hungr O, Fell R, Couture R, and Eberthardt (Eds), Landslide risk management, Taylor and Francis, London:199-235.
- Chick, L M, Healy T and de Lange W P, 2001, Tsunami Hazard in the Firth of Thames, Hauraki Gulf, NZ, Journal of Coastal Research, special issue 34.
- Crozier M J and Paterson M, 1999, Marlborough District Natural Hazard and Risk Study, Prepared for Marlborough District Council, School of Earth Sciences, Victoria University of Wellington Consulting Report 99/1.
- Crozier M J, 1993, Management issues arising from landslides and related activity, New Zealand Geographer 49 (1): 35-37.
- Crozier M J, 2006, Lecture notes for PHYG 412: Natural Hazards, School of Earth Sciences, Victoria University of Wellington.
- de Lange W P and Bell R G, 1998, 'Tsunami risk from the southern flank: Balleny Islands earthquake', Water and Atmosphere 6(3): 13-15.
- de Lange W P and Hull A G, 1994, Tsunami Hazard for the Auckland Region, Auckland Regional Council.
- Defra, 2002, Soft Cliffs Manual for Managers, Defra Flood Management Division, London, UK.
- Department of Building and Housing, 2005, Earthquake-Prone Building Provisions of the Building Act 2004: Policy Guidance for Territorial Authorities, Department of Building and Housing.
- Department of Conservation, 1999, Environmental and risk assessment for mitigation of the hazard from Ruapehu Crater Lake - Assessment of environmental effects.

- Department of Conservation, 2000, Canterbury Conservation Management Strategy, Volumes 1 and 2, Canterbury Conservation Management Planning Series No. 10, ISSN: 1171-5391-10, ISBN: 0-478-01991-2.
- Department of Conservation, 2005a, General Policy for National Parks, April 2005, Produced by the Department of Conservation for the New Zealand Conservation Authority, ISBN 0-478-22685-3 (http://www.doc.govt.nz/About-DOC/Policies-Plans-and-Reports/General-Policy-for-National-Parks-2005/pdf/General-policy-for-National-Parks-2005.pdf)
- Department of Conservation, 2005b, Conservation General Policy, May 2005, ISBN 0-478-22692-6.
- Department of Infrastructure, 2002, Applying the Flood Provisions in Planning Schemes: A Guide for Councils, VPP Practice Note, Victoria, Australia.
- Dowrick D J and Cousins W J, 2002, Historical Incidence of Modified Mercalli Intensity in New Zealand and Comparison with Hazard Models, Bulletin of the New Zealand Society for Earthquake Engineering.
- Dowrick D J and Rhoades D A, 1999, Attenuation of Modified Mercalli Intensity in New Zealand Earthquakes.
- Dowrick D J, Rhoades D A and Davenport, PN, 2001, Damage Ratios for Domestic Property in the Magnitude 7.2 1968 Inangahua, New Zealand, Earthquake, Bulletin of the New Zealand Society for Earthquake Engineering, 34(3): 191-213.
- Environment Bay of Plenty, 1999a, Bay of Plenty Regional Policy Statement, Environment Bay of Plenty Regional Council.
- Environment Bay of Plenty, 1999b, Rotorua Geothermal Regional Plan, Resource Planning Publication 99/02, ISSN 1170 9022, Environment Bay of Plenty Regional Council.
- Environment Bay of Plenty, 2003, Bay of Plenty Regional Coastal Environment Plan, Publication 2003/08, ISSN 1175-9372, Environment Bay of Plenty Regional Council.
- Environment Canterbury, 2005, Regional Coastal Environment Plan for the Canterbury Region, Report No. R04/13/1, Environment Canterbury Regional Council.
- Environment Waikato, 1997a, Earthquake Risk Mitigation Plan, Environment Waikato Policy Series 1997/12, Doc # 487363.
- Environment Waikato, 1997b, Flood Risk Mitigation Plan, Environment Waikato Technical Report 1997/13, Document # 451404.
- Environment Waikato, 1999a, Coastal Erosion Risk Mitigation Strategy For the Waikato Region, Environment Waikato Policy Series 1999/03, Doc # 480281.
- Environment Waikato, 1999b, Coastal Flooding Risk Mitigation Strategy, Environment Waikato Policy Series 1999/06, Doc # 4800895.

- Environment Waikato, 1999c, Volcanic Risk Mitigation Plan, Environment Waikato Policy Series 1999/10, ISSN: 1174-7234.
- Environment Waikato, 2000, Waikato Regional Policy Statement, Environment Waikato Regional Council.
- Environment Waikato, 2002a, Coromandel Beaches: Coastal Hazards and Development Setback Recommendations.
- Environment Waikato, 2002b, The Weather Bomb, Environment Waikato Technical Report 2002/10, 21 June 2002, prepared by Adam Munro for Environment Waikato, ISSN: 1172-4005, Document #: 760464.
- Environment Waikato, 2004, Tsunami Hazard for the Bay of Plenty and Eastern Coromandel Peninsula: Stage 1, Environment Waikato Technical Report TR04/33, ISSN: 1172-4005.
- Gibb, J G, 1984, 'Coastal erosion', In: Speden I and Crozier M J (Eds), 1984, Natural Hazards in New Zealand, UNESCO, New Zealand, pp. 134-158.
- Gibb, J G, 1994, Standards and information requirements for assessing coastal hazard zones for New Zealand, report prepared for Department of Conservation.
- Gisborne District Council, 2005, Gisborne District: Emergency Services Tsunami Contingency Plan, Gisborne District Council.
- Gisborne District Council, 2006, Combined Regional Land and District Plan, Gisborne District Council.
- Glade, T, Anderson M, and Crozier M J, 2005, Landslide Hazard and Risk, Wiley, Chichester.
- Glassey P, 2002, Defining Coastal Hazard - A pilot project in the Auckland Region, Proposal for Manukau City Council.
- Glassey, P, Gibb J, Hoverd J, Jongens R, Alloway B, Coombes K, Benson A, 2003, Establishing a methodology for coastal cliff hazard mapping: An East Coast Bays, Auckland pilot study, In: Coasts & Ports 2003, Proceedings of 16th Australasian Coastal and Ocean Engineering Conference, Auckland.
- Goring D G and Bell R G, 1998, 'Canterbury shelf waves and the PNG tsunami', Water & Atmosphere 6(3): 15-16.
- Greater Wellington, 1995, Regional Policy Statement for the Wellington Region, Publication No. WRC/PP-G-95/28, ISBN 0-909016-31-3, Wellington Regional Council, Greater Wellington Regional Council.
- Hancox G T, Nairn I A, Otway P M, Webby M G, Perrin N D, and Keys J R, 1997, Stability assessment of Mt Ruapehu Crater Rim following the 1995-1996 eruptions, IGNS Client Report 4360B.
- Hancox G T, Perrin N D, Dellow G D, 1997,Earthquake-Induced Landsliding in New Zealand and Implications for MM Intensity and Seismic Hazard Assessment, IGNS (EQC funded project 95/196) - December 1997.
- Hastings District Council, 2003, Hastings District Plan, Hastings District Council.

- Hastings District Council, 2004, District Plan Monitoring: Earthquake Hazard, Section 12.3 - Natural Hazards Review, Hastings District Plan, Report by Nia Belcher, Environmental Planning, Hastings District Council, April 2004.
- Hawke's Bay Regional Council, 2004, Hawke's Bay Regional Coastal Environment Plan (Draft), Hawke's Bay Regional Council.
- Healy and Dean, 2000, Methodology for delineation of CHZ and development setback for open duned coasts, Handbook of Coastal Engineering, McGraw-Hill.
- Horizons Manawatu-Wanganui Regional Council, 1998, Regional Policy Statement for Manawatu-Wanganui, Report No. 98/EXT/324, Horizons Manawatu-Wanganui Regional Council.
- Horizons Manawatu-Wanganui Regional Council, 1999, Hazard Analysis Manual Volume 2, Horizons Manawatu-Wanganui Regional Council, ISBN: 1-877221-45-7.
- Hutt City Council, 2003, City of Lower Hutt District Plan, Hutt City Council.
- Institute of Geological and Nuclear Sciences Ltd, 2005, Review of New Zealand's preparedness tsunami hazard, comparison to risk and recommendations for treatment, compiled by Terry Webb, Client Report 2005/162, Prepared for Ministry of Civil Defence and Emergency Management, December 2005.
- Invercargill City Council, 2005, Invercargill City District Plan, Invercargill City Council.
- Kapiti Coast District Council, 1999, Kapiti Coast District Plan, Kapiti Coast District Council.
- Kay R C, Eriksen N J, Foster G A, Gillgren, Healy T R, Sheffield A T and Warrick R A, 1994, Assessment of Coastal Hazards and their Management for Selected Parts of the Coastal Zone Administered by the Tauranga District Council, A report to the Tauranga District Council and Environment Bay of Plenty.
- Matamata-Piako District Council, 2005, Matamata-Piako District Plan, Matamata-Piako District Council.
- Ministry for Emergency Management, 2000, Managing the Flood Hazard: A Civil Defence Emergency Management Perspective, Information for Local Government, Ministry for Emergency Management, Wellington.
- Ministry for the Environment, 2001, Planning for Climate Change Effects on Coastal Margins, report prepared by NIWA as part of the New Zealand Climate Change Programme.
- Ministry for the Environment, 2003a, Drafting Issues, Objectives, Policies and Methods in Regional Policy Statements and District Plans, Report prepared for the Ministry for the Environment by Gerard Willis, Enfocus

Limited, Ministry for the Environment, July 2003, Ref. ME482, ISBN: 0-478-18902-8.

- Ministry for the Environment, 2003b, Planning for Development of Land on or Close to Active Faults: A guideline to assist resource management planners in New Zealand, Report prepared for the Ministry for the Environment by Janine Kerr, Simon Nathan, Russ Van Dissen, Peter Webb, David Brunsdon and Andrew King, Ministry for Environment, July 2003, Ref. ME565, ISBN: 0-478-18901.
- Ministry for the Environment, Climate Change Guidance Note.
- Ministry of Civil Defence and Emergency Management, 2001, Floods, Tephra 18 For-the-CDEM-Sector-Publications-Tephra-2001-Index?OpenDocument).
- Ministry of Civil Defence and Emergency Management, 2002a, Working Together: Developing a CDEM Group Plan, Director's Guidelines for CDEM Groups, DGL 2/02, ISBN 0-478-25453-9.
- Ministry of Civil Defence and Emergency Management, 2002b, Earth Movements, Tephra 19.
- Ministry of Civil Defence and Emergency Management, 2003, Wet and Wild, Tephra 20.
- Ministry of Civil Defence and Emergency Management, 2004a, Resilient New Zealand: A Aotearoa Manahau: National Civil Defence Emergency Management Strategy 2003-2006, ISBN 0-478-25461-X.
- Ministry of Civil Defence and Emergency Management, 2004b, Living With Volcanoes, Tephra 21.
- Ministry of Civil Defence and Emergency Management, 2005, Proposed National Civil Defence Emergency Management Plan (for consultation), August 2005, ISBN 0-478-25466-0.
- Ministry of Civil Defence and Emergency Management, 2006, The Guide to the National CDEM Plan (Draft Version, 16 February 2006).
- Ministry of Civil Defence, 1994, National Report of New Zealand, Tephra 13(1).
- Ministry of Civil Defence,1995, Volcanic hazards in New Zealand, Tephra 14(2).
- Moon V G and de Lange W P, 2003, Estimating long-term cliff recession rates in soft Flysch Deposits, Waitemata Group, Auckland, New Zealand, Coasts and Ports Australasian Conference, Paper No. 93.
- Moon V G and Healy T, 1994, Mechanisms of Coastal Cliff Retreat and Hazard Zone Delineation in Soft Flysch Deposits, Journal of Coastal Research, 10: 3.
- National Institute for Coastal and Marine Management of the Netherlands et al, 2004, Living With Coastal Erosion in Europe: Sand and Space for Sustainability, Part VII - Guidance Document for Quick Hazard Assessment

of Coastal Erosion and Associated Flooding, April 2004, National Institute for Coastal and Marine Management of the Netherlands (RIKZ) et al.

- National Institute of Water and Atmospheric Research Ltd, 2002, Meteorological Hazards and the Potential Impacts of Climate Change in Wellington Region: A Scoping Study, NIWA Client Report WLG2002/19, WRC Pub. No. WRC/RP-T-02/16, Prepared for Wellington Regional Council.
- National Institute of Water and Atmospheric Research Ltd, 2005, Meteorological Hazards and the Potential Impacts of Climate Change in the Manawatu-Wanganui Region, NIWA Client Report: WLG2005-17, April 2005, NIWA Project: HRC05301, Prepared for Horizons Manawatu-Wanganui Regional Council.
- National Institute of Water and Atmospheric Research, 1998, Potential effects of lahar from Mt. Ruapehu on the Tongariro River and Lake Taupo, NIWA Report, DOC 80219.
- National Institute of Water and Atmospheric Research, 2004, Managing New Zealand's Climate: a Resource and a Hazard, NIWA Information series No. 54. ISSN 1174-264X.
- National Tsunami Hazard Mitigation Program, 2001, Designing for Tsunamis, NOAA, USGS, FEMA, NSF, Alaska, California, Hawaii, Oregon, and Washington, (http://www.pmel.noaa.gov/tsunami-hazard/)
- New Zealand Climate Change Office, 2004a, Coastal Hazards and Climate Change: A guidance manual for local government in New Zealand, ME512, New Zealand Climate Change Office, Ministry for the Environment, Wellington.
- New Zealand Climate Change Office, 2004b, Climate Change Effects and Impact Assessment: A guidance manual for Local Government in New Zealand, ME513, New Zealand Climate Change Office, Ministry for the Environment, Wellington.
- New Zealand Society for Earthquake Engineering, 2005, Assessment and Improvement of the Structural Performance of Buildings in Earthquakes: Initial Evaluation, Detailed Assessment, Improvement Measures, Study Group Draft, December 2005. (http://www.nzsee.org.nz/PUBS/2005Paise-beguide_whole.pdf)
- NZIER, 2002, The Waikato Weather Bomb: Understanding the impact, March 2004, A report commissioned by the New Zealand Climate Change Office (Ministry for the Environment) in conjunction with Environment Waikato and the Ministry of Civil Defence and Emergency Management (http://www.climatechange.govt.nz/resources/reports/waikato-weather-mar-04/waikato-weather-bomb-mar04.pdf)
- OFDA/CRED EM-DAT, 2005, International Disaster Database, Centre for Research on the epidemiology of disasters.

- Palmerston North City Council, 2000, Palmerston North City Council District Plan, Palmerston North City Council.
- Patel J, 1997, Engineering geology of coastal cliff stability along the northern Manukau Harbour, Masters Thesis, University of Auckland.
- Porirua City Council, 1999, Porirua City District Plan, Porirua City Council.
- Reeve D E, 1998, Coastal Flood Risk Assessment, Journal of Waterway, Port, Coastal and Ocean Engineering, Sept/Oct. p. 219-228.
- Rodney District Council, 2003, Omaha Coastal Compartment Management Plan, Rodney District Council.
- Rotorua District Council, 1996, Rotorua District Plan, Rotorua District Council.
- Ruapehu District Council, 2000, Ruapehu District Plan, Ruapehu District Council.
- SAA/SNZ, 1999, Guidelines for Managing Risk in the Australian and New Zealand Public Sector, HB 1343.
- SCOR Working Group 89, 1991, The response of beaches to sea-level changes: A review of predictive models, Journal of Coastal Research 7(3): 895-921.
- Smith K, 2004, Environmental Hazards: Assessing Risk and Reducing Disaster, (Fourth Edition) Routledge, London.
- Speden I and Crozier M J (Eds), 1984, Natural Hazards in New Zealand, UNESCO, New Zealand, 500 pp.
- Taranaki Regional Council, 1991, Preliminary Hazard Analysis, Internal Report.
- Taranaki Regional Council, 1992a, Regional Policy Statement Working Paper: Natural Hazards, Taranaki Regional Council.
- Taranaki Regional Council, 1992b, Regional Policy Statement - Natural Hazards: Preferred Goals, Objectives, Policies and Methods of Implementation, (Working Draft), as amended subsequent to peer review, December 1992.
- Taranaki Regional Council, 1994, Regional Policy Statement, Taranaki Regional Council.
- Taranaki Regional Council, 2004a, Civil Defence Emergency Management Group Plan for Taranaki, prepared by Taranaki Regional Council on behalf of the Taranaki CDEM Group.
- Taranaki Regional Council, 2004b, Taranaki Civil Defence Emergency Management Group: Hazard and Risk Analysis: Explanatory Notes.
- Tauranga District Council, 2006, Tauranga District Plan, Tauranga District Council.
- Timaru District Council, 2005, Timaru District Plan, Timaru District Council.

- Tomlinson, 1980, The frequency of high intensity rainfalls in New Zealand, Water and Soil Technical Publication 19, National Water and Soil Conservation Organisation.
- Tonkin & Taylor Ltd, 1998, Lower Tongariro Natural Hazard Management Plan, Auckland.
- Tonkin & Taylor Ltd, 2002a, Options for Managing Risks from Tsunami in the Wellington Region, report for Wellington Regional Council, WRC Publication No. WRC/RP-T-02/17, (http://www.gw.govt.nz/council-publications/pdfs/Environment%20Management_20020829_091412.pdf)
- Tonkin & Taylor, 2002b, Coastal Hazard Analysis, Unpublished report for Whakatane District Council, Tonkin & Taylor Report Ref. 18731, Auckland, November 2002.
- Tonkin & Taylor, 2003, Regional Coastal Hazard Assessment, Unpublished report for Hawke's Bay Regional Council, Tonkin & Taylor Report Ref 20514, Auckland.
- Tonkin & Taylor, 2005, Regional Coastal Erosion Hazard Assessment (Draft), Unpublished report for Auckland Regional Council, Tonkin & Taylor Report 19891.100, September 2005.
- Waikato District Council, 1997, Waikato District Plan, Waikato District Council.
- Wairoa District Council, 2004, Wairoa Coastal Strategy: Te Maahere Taatahi ki te Wairoa, prepared by Beca Planning for Wairoa District Council, Wairoa District Council.
- Walters R A, 2002, Long wave resonance on the New Zealand coast, NIWA Technical Report 109.32.
- Wellington City Council, 2000, Wellington City District Plan, Wellington City Council.
- Wellington Regional Council, 1993, Seismic Hazard Map Series, Wellington Regional Council publication WRC/PP-T-93/74.
- Wellington Regional Council, 1995, Natural hazards, Section 11, In: Regional Policy Statement for the Wellington Region, Publication number WRC/PP-G-95/28.:193-205.
- Wellington Regional Council, 2001, Hutt River Floodplain Management Plan: For the Hutt River and its Environment, Publication No. WRC/FPSA-G-01/32, ISBN: 0-909016-76-3, Flood Protection Group Landcare Division, Wellington Regional Council (http://www.gw.govt.nz/story_images/1390_HuttFMP_s2716.pdf)
- Wilson H and Crozier M, 2000, 'Quantitative hazard assessment: rainfall-triggered landslides', In Bromhead, Dixon, and Ibsen (Eds), 2000, Landslides in Research Theory and Practice, Vol. 3, Thomas Telford: 1575 -1581.

End Note

1. ARTRAC Doctrine Op cit, pp. 1-6.
2. ARTRAC Doctrine Op cit, p. 3.
3. ARTRAC Policy Op cit pp. 4-9.
4. ARTRAC Policy Op cit p. 5.
5. ARTRAC Policy Op cit p. 5.
6. ARTRAC Policy Op cit p. 15.
7. ARTRAC Policy Op cit pp. 9-10.
8. Doctor Indu Prakash Disaster Management, pp. 60-110.
9. Coping with Natural Calamities. The Hindu. 25 May 1991.
10. Disaster Management Institute (DMI) Bhopal Reference Document Vol I, Emergency Management: Basic Concepts and Approach, p. 50.
11. DMI Document Op cit, p. 53.
12. DMI Document Op cit, p. 56.
13. ARTRAC Policy, p. 21.
14. DMI Bhopal Document Op Cit, pp. 1-8.
15. The Hindu- op. cit. 10 October.

Conclusion

"It sufficient number of management layers are superimposed on top of each other it can be assured that disaster is not left to chance."

– Norman R Augustine

General

Disaster are not new to mankind. However, in recent times, owing to their increased frequency as well as the intensity, disaster management has attracted immense public interest at the national and international level. Almost half of the disasters in the world occur in Asia, making this region the world's most vulnerable area. Some of the reason for increase in the frequency of natural disasters are population explosion, uncontrolled urbanisation, unplanned land use and global warming. Rapid industrialisation and the menace of terrorism have also added new dimensions to man-made disasters.

Global Trends

Keeping in view the death and destruction wrought by devastating disasters, the decade of 1990s was observed, the United Nations, as the International Decade for Natural Disaster Reduction. A number of initiatives were taken globally, prominent along them being the Kyoto protocol, under which the United Nations Framework convention on climate change has been ratified by 175 countries. Under this protocol, industrialised countries were to reduce the collective emissions of green house gases by 52 per cent compared to the year 1990. The new millennium began with the touch of international Strategy for Disaster Reduction to build up disaster resilience in vulnerable areas. The Hyogo

Framework for Action (2005-2015) was adopted by 168 Governments at the world conference on Disaster Reduction at Kobe, Japan in Jan 2005. India is one of the signatories to these declarations.

The Transition in India

Government of India in recognition of the importance of disaster management as a national priority, had set up a High Powered Committee (HPC) in August 1999 and a National Committee on Disaster Management (DM) after the Gujarat Earthquake for making recommendations on the preparation of DM plans and for suggesting effective mitigation mechanism. Recommendations of the HPC laid the foundation for DM framework in India. Indian Ocean Tsunami acted as the catalyst and the Government of India (GoI took a defining stem in the legislative history of the country by enacting DM Act 2005).

The Disaster Management Act 2005

The DM Act (2005) was unanimously passed by both houses of parliament and received the assent of the President of India on 23rd December 2005. Under this Act, the National Disaster Management Authority (NDMA) was created chaired by the Hon'ble Prime Minister of India as the Apex Body for DM in the country. Similarly State Disaster Management Authorities are headed by the respective chief ministers/ Lt Governors, as the case may be. The fact that these authorities are being headed by the heads of the Government themselves exhibits the national to tackle this problem most seriously. Another interesting aspect of this Act is that the District Disaster Management Authorities are being headed by the respective district collectors and co-chaired by the elected representatives of the respective districts. This brings in the much required public interface at the cutting edge level.

The Act envisages a paradigm shift, from the erstwhile response-centric syndrome to a pro-active, holistic and integrated management of disasters with emphasis on prevention, preparedness and mitigation. These efforts are aimed at conserving developmental gains and also minimising losses to lives, livelihood and property. The Act also mandates the creation of the National Disaster Response Force (NDRF) for specialised response and the National Institute of Disaster Management (NIDM) for institutional capacity development.

The NIDM works within the broad guidelines of the NDMA which ensures completes synergy at the national level. The entire DM arrangement is backed by institutional, financial and legal mechanism.

National Vision

The national vision is to build a safer and disaster resilient India by developing a holistic proactive multi-disaster and technology driven strategy for DM. This will be achieved through a culture of prevention, mitigation and preparedness to senate a prompt and efficient response at the time of disasters. The entire process will centre stage the community and will be provided momentum and sustenance through the collective effort of all government agencies and Non-Governmental Organisatoin (NGOs)

Centre-staging Communities

Civil society stakeholders like NGOs Corporate Sector, National Service Scheme, Nehru Yuva Kendra Sangathan, Volunteers and Youth belonging to the Indian Red Cross Society, National Cadet Corps, Scouts and Guides, Civil Defence and Home Guards and elected representatives from Panchayati Raj Institutions etc, are being encouraged to actively participate in various aspects of DM in a proactive manner.

To inculcate of preparedness and secure effective participation of the community and other stakeholders, a number of mock exercises, are being carried out by DM authorities, throughout the country on earthquakes, cyclones, floods, fire and chemical (industrial) disasters. These exercises have not only enhanced the level of public awareness but also have honed the level of preparedness of the administration at the district level.

National Disaster Response Force (NDRF)

For the purpose of specialised response, a deputation force of eight battalions is to be operationalised. Presently, seven of these battalions have been positioned at eight different locations in the country based on the vulnerability profile of the states. During the pre-disaster phase, this force will impart basic level training the State Disaster Response Forces, Civil Defence, Home Guards and assist in community capacity building and awareness-cum-preparedness activities including conduct of mock exercises. This force is being equipped with state-of-the-art equipments.

NDRF units will maintain close liaison with the various state governments and be available to them proactively.

Mitigation Measures and Role of Science and Technology

In order to realise the national vision, a number of mitigation projects have been initiated. The National Cyclone Risk Mitigation Project in partnership with the World Bank will cover 13 cyclone-prone states and Union Territories. Other mitigation projects on the anvil include those dealing with Earthquakes, Floods, Medical Preparedness and Mass Causality Management and the Mitigation Reserves and Information and Communication Network. Studies are also progress on microzonation, risk assessment and vulnerability analysis.

The strengthening of the early warning systems, research and development and the applications of modern state-of-the-art science and technology solutions for improving the mitigation and preparedness measures, are being accorded high priority. Efforts are also being made to integrate the indigenous traditional knowledge among the disaster prone communities and document the coping strategies of communities facing recurring disasters. A National Database for Emergency Management is being created in coordination with National Spatial Data Infrastructure of the Department of Science and Technology. 241 multi-disaster prone districts in the country will be accorded priority. Guidelines and formulation of plans.

The prime responsibility for the management of disasters rests with the States. To facilitate the central Ministries and States in the formulation of their plans, NDMA has initiated the process of issuing guidelines in an inclusive and participatory process in coordination with all the stakeholders. The Guidelines on Earthquakes, Chemical (industrial) Disasters and Preparation of State Plans have already been released. The guidelines on Floods, Cyclones, Medical Preparedness and Biological Hazards will follow very shortly. Urban Flooding, Tsunami, Landslides, Micro-Finance and Insurance and Community Based Disaster Preparedness are some of the other subjects on which work is in progress.

Techno-legal and Techno-financial Regime

Action is already afoot states to revise and update the town planning bye-laws and thereby create both a regime for regulation and a mechanism for enforcement to promote and monitor the compliance of safe construction in multi-hazard locations. The codes and standards for the construction of earthquake resistant buildings and structures are also being revised and updated. Innovative financial instruments for risk sharing, risk avoidance and risk transfer like insurance, re-insurance and micro-finance are also being explored for their suitability in disaster prone areas for ensuring disaster resilience among vulnerable communities.

Regional and International Co-operation

Disaster do not recognise geographical boundaries. Majors disasters may often simultaneously affect several states or even countries. It will be the national endeavour to develop close cooperation and coordination at the international level in all spheres of DM. The establishment of the SAARC DM Centre as Centre of Excellence at the National Institute of Disaster Management, New Delhi is a major step in this direction. Similar arrangements will also be worked out with other nations in the world. India will also continue to actively participate and render assistance internationally during disasters.

To conclude, our ultimate aim should be to work together at all levels and build a disaster resilient India in which there will be minimal loss to property and zero tolerance to avoidable deaths.

EARTHQUAKE RISK MITIGATION IN INDIA

Backgournd

58.6 per cent of India's Geographical area is vulnerable to moderate or serve earthquakes. The vulnerability Atlas prepared by the Building Materials Technology Promotion Council (BMTPC) indicates that 299 districts from 21 states and Union Territories of the country falls within the seismic zones IV and V. During the decade of 1990s India witnessed several devastating earthquakes like the Uttarkashi earthquakes of 1991, Latur earthquakes of 1993, Jabalpur earthquakes of 1997 and Chamoli earthquakes of 1999. These are followed the Bhuj Earthquakes of 2001, the Andaman and Nicobar earthquakes of 2004 and the Jammu and

Kashmir earthquakes of October 2005. These earthquakes resulted in enormous loss of life and damage to property, assets and infrastructure. India has witnessed for major earthquakes of magnitude exceeding 8.0 in the Richter Scale in Shillong, 1897 (M 8.7), Kangra 1905 (M 8.0), Bihar Nepal 1934 (M 8.3) and Assam Tibet, 1950 (M 8.6), indicating that the entire Himalayan Region is vulnerable to high intensity earthquakes.

Critical Gaps

The critical gaps for the effective management of the earthquakes in India include the:

1. Lack of formal training among construction professionals in earthquake resistant construction practices.
2. Lack of awareness among various stakeholders about the seismic risk and vulnerability.
3. Inadequate monitoring and enforcement of earthquake-resistant building codes and town planning bye-laws.
4. Absence of systems of licensing of engineers and masons.
5. Absence of earthquake resistant features in non-engineered construction in suburban and rural areas, and
6. Lack of adequate preparedness and response capacity among various stakeholder groups.

NDMA Guidelines for Management of Earthquakes

Ever since its inception in Sep 2005 NDMA initiated its efforts in identifying the critical gaps of the management of earthquakes in India through a series of workshops and consultation with eminent academics, earthquake management experts, representatives government agencies and volunteer organisation for formulation guidelines for the effective management in earthquakes in India. Over 300 earthquake management specialists contributed to this process which evolved a comprehensive strategy for the management of earthquakes in India. These activities identified as priorities included the following :-

1. Earthquake resistant design and construction of new structures in compliance with earthquake resistant building codes and other safety codes in villages, towns and cities in Zones III, IV and V.

2. Selective seismic strengthening and retrofitting of lifeline and priority structures with special emphasis on buildings of national importance, critical facilities like hospitals and schools, public utility structures like reservoirs and dams, bridges and flyover, ports and harbours, airports, railway stations and bus station complexes, important buildings that ensure governance and business continuity and multistoried buildings with five or more floors in residential apartments, office and commercial complexes etc.
3. Strengthening techno-legal regime through more effective regulations and enforcement of town planning bye-laws, earthquake resistance building codes and other safety codes and regulations.
4. Strengthening the public awareness and earthquake preparedness through appropriate campaigns for wider dissemination of information on earthquake risk and vulnerability and on earthquake mitigation and risk reduction activities.
5. Enhancing the capacity development of stakeholders including education, training research and development and documentation, and
6. Strengthening the emergency response capabilities in earthquake prone areas.

Proposed National Earthquake Risk Mitigation Project (NERMP)

The NDMA proposes to launch the National Earthquake Risk Mitigation Project during the Eleventh Five Year Plan period, in close cooperation with the concerned ministries and departments of the Government of India and State Governments to address some of the critical gaps identified during the formulation of the guidelines for management of earthquakes. Many State Governments have already initiated their efforts in improving school safety, medical preparedness and for strengthening the emergency preparedness and response capabilities of the stakeholder groups. The National Disaster Management Authority and the Government of India seek the support and cooperation of the various stakeholder groups, especially the public at large, in ensuring that an enabling environment is created for the institutionalisation of earthquake risk reduction initiatives in the country.

CYCLONE

Cyclone, also known as Tropical Cyclone (TC), is the term used globally to cover tropical law pressure system in which wind speed exceeds gale force (minimum of 34 knot i.e. 63 kmph). These are intense low pressure areas around which fierce winds circulate in an anti-clockwise manner in the Northern Hemisphere.

Cyclones are destructive because of their associated hazards like strong winds, very heavy rainfall and storm surge. It is more so when they strike coasts of countries/states bordering the North Bay of Bengal. In the past about two and a half century, 21 out of 24 cyclones with heavy loss of lives (human deaths 10,000 or more) in the globe took place in these areas. This was due to very serious storm surge problem of the region. Orissa super cyclone of 1999, when about 10,000 people died, is the most recent case of cyclone disaster in India. Shallow Bay, low flat zigzag terrain, high astronomical tide, high density of population, socio-economic conditions, lack of awareness, inadequate preparedness and absence of hedging mechanisms add to the problem. Every year, on an average five to six cyclones form in the Bay of Bengal and the Arabian Sea, of which two to three may become severe. Incidentally, more cyclones ($:1) form in the Bay of Bengal than the Arabian Sea. Cyclones are seasonal phenomena. Severe cyclones, generally, occur in the months of May, June, October and November.

Although cyclones affect the entire coastline of India, the east coast is more vulnerable compared to the west coast. thirteen coastal States and Union Territories (UTs) with 84 coastal districts are directly affected by tropical cyclones.

Fortunately, a cyclone can be detected and predicted some time in advance before it affects the population and hence losses can be minimised by organising early warnings and adequate response and preparedness.

In India, India Meteorological Department (IMD) provides cyclone warnings to various users through its six Area Cyclone Warning Centres/ Cyclone Warning Centres and two co-ordination centres located at Pune and New Delhi. Cyclones are tracked with the help of conventional observations, ship's reports, ocean data buoy, cyclone detection radars,

Indian Geo-Stationary Satellites (INSAT) and polar orbiting satellites. Aircraft reconnaissance facilities, which are one of the important tools for cyclone observations and tracking, are currently not available in this region.

Warning are communicated through various communication modes like teleprinter, telex, telephone, fax frequent radio broadcast, television, press, wireless including police wireless, internet and though satellite based Cyclone Warning Dissemination System (CWDS). CWDS is a unique system in India to communicate cyclone warnings direct to the community from the source (IMD).

Warnings to Disaster Management Officials such as Central and State Government officials, districts collectors, etc, are issued in four stages, namely Cyclone Watch, Cyclone Alert (48 hour before), Cyclone Warning (24 hours before landfall), and post landfall outlook (12 hours before landfall). Warnings contain various information related to cyclone like its position, speed, direction of movement, anticipated adverse weather etc impact of cylone on common objects on land is also included when cylones landfall is imminent. IMD has a plan for further strengthening/modernisation of cyclone warning tools and infrastructure for providing improved services.

High Power Committees have been constituted at the Centre as well as in States up to district level for taking appropriate action on receipt of warnings. Natural Disaster Management Division in the Ministry of Home Affairs through its 24x7 Control Room, coordinates all activities at the central level and with States when cyclone warnings are issued. There is a Contingency Action Plan spelling out the actions that need to be taken by various agencies at the time of cyclone threat.

To facilitate the paradigm shift from the hitherto relief-centric approach to a more pro-active, holistic and integrated approach of strengthening disaster preparedness, mitigation and emergency response, Government of India has taken path breaking steps in notifying the DM Act, 2005, and establishing the National Disaster Management Authority (NDMA) under the chairmanship of the Prime Minister at the Central level. Disaster Management Authorities are also being constituted in the States as well as in the Districts. At present, NDMA in inter-allia engaged in preparation of the Comprehensive Guidelines for the management of cyclones in the country.

A comprehensive project knows as National Cyclone Risk Mitigation Project (NCRMP), has been the drawn up with a view of mitigate the cyclone risk in all the coastal States and Union Territories (13 in number) of the country. This project is proposed to be implemented with the World Bank assistance.

NDMA is arranging Awareness Programmes and Mock Drills from time to time for building capacity of the community to fight cyclone disasters. Government of India has undertaken a Comprehensive Disaster Risk Mitigation (DRM) programme in association with UNDP in 169 most hazard prone districts in the country for capacity building and training at grass root level. Arrangements also exist to train Disaster Management Officials through the Institutes, such as the National Institute of Disaster Management (NDM) at the Central level and ATIs/ Disaster Management Institutes in the States. Specific programmes are also organised from time to time to educate public on the meteorological and warning aspects of cyclones.

Experience gained from the past events is that the maximum benefit can be obtained by developing better coordination between various organisations managing cylone warning, response and preparedness and the community. To handle an emergency like tropical cyclone, which affects millions of people, essential requirement like shelter, food, transportation etc need to be identified in advance. It may be stated that the only prescribed measures to save vulnerable population from the onslaught of storm surges are to temporarily evacuate the people on receipt of warnings and to look after them for two to three days by arranging shelters, food, healthcare facilities etc. This practice is followed even in advanced countries like USA and Japan where infrastructures and houses are built strictly following the building codes.

For better response to tropical cyclone warning, adequate preparedness and risk mitigation measures are a must. Meteorologists, Disaster Management Officials, Media and Public would need to come together and fight collectively to reduce the harmful effects to tropical cyclones.

URBAN FLOOD DISASTER MANAGEMENT

Urban flood disaster are now affecting a large number of people living in urban areas in India. Major cities in India have witness loss of life and property, disruption to transport and power and incidents of epidemics during the monsoons, most notable amongst them being Mumbai in 2005, Surat in 2006 and Kolkata in 2007. The annual losses from urban flooding are now much greater than the annual economic losses due to other disasters in urban areas.

Background

In 2001, there were 285 million people residing in 35 metro cities (have a population of one million plus). This is estimated to exceed 600 million by 2021 in over a hundred metro cities. There is a marked impact of globalisation on city growth and most growths increasingly concentrated and around dynamic urban areas, large and small. Rapid urban development the pressure of population have resulted in construction in flood-prone areas and the urban population is now more vulnerable to urban flooding.

A special in future India is heavy rainfall occurs mainly during the monsoons, hence unique solutions and approach need for Indian cities. In addition the urban heat island effect has resulted in as increase in the rainfall over urban areas. Global climate change is resulting in changed weather patterns and increased intensities of rainfall in lesser number of rainfall events on river banks on downstream of major dams and even otherwise need to have special provision for mitigation of urban flood disasters. To survive in a global economy, our urban centres should quickly recover from flotoding incidences through adequate flood disaster mitigation measures.

URBAN FLOODING IS DIFFERENT

Urban flooding is significantly different from rural flooding as urbanisation increases flood risk by up to three times peak flows result in flooding very quickly due to faster flow times (in a matter of minutes a large number of people are affected in dense population clusters and result in severe economic and infrastructure loss to industry and commerce. Urban flood can be reduced through a variety of measures like maintenance of existing drainage channels, provision of alternate drainage paths (may be underground). On-site storage of rainwater control of solid waste entering the drainage systems provision of porous pavements to allow infiltration of rainwater reservation of low-lying areas for playgrounds and parks, utilisation of state-of-the-art technologies to address current problems etc.

RUNNING URBAN CENTRES 24X7

To keep the urban centres running 24×7, flood damages need to be minimised through proper planning and enforcement. Four main objectives have to be achieved which include: (a) warning the people of an impending flooding, (b) protecting the existing infrastructure, (c) maintaining the transport and communication through the worst possible event special emphasis on air transport and communication to be 24×7 and, (d) minimising urban flooding in future cities/suburbs through improved master drainage plans.

National guidelines from NDMA

Recognising the fact that urban flooding is now a major disaster which affects a large number of people, National Disaster Management Authority (NDMA) is now dealing with this as a separate subject delinking it from (rural) flooding, NDMA has initiated the process for evolving National Guidelines for Management of urban flooding with the involvement of all stakeholders. NDMA will review the present status of Urban Flood Management, identify gaps and challenges and formulate guidelines for urban flood disaster management.

The guidelines will focus on S and T Tools for more effective early warning and monitoring based on state-of-the-art equipment, impact assessment from work and climate change impact.

FLOOD MANAGEMENT – AN OVERVIEW

The Flood Hazard

Floods have been a recurrent phenomenon in India for times immemorial. The annual average precipitation including snowfall over India is estimated at 1200 mm, 80 per cent of which occurs in the monsoon. Rainfall varies widely across the length and breadth of the country. The result is devastating floods in some parts of the country and drought conditions in other parts.

Inadequate capacity of the rivers to contain within their banks, the high flows following heavy rainfall, leads to flooding. Areas with poor-drainage characteristics get flooded by accumulation of water from heavy rainfall.

Hilly and not too regions with heavy rainfall/thunderstorms/ cloudbursts are prone to flash floods. Depressions, cyclonic storms, sudden release of waters from the reservoirs, breaches in flood embankments, dams and landslide dams and release of water due to melting of glacial ice jams may also cause flash floods.

The problem of flooding and drainage congestion in urban areas is a recent phenomenon and is a result of encroachments in flood plains and waterways and lack of drainage network.

River erosion is a result of the tendency of rivers to braid, meander and split into branches.

As reported by the state governments, the area prone to floods, works out to 46.56 mha and area prone to water logging/drainage congestion as 9 mha. Heavy floods occur in the country with a marked periodicity. On an average, every year, an area of 7.51 mha is affected by floods and monetary loss is of the order of Rs 1800 crore.

The rivers originating in China, Nepal and Bhutan cause severe floods in the states of Jammu and Kashmir, Himachal Pradesh, Uttar Pradesh, Bihar, West Bengal, Arunachal Pradesh and Assam.

Past Initiatives by the Government of India

The Government of India have, from time to time, appointed several Committees to look into the problem of floods and their management. The most important ones are the Policy Statement of 1954, the Rasthriya Baarh Ayog (1978) and the Task Force on Flood Management/ Erosion Control (2004). The implementation of their recommendations has been rather slow.

Institutional Mechanism

As per provisions of the Constitution of India, the primary responsibility for flood control lies with the States. At the central level, the Ministry of Home Affairs, the Ministry of Water Resources along with Central Water Commission, Brahmaputra Board, Ganga Flood Control Commission, Indian Meteorological Department and National Remote Sensing Agency look after various aspects of flood management. Recently the GOI has established the National Disaster Management Authority (NDMA) with the responsibility of prevention, preparedness, mitigation, rehabilitation, reconstruction and recovery and formulation of appropriate policies and guidelines for disaster management. The National Disaster Response Force (NDRF) provides specialised response to disasters.

At the State level, disaster management departments/ Relief Commissioners, State Disaster Management Authority headed by the Chief Minister, the District Disaster Management Authority headed by the District Magistrate, besides irrigation/ Water Resources/ Flood Control/ Public Works Departments deal with flood management.

Out of the loans and grants by the centre, allocations for the flood sector are made by state governments themselves. There are also a few centrally sponsored/ central sector schemes to assist them in this field. Under calamity Relief Fund, provision is made for urgent relief and immediate repairs to the infrastructure damaged in floods. The National Flood Mitigation Project is proposed in the XI Plan to assist them in flood management.

Flood Management Measures

Structural measure are physical in nature and aim to prevent flood waters from reaching potential damage centres. The important ones are flood embankments, dams, reservoirs, dention basing, channel improvement works like desilting/dredging of rivers, drainage improvement works, diversion of flood water, catchments area treatment/ aforestation measures, anti-erosion works etc. Flood embankments, roads and railway lines are required to be aligned, located and designed properly and provided with adequate waterway. The effectiveness of reservoirs in moderating floods can be optimised by having proper arrangements laid down procedures. So far 33,923 km of embankments, 38,809 km of drainage channels, 2,450 town protection works and raising of 4,721 villages above flood level have been completed. Barring occasional breaches, these works have given reasonable protection to an area of about 18.22 mha. Periodic and systematic inspection, rehabilitation and maintenance of these works are required in accordance with prescribed standards and guidelines.

Non-structural measures aim at keeping the people away from flood waters. Important once are flood plain zoning, flood proofing, flood forecasting and warning. The flood plain zoning aims at regulating the land use in the flood plains. A model draft bill for flood plain zoning legislation was also circulated by the Union Government in 1975 to all the States but their response has not been satisfactory. This along with other legal framework will be introduced to make building, public utility installations and infrastructure flood safe in the flood prone areas.

Providing raised platforms for the people to take shelter in floods is an important aspect of flood proofing. Flood forecasting enables us to be forewarned about the likely depth, duration and extent of flooding. A nation wide network of 176 flood forecasting stations operated by the CWC needs to be expanded and modernised.

The best available technical and non-technical inputs on flood management will be incorporated in educational curricula of all academic and professional institutions. Films, manuals and other documents need to be prepared and circulated among various stakeholders.

Flood Response

The setting up of relief camps and providing basic amenities in them and creating awareness among all the stakeholders about the type of illness and other health problems likely to arise during and after floods and simple methods of their prevention, making arrangements for keeping dead bodies, their proper identification and disposal are important aspect of preparedness for prompt flood response.

Management and control of the adverse consequences of floods require coordinated and effective response systems at all levels. The local community in the affected neighbourhood is always the first responder and as such trained and equipped teams consisting of local people are to be set up in flood prone areas. All response activities will be coordinated through a suitably devised incident command system headed by the district magistrate. The corporate sector has to be motivated in making available their resources to the government after the flood.

Prompt and efficient emergency medical response will be provided by well equipped quick relief medical teams and other mobile land, water and airborne field hospitals.

Flood Management Plans

The NDMA is formulating guidelines for flood management which will be issued shortly. Reservoir safety, their operations and inter-state coordination constitute important parts of these guidelines. Following these, the Central Ministries and Departments concerned and State Governments and other stakeholders will formulate their Flood Management Plans (FMPs) which will be approved by the NDMA so as to fit into overall national disaster management plan. Their implementation will be monitored closely and corrective measures, as necessary, will be taken from time to time.

STRENGTHENING DISASTER RESPONSE IN INDIA

The steadily increasing frequency and intensity of disasters in the country, particularly during the last decade, has underscored the need for a prompt and effective response mechanism to minimise the loss of life and property in any disaster this important issue has been given due weightage in the Disaster Response Force (NDRF) for the purpose of specialised response to any disaster situation. The general super-intendence, direction and control this force has been vested in the National Disaster Management Authority (NDMA), the apex body for disaster management in the country.

Presently, the NDRF is to comprise eight battalions, positioned at different locations in the country based on the vulnerability profile. Seven of these battalions have already been located at Guwahati, Kolkata, Mundali (Bhubaneshwar), Akrakonam (Chennai), Talegaon (Pune), Gandhinagar (Gujarat) and Chandigarh are already in position. This force, comprising specially chosen personnel from the Central Para Military Forces is being provided high skill training and state-of-the-art equipment. The field of specialised training of this force include, training in collapsed structure search and rescue, water rescue and Diving, medical first Response, Heli-slithering and chemical, Bio-logical, Radiological and Nuclear (CBRN). While all the eight Battalions are being equipped and trained for all natural disasters, four of these Battalions are specially trained for CBRN. While all the eight Bns are being equipped and trained for all natural disasters, four of these Bns are specially trained for CBRN Emergencies. The assistance of Bhabha Atomic Research Centre (BARC) Mumbai, Defence Research Development Estabilishment (DRDE) Gwalior and College of Military Engineering (CME) Pune is being taken for training them in these scenarios.

NDRF is being groomed as multi-disciplinary, multi-skilled and hi-tech force for all types of disasters capable of insertion by air, land and sea. The personnel of this force are being trained for heli-insertion in impact area with the help of the Indian Air Force. The process of setting up state-of-the-art training institutions in Disaster Response for the NDRF personnel has already started. The facilities of these institutions, as also the infrastructure of NDRF battalions, would be available to the police force and other stakeholders in the states for training in Disaster Response. The NDRF Units are to maintain close liaison with the state administration and will be available to them proactively in the event of any serious disaster situation developing.

Community being the first responder in any disaster situation, Community Capacity Building and Public Awareness is of utmost importance in any initiative towards saving life and property in a disaster. This important issue has been given due priority in the role and responsibility of NDRF. The force has been trained and equipped to carry out Community Capacity building and Public Awareness programme, particularly for the vulnerable groups This force has already won much appreciation for its work in the field of fold preparedness and flood response this year.

While the NDRF is being trained and equipped as a specialist Force for major disasters, it is equally important to ensure training of State Police personnel, who are also to be one of the important first responders in any natural or man-made situation. To ensure this, a two pronged strategy is being suggested to the States firstly, to familiarise the Police Personnel in the states with the basic of Disaster management and secondly, to train at least one battalion equivalent to some of the Armed Police battalions in each state in Disaster Management in a progressive manner as a specialist force aimed at raising the State Disaster Response Force (SDRF) on the lines of NDRF. Ten per cent of the funds out of calamity Relief Fund being given to the states by the centre, can be utilised for purchase of the specialist equipment. For this purpose, NDMA is assisting the states in Training of Trainers' aimed at encouraging the states to set up Disaster Management traing facilities in their respective Police Training Colleges for including Disaster Management training in the Basic and In-service courses for all ranks of police personnel.

The other organisations which have tremendous role and potential as force multipliers in Disaster Response are Fire Services and Civil Defence. In most countries in the world, the primary responsibility to respond to any major disaster situation vests with the Fire Services or Civil Defence. However, in India, the Fire Services are handicapped on account of gross inadequacies in terms of resources and infrastructure and this is now being given a major upgradation. Similarly, Civil Defence as a community-based voluntary organisation can play a very important role in community capacity building and response at grassroot level. This is proposed to be organised by extending the Civil Defence coverage to all the districts in the country in a phased manner and by integrating them in the Disaster Management framework by training and assigning the Civil Defence volunteer a role in Community Capacity Building and Public Awareness, besides that of response during disasters.

Thus, while NDRF is a major national initiative toward ensuring an effective and prompt response to any disaster situation, similar initiative towards training and equipping the other agencies like police, Civil Defence, Home Guards, Fire Services as youth organisations like NCC, NSS, NYKS etc to play a complementary role as force multipliers in Disaster Response would go a long way towards building disaster resilience in the country.

DISASTER MANAGEMENT: SHIFTING AXIS FROM VISIBLE TO INVISIBLE

Looking at the disaster scenario in India and across the region, it has become inevitable that everybody should get prepared for future disaster risks. Earlier, disasters were one time phenomenon in ten years, but now the scenario has changed drastically and it has reversed its feature to ten disasters in one year and it is no more a distant but a more frequent phenomenon and in a more intensified form. We human beings are emotional and have the characteristics of being benevolent and so, soon after any crisis, we are ready to offer help in any and every possible way but, unfortunately when it comes to the pre-planning support for disaster risk reduction, our attitude is more of a casual approach and therefore, since ages, we are still focusing on post-disaster management only. Again, the large investments of disaster management and of development agencies both, including the government, are more in the post-disaster activities because it gets noticed and is more visible whereas, the pre-disaster risk reduction planning remains almost invisible (although is effective in the long run). The time has come, if we are really interested in reducing the impact of disasters, i.e. to change our attitude and shift the axix from the "visible to invisible".

We, therefore, must plan for this invisible investment, leading to safer development and ensure that our plan does not get imprisoned in the paper alone, but is translated at the ground.

Disasters are not natural but, human induced. Cyclones, floods, earthquakes, tsunami are all natural hazards and they have the potential to damage life and property whenever there is human interface with them. Our development activities have not been planned to sustain the force and also we, by design or default, are gradually deducing our capacity to cope or rather facilitate them to take a violent shape. To justify we has the Gujarat earthquake (poor infrastructure and residential buildings), Mumbai floods (drainage and city water carrying capacity), Tsunami (No warning system and weak infrastructure) These examples corroborate the fact that it is our inadequate capacity or negligence that converts natural activities into disasters. Poorly- planned development and inappropriate poverty reduction measures can increase vulnerability to external natural shocks. Economic poverty can force people to settle in areas that are more prone to natural hazards and again, their affordability and accessibility to safe locations is almost unthinkable in both, rural as well as in urban areas, this vulnerable population settle themselves in hazard prone areas and their exposure to natural hazards is augmented. Poor then become more vulnerable within the parameters of the protective dimension of poverty. The dream of MDG (Millennium Development Goal) and Hygo framework of action, a global initiatives for disaster risk deduction, might just remain a pipes dream if, we do not address the issue of poverty, development and disasters in a more integrated manner.

All the institutional policies, tools, framework are designed and institutionalised over the years for managing post-disaster crisis. The efforts roped in so far, by different stakeholders (government, community, civil societies, NGOs multilateral and bilateral agencies, UN organisations) are unfortunately not yet enough for disaster risk reduction. Disaster Prevention and mitigation is still a word reflecting a flabbergasted look for many. There is need to inculcate the habit of risk reduction not only in the minds and approach of the common man but, in the complete circle of development institutions and governance, many states in the country are still blissfully ignorant about disaster risks for the safety of the future generations, we need to ensure that all the development initiatives must have disaster risk auditing as its safeguard in development projects, at least, in the vulnerable states.

The World Disaster Report 2001 indicates that 97 per cent of all disaster-related death occur in the poorest of the developing countries, while only two per cent took place in the industrialised nations. Moreover, as a percentage of GNP disaster losses in developing countries are an estimated 20 per cent higher in developing than in developed countries in India, the states which are less developed are in high vulnerable zone and have low capacity to respond. States like Bihar, Assam, Rajasthan, UP, West Bengal, Odisha, North-Eastern States, Uttaranchal, Himachal Pradesh are vulnerable to frequent disasters such as floods, cyclone, earthquake and drought. The only weapon on which states are dependant is the relief money (Calamity Relief Fund, National Calamity Contingency Fund, PM Relief Fund, donations, grants, loan etc.). With these funds, we recover infrastructure and housing losses but, financial and economic losses still remain unattended. Natural disasters can cause sharp increase in poverty and slow the pace of human development. The states who are poor but in developing stage, therefore, again remain poor and this recognises the need to develop multiple tools which can address post-disaster recovery-infrastructure and financial loss, pre-disaster risk reduction and during disasters, an effective response system.

Let's face the fact that OUR future is not safe and the world is bound to be enveloped by disaster risks if we do not address the issue in time. If we monitor risks and risk reduction on a daily basis we will find that, rate of increase in disaster risk is much higher than the rate of risk reduction. Urbanisatoin climate change population boom, environmental degradation industrialisation unsafe development etc coupled with terrorism and other blasphemous activities are gradually adding to the existing risk. Also, globally, vulnerability has increased and it will continue to expand, hence, the challenge for a safer tomorrow is not just to ameliorate disaster risk reduction activities but also of containing the existing risks and not allowing them to proliferate. Again, since disasters do not demarcate between national and international or political boundaries so, we must tackle this with a more regional and international synergistic approach. Initiatives taken so far at the global, national and state levels are a welcome step but, are not enough. We have set the ball rolling and now must have the momentum ongoing and take this from reach to the un-reach and make disaster risk reduction as the people's movement.

MEDICAL PREPAREDNESS FOR DISASTER MANAGEMENT

The Indian subcontinent is one of the most vulnerable region for both natural and man-made disasters which result into extensive damage and large number of casualties. The incidents of natural catastrophes have increased from about 100 per year in 1975 to 395 by the year in 2006, according to a UN Report. An estimate revealed that the 10 nations hardest hit by natural disasters in 2006, in terms of the number of people killed or otherwise affected, were all developing countries. The increasing geological and hydrological events, deforestation, population explosion, poverty and uncontrolled urbanisation further increases the vulnerability with high degree of mass casualty potential. It clearly indicates the requirement of an institutionalised mechanism for disaster management and furthermore, a well organised and elaborate medical preparedness in every country. There is also a need for regional operation and knowledge sharing amongst the countries of the region facing similar types of disasters.

The medical preparedness should aim at minimising the loss of life and prevention of disabilities. The incidence of mortality and morbidity can be substantially reduced by proper planning and preparedness at all levels based on a comprehensive, integrated and all hazard approach. The necessary measures include capacity development, augmentation of infrastructure and a coordinated network of all emergency responders, hospital managers and other stakeholders. The important elements include incident site management, hospital care and long-term management of delayed health effects including psychosocial support.

An alert mechanism is required to be developed for activation of the emergency protocols at the incident site depending upon the severity of disaster. An Integrated Disease Surveillance Programme has been initiated that gives early warning signals of the impending outbreaks of epidemics to adopt preventive measures like vector control and immunisation programmes and other measures to maintain the sanitation and hygiene of the region. The other preventive strategies like measures for containment of hazardous chemicals within the major accident hazard units and other activities based upon the risk assessment of the area needs to be undertaken. Further it is essential to train and equip the MFRs/QRMTs with an organised Integrated Ambulance Network including ARMVs, Heli-Ambulances to provide Basic life support, triage, resuscitation and immediate care to the seriously injured ones.

Our experience during Bhuj Earthquake established the requirement of full-fledged containerised hospitals, public-private partnership and integrated role of NGOs and community at all levels. The growth rate of public health sector requires a pro-active involvement of private healthcare providers to fulfil the gaps especially for effective medical management of mass casualty incidences. Another important issue is development of disaster resilient intra/inter-medical communication network with other emergency functionaries. All the emergency practices at the incident site need to be in harmony with the emergency protocols laid down in hospital disaster management plans. It is important to formulate and maintain resource inventories/crisis expansion of beds; intensive care units; emergency departments; operating rooms; doctors, nurses, paramedics and other health professionals; transportation assets such as ambulances and other emergency medical services units. Such plans should be tested twice a year by conducting mock exercises. The medical management should also include development of adequate mechanism for long-term medical follow up of delayed health effects.

The medical problems posed by different disaster situations are varied and there is a need for the development of specialised facilities and disaster specific modules. It is necessary to develop apex and zonal trauma centres at State level and designated trauma beds at district hospitals. In addition, there is a need to develop burn facilities, poison information units, upgraded network of advance blood banks, various types of laboratories including DNA fingerprinting laboratories, biosafety and public health laboratories. Necessary planning to surge the capacity to provide mortuary services is also required. Another area is to identify the vulnerable groups and to integrate the psychosocial support and mental health services with general healthcare services. The medical preparedness for Chemical, Biological, Radiological and Nuclear (RBN) management necessitates development of SOPs for CBRN management at the incident site for triage, personal protection, decontamination, resuscitation, casualty evacuation followed by treatment of exposed victims at the hospital level. The critical infrastructure for medical management includes CBRN casualty treatment centres/wards and training facilities for specialised response to deal with covert CBRN attacks.

The above preparedness measures are with a view to institutionalise a system for prompt and effective emergency medical response at the site so that casualties are provided with basic life support measures, triage and resuscitation, followed by safe evacuation to the earmarked hospitals. The hospital care also needs to be provided in accordance with the Standard Operating Procedures (SOPs) laid down in hospital disaster management plans.

The relief and rehabilitation phases need minimum standards for food, water, shelter and hygiene to be laid down at the National and State level. It is also important to understand and respect the sentiments of local community, religious issues, food habits and major livelihood of occupation while deciding the course of action during these phases. The role of public information officer from the medical fraternity is very crucial in media management. Research and Development (R&D) will focus on regular upgradation of technologies by either adoption of best global practices and time tested technologies or development of the indigenous cost effective alternatives for medical management based upon the lessons learnt.

National Disaster Management Authority, Government of India, in partnership with all stakeholders and experts in the country, has already taken a proactive initiative towards institutionalisation of the medical management framework by formulating national guidelines for all stakeholders and will soon be available in the public domain. These guidelines will form a basis for the development of various action plans by different ministries and departments concerned. Medical preparedness plans will also be prepared at the district level as a part of district DM plan.

In conclusion, the major objective of medical preparedness is to convert our capabilities in terms of human resource and supportive infrastructure into capacities for quick and efficient medical response. This can be achieved only through a participative approach of all stakeholders. It is most necessary to establish suitable mechanism for proper coordination and implementation of all the activities required for medical preparedness and mass casualty management.

ROLE OF LABORATORY IN DISASTER MANAGEMENT

Disaster can be defined as a calamity taking place in the society causing disruption of its function and widespread human, material or environmental losses, including loss of lives and deterioration of health and health services.

Natural disasters occur frequently affecting large population and are generally accompanied by number of outbreaks. These disasters may lead to insurgence of many infections and trigger off their spread to the community, thus facilitating the risk of any kind of outbreak. Also large masses are affected by NBC agents or radiological injuries which may pose a great risk to the mankind. This has to be prevented and immediate screening of sample population should be done for conformity of root cause of the incidence. All clinical diagnosis and course of treatment procedures are based upon the accuracy of these investigations, though this sector is developed but not organised and harmonised. The introduction of laboratory support in epidemiological services has revolutionised the concept as well as scope of disease surveillance, which means, laboratory support is an integral components of any surveillance system. Laboratories can support the public health surveillance activities in disaster including NBC and emergency situations, including prevention and control of outbreaks due to communicable diseases.

To perform these vital functions and on the basis of need assessment analysis of a particular area, the laboratories are to be established. In addition, there are National laboratories including ICMR, NICD, DRDO etc. that are able to handle the various levels of functioning like identification of new biological agents, chemical agents. The diagnostic procedures to be adopted for identification will be developed as the came decision-making laboratories of National Laboratory Network. The laboratories at the hospitals and medical colleges need to be upgraded along with specialised departments in accordance with the requirements of the particular area.

Setting up Laboratory Support to Disease Surveillance Post Disaster Situations

The setting up this support system requires the prior identification of the important communicable diseases, possible etiology/ causative agents and the tests to be performed at various levels of laboratories. These laboratories will prioritise the communicable diseases of public health importance of the local region. The list of tests to be performed at each level of laboratories for the priority diseases (to be determined by the local situation) will be defined. The existing laboratory facilities and available manpower will be assessed and mapped out followed by identification of referral laboratories that can provide a back up to the other laboratories. The networking of these laboratories will be ensured for its optimal use in an emergency situation. A focal laboratory person will be identified at the district level to coordinate the activities. The flow of information will also be defined. The standard guidelines for formats samples to be collected and common strategy for testing will be issued. The supplies for collection, transport and storage of clinical samples will also be ensured. It is important to focus on proper collection, storage tests that require minimal expertise and have high sensitivity. Outbreak investigation kits should be made available to the Rapid Response Team (RRTs) and constantly replenished and restocked. It is necessary to send only representative samples which need to be tested in order to avoid unnecessary burden on the laboratory services. The results, trends and useful findings serving as early warning signals will be monitored. The rapid communication and regular reporting of results to be epistemologists for initiating action will be ensured.

Laboratory Support for Disaster Management

A special attention is required to tackle the probable epidemics and public health emergencies arising out of various disasters. This includes development of specialised medical facility and laboratory support. Development of disaster research centre at the National level capable to handle the screening of large number of samples at a time as well as core research laboratory to develop protection and detection equipments and prophylactic drugs and treatment modalities is necessary. It is also essential to develop models based on novel biomarkers able to provide necessary information about the damage caused due to disaster including agents or radiation dose to which victim is exposed. Treatment modalities needs to be laid down and also the tests to be conducted for monitoring the situation of the victim for evaluation of short and long-term effects including bone marrow transplantation. The available detection techniques need to be integrated at one place and develop mobile laboratories wherever required. At state level, the similar centres are required to be replicated in due course of time. At district levels, the regional centres and mobile laboratories will be developed in the initial phase and also its integration with advanced ambulance services to eventually develop the single van concept able to take care of the victims immediately after the disasters. All these laboratories will be connected by an intra-laboratory network and inter-and inter-laboratory network under a single umbrella of EMS (Emergency Medical Services) at the district level. The hospital network will become the front end of the EMS databases with laboratory support as back end along with horizontal interfaces of medical and logistics supplies and other required logistics for EMS. It will also integrate with other component of EMS and other emergency services like police, fire etc.

All the laboratories include biochemical and laboratories, pathological clinics and will be integrated into a single laboratory network with National, State, District and local level. Some major guidelines for development of an efficient network of such laboratories include defining of the functional status of the laboratory in terms of its primary function i.e. CBRN type or epidemiological services. The secondary function i.e. any extendable function its can perform for EMS in case of mass casualty event will also be defined. It is essential to develop laboratories for identification of the dead based upon the DNA technology at all levels. The capacity need to be enhanced to deal with identification of large number of samples during a mass causality event. It is also essential to develop trained manpower at the local level who are able to collect and dispatch the biological samples, as per in accordance with the laid down standardised procedures, to the referral laboratories for rapid identification of the dead.

An accreditation system of laboratories is being done by National Accreditation Board for laboratories under Ministry of Science and Technology and its strict implementation needs to be ensured by the states. To develop these laboratories as self sustain units, research components, and state centre sponsored projects and clinical supports for diagnosis will to be encouraged and developed. SOPs for standardised testing procedures, reporting system, cost effective rates of the tests and authenticity of scientific manpower will be laid down for harmonisation of these activities.

A mutual aid on line information exchange network will also be developed and dovetailed into this laboratory network. RRTs will be developed, trained and re-trained for their vital usage at the time of disasters. Well equipped detection vans will also be developed for On Site management of the disasters. PPEs will be provided to the RRTs and QRMTs. The various combinations of kits for tacking multi-hazard eventualities will be developed and readily available for rapid mobilisation to the incident site. SOPs for backup support in case of laboratories being victim of disasters also need to be outlined. Backup communication system and power, resource pooling and harmony in results will be tested periodically using mock drills. Biomedical waste managements practices as per pollution control guidelines shall be strictly implemented to reduce the occurrence of any secondary disasters. It is the responsibility of nodal hospital and nodal laboratory to closely monitor the site for a sufficient longer period of time till they declared it as safe zone.

Networking of laboratories under Integrated Disease Surveillance Programme (IDSP)

Under the IDSP of Government of India, a laboratory network has been established at various levels of healthcare as given below and this network is to be used for disease surveillance/outbreak investigation even during disaster. The network comprises of Peripheral Laboratories and Microscopy Centres (L1 Labs); District Public Health Laboratories (L2 Lab); State Laboratories (L3 Lab); Regional and Quality Assurance Laboratories (L4); Disease based reference Laboratories (L5); There are 8-10 laboratories of repute in the country which will be acting as national Reference Labs. The IDSP has been initiated three years back and is in stage of implementation. It will support the biological disaster management also. In order to set up the district laboratories initially there will be strengthening of three to four priority laboratories for each state and model district labs will be set up which will later on expanded to all district laboratories.

e-Governance Suggestions

In simple terms Electronic Governance can be defined as giving Citizens the choice of when and where they access government information and services. Putting the Citizen at the centre of government means taking a delivery channel view. This would mean using more and more of Electronics and Information Technology in many of the government functions.

Electronic Governance thus, is the application of Information Technology to the processes of government functioning to bring about

- Simple
- Moral
- Accountable
- Responsive and
- Transparent Governance

The objective of achieving Electronic Governance (EG) goes far beyond mere computerisation of stand alone back office operations. It means to fundamentally change as to how the government operates and this implies a new set of responsibilities for the executive, legislature and the citizenry. The effort should aim to bring about a social catharsis, which needs to be orchestrated in a comprehensive, concerted and planned fashion.

Electronic government has emerged as one of the flagship applications with aspiration to employ multimedia and network technologies to re-invent the way the government works. This IT enabled government will ensure better transparency and services to the public.

Major Areas of Implementation

Identification of Government Departments with maximum citizen interface: Government departments, which have maximum interaction with the public, must be identified for the use of IT. Listed below are a few such departments that can be considered:

Public Grievances

Electricity, Water, Telephone, Ration Card, Sanitation, Public Transport, Police.

Rural. Services

Land Records, Below Poverty Line (BPL) /EWS Families

Police

- FIR Registration, Lost and Found
- Valuables, Persons, Dead Bodies

Social Services: Pension

- Old Age, Widows, Exgratia Scheme
- Acquisition/Rehabilitation and Compensation
- Registration of Licenses and Certificates
- Ration Cards, Birth Certificates, Death Certificate, Domicile Certificate, Caste/Tribe Certificate, Arms Renewal, Registration of Documents, School Registration, University Registration, Motor Vehicle Registration, Driving License.

Public Information

Employment Exchange Registration, Employment Opportunities, Examination Results, Hospitals / Beds Availability / Services, Railway Time Tables, Airline Time Tables, Road Transport Time Tables, Charitable Trusts, Government Notifications, Government Forms, Government Schemes.

EWS Services

Civil supplies, Old Age Pension, Widow Pension, Handicapped Pension/Services, Ex Gratia Payment.

Agriculture Sector

Speeds Information, Pesticides, Fertilizers, Crop disease, Weather Forecast - short range/District-wise, Market Price.

Utility Payments/Billing

Electricity, Water, Telephone.

Commercial

Taxation and Return Filing, Income Tax, Corporate Tax, Custom Duty, Central/State Excise Duty, Sales Tax, House Tax, Property Tax, Octroi, Road Tax, Company Returns.

Government

Electronic Procurement, Education University Model for E-Governance. e-Zest is committed towards e-governance implementation at every level of government. e-Zest has dedicated research and development team for making e-Governance reality.

SUGGESTIONS

We have seen that the district magistrate is generally over-burdened while coordinating all disaster management activities in his district. So I recommend that the Relief Commissioner should be made the nodal officer for efficient management of funds. To ensure this, the Relief Commissioner should have access to complete information database pertaining to relief and rehabilition activities in the disaster struck state. The utilisation of funds can be audited at a later stage.

Primary purpose of UNDMT is to ensure prompt and effective response at country level. Further, UNDP focuses on development-related aspects of disaster risks and on providing technical assistance. It supported initiatives in India in the aftermath of major disasters of Gujarat in 2001 and Tsunami in 2004. The UNICEF, WFP, World Health Organisation ensuring that the immediate and particular needs of victims are met. Field Coordination Units are deployed in the event of an emergency such and the Emergency Relief Co-ordinator who is the Head of OCHA coordinates all actions.

OCHA stands for Office for Coordination of Humanitarian Affairs and is headed by a disaster relief coordinator who reports directly to the UN Secretary-General and works closely with UN Development Programme. OCHA directs UN assistance and mobilises aid from NGOs such as the International Red Cross. It also functions as an information coordination centre. But what the audience is really waiting for Peush is for us to tell them how to manage the aftermath of these disasters. Reducing loss to life and property as well as natural resources and reaching out to provide relief to maximum number of affected people should be our prime focus. Let us give a broad overview of the concept of Disaster Management. So much for various disasters and their effects. Disaster Management has three stages:

(a) Preparatory Stage

(b) Emergency and Response Stage

(c) Rehabilitation and Reconstruction Stage

Preparatory Stage corresponds to the pre-disaster period and includes disaster prediction, warning and alert systems, preventive measures and preparing for contingencies.

The Emergency and Response Stage would commence immediately before and after the disaster strikes. This includes reaction to warnings and emergency relief activities.

While the *rehabilitation phase* may last for a few weeks or months, the reconstruction may even take years.

And of course the third stage is that of Rehabilitation and Reconstruction. This would involve short and long-term measures to restore essential services, communication and normalcy.

Weaknesses

(i) ***Inadequate equipments and trained people.*** The Army and the local civilian organisations carried out the initial search and rescue work with available tools and equipment which were inadequate and unwieldy. On the other hand, well trained Swiss team arrived on 28 January with better equipment. They could save valuable lives because of this factor. This aspect is being addressed on a war footing by the government, as was evident during the recent earthquake in Jammu & Kashmir.

(ii) ***Lack of Emergency Medical Response System.*** The next weakness noticed was the lack of emergency medical response system. Many hospital emergency plans focus on the hospital as a disaster responder, able to receive and treat mass casualties from an incident. However, at times the hospital may itself become a victim of the disaster, as it happened in Bhuj. In such cases, the process of evacuation, care of patients and treatment of casualties can be efficiently managed only through proper planning and training.

(iii) Construction of buildings by ignoring the building bye-laws. Violation of the building bye-laws caused avoidable casualties. Strict action should be taken against builders and officials, without whose patronage, construction of such weak structures would not have been possible.

Threats

(i) ***Casual Approach.*** The first is the casual approach. To highlight this aspect an incident which happened prior to the quake. Sometime in Dec 2000, Gujarat's Principal Secy, Mr CK Koshy, wrote to all 25 district collectors. His memo read, "Take out the Inmarsat satellite phones, dust them, check if they are working and report back." A week later, Mr Koshy found that only four collectors had responded. A second letter with a stern warning was dispatched. This time around, without exception, all responded positively. However, on that fateful day, the satellite phones, simply did not work.

(ii) ***Lack of a Pro-Active Approach Towards Disaster Mitigation and Preparedness.*** Another threat is the lack of a pro-active approach by the state, towards disaster preparedness and mitigation.

Conclusion

It would be presumptuous to suggest that disasters can be totally managed by technology. A well-oiled disaster management machinery will help save a number of precious lives. The three crucial components are–evolving a structure, an implementation mechanism and blending technology in the process. All these three facets can evolve a worthwhile synergy provided they are leveraged through sincere element of participation at every step. Participation in evolving the structure shall essentially promulgate sustainability and reliability. Local involvement is crucial in implementation and finally any technology that is based on the beneficiaries contribution has the best change of acceptance.

Index

A

Accountability, 121
Africa, 57
African plates, 168
Agriculture Advancing Australia (AAA), 160
Agriculture Ministry, 33, 65, 182
Agriculture, 69, 124
Agri-Food Canada, 56
Ahmedabad, 35, 126
Airline Time Tables, 245
Akrakonam (Chennai), 232
Alabama, 162
Alaska, 22, 162
Amateur Radio Operators, 196
Andaman and Nicobar earthquakes, 221
Andaman and Nicobar, 69, 78
Andaman, 73
Andhra Pradesh, 34, 54, 81, 89
Arabian Sea, 30, 54, 74, 224
Arkansas, 162
Arthasastra, 114
Arunachal Pradesh, 69, 229
Asia Pacific, 123
Assam, 72, 81, 229, 236
Australia, 43, 56, 144, 147, 154, 155, 156, 157, 159, 161
Australian Central Government, 157
Australian Counter Disaster College (ACDC), 145
Australian Emergency Management Committee, 158
Australian Emergency Management Organisation, 158
Australian Government Department of Health, 159
Australian Government, 157, 158, 159, 161
Australian Local Government Association (ALGA) 161
Australian Maritime Safety Authority (AMSA), 160
Australian, 158
Austria, 167, 171

B

Bahamas, 162
Bangalore, 31, 33, 118
Bangladesh, 23, 26, 87
Bay of Bengal, 27, 30, 54, 74, 224
Bhabha Atomic Research Centre (BARC) Mumbai, 232
Bhavnagar, 127
Bhoomi, 118
Bhopal Gas Tragedy, 31, 87, 103
Bhubaneswar, 121
Bhuj earthquake, 74, 82
Bhutan, 229

Bihar (Floods), 81
Bihar, 70, 72, 229, 236
Bikaner, 205
Biological, 238
Block and District Rural Development Agencies, 122
Brahmaputra Board, 229
British Columbia Canada, 51
Brussels, 170
Bureau of Meteorology, 160
Burundi, 26

C

Calamity Relief Fund (CRF), 71, 94, 186, 187, 230, 233, 236
Canadian Prairies, 56
Cardio Pulmonary Resuscitation (CPR), 39
Caribbean, 23, 53
C-band, 121
Central America, 23
Central European Initiative (CEI), 171
Central Government, 64, 66
Central Water Commission, 73, 229
Chamoli earthquakes, 221
Chandigarh Administration, 69
Chandigarh, 232
Charitable Trusts, 245
Chemical Emergency Teams, 101
Chemical, 219, 220, 238
Chennai, 78, 93
Chhattisgarh, 72
China killing, 17
China, 23, 229
Citizen Convenience Centres, 126
City Civic Bodies, 126
City Civic Centres, 126
Civil Defence, 219
Civil supplies, 245
Committee on Earth Observation Satellites Disaster Information Server (CEOSDIS), 171
Common Entrance Test Karnataka, 118
Commonwealth Counter-Disaster Task Force (CCDTF), 158
Communication Infrastructure, 44
Community Capacity Building, 233
Comprehensive Case Information System (CCIS), 129
Comprehensive Emergency Management (CEM), 200
Confederation of Indian Industry (CII), 117
Consultative Committees (CCC), 116
Contingency Action Plan for Natural Calamities, 31, 33
Contingency Action Plan, 225
Co-ordination of Humanitarian Affairs (OCHA), 147
Coriolis Effect, 21
Court Case Monitoring System (CCMS), 129
Crisis Management Group (CMG), 64, 105
Croatia, 171
Crop Assessment Missions, 57
Crop disease, 245
Cross-border co-ordination, 166
Cyclone Warning Centres, 224
Cyclone Warning Dissemination System (CWDS), 225
Cyclones or Typhoons, 21
Cyclones, 19, 25, 32, 219

D

Database servers, 124
Database, 44
Deccan plateau, 34

Decision Information Distributing System, 146

Defence and State Civil Preparedness Agencies, 145

Defence Research Development Estabilishment (DRDE), 232

Defence Support of Civil Authorities (DSCA), 164

Delhi, 69, 72

Department of Agriculture & Cooperation (DAC), 186

Department of Defence (DOD), 164

Department of Defence, 144, 145, 160

Department of Homeland Security (DHS), 164

Department of Space (DOS), 187

Department of Transport and Regional Services (DOTARS), 159

Departmental LANs, 125

Develop national database system, 166

Dharwad, 118

Digital Signature Certificates, 125

Direct Reception System (DRS), 121, 122

Disaster Management (DM), 218

Disaster Management and Education, 124

Disaster Management Authorities (DMA), 36, 59, 218, 225

Disaster Management Committee, 70

Disaster Management Information System, 35, 36

Disaster Management Institutes, 226

Disaster Management Plan, 37, 69, 70, 72, 81, 96, 104, 182, 189, 239

Disaster Management Programme (DMP), 148

Disaster Management Structure, 157

Disaster Management Training Programme (DTMP), 149

Disaster Management, 69

Disaster Medical Assistance teams, 101

Disaster Mitigation and Emergency Preparedness, 36

Disaster Mortuary Assistance Teams, 101

Disaster Risk Management Programme, 125

Disaster Risk Mitigation (DRM), 226

Disaster Service Liaison Officer (DSLOs), 145

Disaster warning, 121

District Disaster Management Authority, 68, 218, 230

District Management Information System, 189

District Panchayat, 130

DNS servers, 124

Dominican Republic, 26

Donations, 236

Dr Manmohan Singh, 68

Dr Walter Fernandes, 34

DRDO, 240

Drinking Water Supply, 69

Droughts, 32

E

Earth observation (EO), 171

Earthquake Risk Mitigation, 72, 221

Earthquakes, 17, 19, 20, 21, 22, 23, 24, 25, 29, 31, 32, 34, 52, 72, 92, 146, 162, 197, 219, 220, 222, 223, 235

East Pakistan, 23

Eastern Pacific Ocean, 21

Education and Training, 59

El Niño/ Southern Oscillation (ENSO), 57

El Salvador, 26

Electronic Governance (EG), 244
Eleventh Finance Commission, 71, 94, 130
Emergency Information Centre (EIC), 101
Emergency Information Infrastructure Partnership (EIIP), 59
Emergency Management Australia (DGEMA), 159
Emergency Management Australia (EMA), 157, 158
Emergency Management Liaison Officers (EMLOs), 159
Emergency Management Liaison Officers, 158
Emergency Management Systems, 59
Emergency Medical Relief Division, 33
Emergency Medical Services (EMS), 242
Emergency Operation Centre (EOC), 100
Emergency Operation Centre, 76, 94, 101, 189
Emergency Preparedness, 44
Emergency Relief Coordinator (ERC), 153
Emergency Support Function (ESF) Plans, 76
Emergency Support Function, 105, 165
Emergency, 201
Employment Exchange Registration, 245
Employment Opportunities, 245
Environment and Forests, 69
Eurasian, 168
Euro-Canadian Space Programme, 172
Euro-Mediterranean area, 171
EUR-OPA Major Hazards Agreement, 171
Europe as a Union, 166
Europe, 23, 147, 155, 166, 172
European Commission, 170, 171
European Commission's Humanitarian Aid (ECHO), 172
European Community, 169
European Space Agency (ESA), 172
European Union Civil Protection Monitoring and Information Center (ECPMIC), 170
European Union, 166, 167, 172
European-Mediterranean Seismological Centre (EMSC), 53
Ex Gratia Payment, 245
Examination Results, 245
Executive Committee on Humanitarian Affairs (ECHA), 153
Exxon Valdez, 162

F

Family and Community Services (FaCS), 160
Ferozabad Railway accident, 31
Fertilizers, 245
Field Coordination Units (FCU), 152
Fire, 219
Flash floods, 19
Flood Management Measures, 230
Flood Management Plans (FMPs), 231
Floods, 20, 25, 32, 219
Florida, 162
Food and Agriculture Organisation, 141
Food and Civil Supplies, 192
Forecasting, 44
Forestry, 124
France, 20, 167

G

Gandhinagar (Gujarat), 232
Ganga Flood Control Commission, 229
Geneva, 102
Geographic information system (GIS), 172
Geographical Information System (GIS), 77
Geological Survey of India (GSI), 74
GIS Software, 59
Global Information and Early Warning System on Food and Agriculture (GIEWS), 57
Global Risk Analysis, 25
Good Governance Kautilya, 114
Government and Non-governmental, 194
Government Forms, 245
Government Notifications, 245
Government to Citizens, 123
Gram Panchayat, 130
Gramsat Pilot Project, 121
Grants, 236
Great Chicago Fire, 21
Great Fire of London, 21
Greater Horn Information Exchange (GHIE), 57
Greece, 167
GSWAN, 125
Gujarat earthquake, 23, 153, 235
Gujarat State Wide Area Network, 123
Gujarat, 35, 69, 70, 81, 93, 123, 151, 246
Guwahati, 232
Gwalior and College of Military Engineering (CME) Pune, 232
Gyan Ganga, 126, 127

H

Habitat Agenda, 148
Haiti, 26
Handicapped, 245
Harbour Centre campus, 51
Hazard Safety Cells (HSC), 72
Health Department, 192
Health Ministry, 33
High Level Committee on Relief (HLCR), 187
High Level Group (HLG), 161
Himachal Pradesh, 229, 236
Himalayan region, 24, 34, 222
Himalayas, 30
Home Guards, 192, 219
Honduras, 26
Hospital Management Information System (HMIS), 130
Hospitals / Beds Availability / Services, 245
Household inventory, 40, 41, 42
Housing, 192
Human Resource Development, 63, 98, 103
Hungary, 171
Hunraken, 53
Hurricane Katrina, 21

I

IAS officer, 78
ICMR, 240
IIT-Madras, 126
Image Processing Software and SDIS, 124
Implementation Mechanisms, 93
India Disaster Resource Network (IDRN), 76
India Meteorological Department (IMD), 224

India, 52
Indian Institute of Management, 35
Indian Meteorological Department (IMD), 187
Indian Meteorological Department, 73, 229
Indian Ocean Earthquake, 22
Indian Ocean Tsunami, 218
Indian Ocean, 21, 30, 53
Indian Red Cross Society, 219
Indian Space Research Organisation, 73
Indo-Pak War, 87
Information Gathering/Processing System, 204
Information Technology (IT), 130, 132
Information Technology Tools for Natural Disaster Risk, 59
Information Technology, 125, 244
Initiative to Nurture a Vibrant Information Technology Ecosystem (INVITE), 130
INSAT-1B satellite, 188
INSAT-3B, 121
Institute of Disaster Management (NDM), 226
Integrated Disease Surveillance Programme, 237
Integrated Disease Surveillance System (IDS), 129
Integrated Workflow and Document Management System (IWDMS), 125
Interactive Weather Information Network (IWIN), 50
Inter-Agency Standing Committee (IASC), 153
Internally Displaced People (IDP), 34
International Committee of the Red Cross (ICRC), 142
International Cooperation, 102
International Decade for Natural Disaster Reduction, 23, 217
International decade of natural disaster reduction (IDNDR), 30
International Relief System, 139
Irrigation, 192
Italy, 167, 171
Izmit earthquake, 168

J

Jabalpur earthquakes, 221
Jabalpur, 34
Jammu and Kashmir earthquakes, 81, 221
Jammu and Kashmir, 229
Jan Sampark, 128
Japan, 23

K

Karma Yogi Maha Abhiyaan, 123
Karma Yogis, 123
Karnataka, 113, 117, 119
Kashmir valley, 34
Kashmir, 151
Kerala, 69, 113
Kolkata, 227, 232
Koyna, 89
Krakatoa, 22
Kutch, 35

L

Lack of Emergency Medical Response System, 247
Lal Bahadur Shastri National Academy of Administration, 100
Land and Water Resource Management, 124
Landslide Hazard Mitigation, 74
Landslides, 220

Latur earthquakes, 221
Latur, 89
League of Red Cross Societies (LORCS), 142
League of Red Cross Societies, 141
Liechtenstein, 167
Lituya Bay, 22
Loan, 236
Local Area Network (LAN), 117
Local Civil Preparedness Agencies, 145
Lodhika Taluka, 128
Logistics, 44
Lok Sabha, 68

M

Madhya Pradesh, 69
Maharashtra earthquake, 150
Maharashtra Emergency Earthquake, 150
Maharashtra, 89, 93, 189
Mail servers, 124
Major Disaster Area, 146
Malaria, 87
Malawi, 26
Malaysia, 154
Market Price, 245
Massachusetts Institute of Technology (MIT), 115, 117
Media Lab-Asia, 117
Micro-Finance, 220
Millennium Development Goal (MDG), 235
Ministries Consultative Committees (MCC), 116
Ministry of Information Technology, 117
Mississippi, 162
Mitigation, 59
Montroc, 20
Mount St. Helens, 22
Mr B Someshwar Rao, 78
Mr CK Koshy, 248
Mr J Dunant, 142
Mr Koshy, 248
Ms Ann-Louise Eksborg, 166
Mukhya Vahini, 118
Mumbai, 227
Mundali (Bhubaneshwar), 232
Mussoorie, 100

N

Nagaland, 69
Nagarpalikas, 126
National Award, 124
National Cadet Corps, 219
National Calamity Contingency Fund (NCCF), 71, 236
National Centre for Disaster Management (NCDM), 150
National Centre for Medium Range Weather Forecasting, 73
National Contingency Action Plan (CAP), 186
National Core Group for Earthquake Risk Mitigation, 72
National Core Group, 74
National Crisis Management Committee (NCMC), 33, 64, 184
National Cyclone Risk Mitigation Project (NCRMP), 226
National Database for Emergency Management, 220
National Disaster Management Authority (NDMA), 64, 68, 218, 225, 228, 229, 232

National disaster management plan, 232
National Disaster Response Force (NDRF), 218, 219, 229
National Disaster Risk Management Programme, 72
National Emergency Communication Network, 77
National Emergency Operation Centre (NEOC), 77
National Emergency Operations Centre (NEOC), 144
National emergency operations centre, 105
National Finance Commission, 186
National Institute of Disaster Management (NIDM), 204, 218, 221
National Laboratory Network, 240
National Organisation of Civil Defence, 145
National Registration and Inquiry System, 159
National Remote Sensing Agency, 73, 188, 229
National Resources Evaluation Centre, 145
National response plan (NRP), 162
National Service Scheme, 219
National Weather Service Disaster Survey Reports, 55
Natural Disaster Hotspots, 25
Natural Disaster Management Division, 33, 225
Natural Disaster Mitigation Programme, 161
Natural Disasters in Australia, 156
Natural Disasters Organisation (NDO), 144
NCC, 234
Nehru Yuva Kendra Sangathan, 219
Nepal, 26, 229
New Delhi, 221
NGOs Corporate Sector, 219
NICD, 240
NIMHANS, 31, 33
Non Government Organisations (NGOs), 66
Nondani, 118
Nongovernmental and Volunteer Organisations, 165
Non-governmental organisations (NGOs), 147, 149, 169, 219
North Bay of Bengal, 224
North East Monsoons, 89
North-Eastern States, 236
Northern Hemisphere, 31, 224
NSS, 234
Nuclear bomb, 17
Nuclear Emergency Teams, 101
Nuclear, 238
NYKS, 234

O

Observing, 59
Odisha (Cyclones), 81, 82
Odisha, 34, 69, 72, 89, 93, 113, 236
Office of Emergency Preparedness (OEP), 145
Old Age Pension, 245
One-Day Governance model, 126
Orissa State Disaster Mitigation Authority (OSDMA), 154
Orissa Super-cyclone, 153
Orissa, 150

P

Pakistan, 153
Panchayati Raj Department, 122

Panchayati Raj Institutions, 219
Pay and Account Offices (PAOs), 128
Pension/Services, 245
Peoples participation, 121
Permanent Network of National Correspondents (PNNC), 170
Peru, 52
Pesticides, 245
Philippines, 23
Plague in Surat, 87
PM Relief Fund, 236
Poland, 171
Police Training Colleges, 233
Portugal, 167
PRAGATI, 124
Preparedness, 59
Primacy of Civil Administration, 199
Project planning, 121
Proposed National Earthquake Risk Mitigation Project (NERMP), 223
Public Awareness, 233
Public Distribution System, 183
Public Health Engineering, 192
Pune, 154

R

Railway Time Tables, 245
Rajasthan, 34, 72, 87, 205, 236
Rajkot District, 128
Rajya Sabha, 68
Rapid Response Team (RRTs), 241
Rasthriya Baarh Ayog (1978), 229
Recovery, 59
Reduction of corruption, 121
Regional Response Centres (RRC), 75
Relief, 59
Research, 59
Response, 59
Responsiveness, 121
Richter scale struck Gujarat, 35
Road Transport Time Tables, 245
Rural Development, 69

S

Sachivalaya Integrated Communication Network (SICN), 124
Sahel Report, 56
Sarpanch, 130
Scouts and Guides, 219
Search and Rescue teams, 101
Self Reliance, 44
Seventh Schedule of the Indian Constitution 64
Sher-e-Khoshed, 146, 147
Simon Fraser University (SFU), 51
Singapore, 154
Slovenia, 171
Society for Research and Initiatives for Sustainable Technologies and Institutions (SRISTI), 35
South Asia, 23, 30
South East Asia, 20
Southern France, 167
Southern Germany, 167
Southern Peninsula, 89
Spain, 167
Special Sensor Microwave Imager (SSMI), 56
Specialised Emergency Operation Teams, 101
Specialist Response Teams (SRT), 75
Speeds Information, 245
SRISTI volunteers, 36
Standard Operating Procedures (SOPs), 239

State Crisis Management Group (SCMG), 65
State Disaster Management Unit, 205
State Disaster Resource Network (SDRN), 125
State Disaster Response Force (SDRF), 233
State Disaster Response Forces, 219
State Emergency Services (SES), 145
State Governments, 31, 64, 65, 66, 69, 70, 74, 75, 82, 93, 116, 150, 181, 194, 223, 229, 230
State Level Control Room, 65
State Search and Rescue (SAR) Teams, 75
State Wide Information on Financial Transactions (SWIFT), 128
States/Union Territories, 26, 68
Storm Warning Centre, 55
Storm winds, 20
Strengthening of Civil Defence, 78
Sumatra region, 73
Super Cyclone, 150
Surat, 227
Swedish Emergency Management Agency, 166
Switzerland, 167
System of Disaster Management, 157
Systems, 59

T

Taiwan, 26
Talatis, 130
Talegaon (Pune), 232
Talim Rojgar, 128
Taluka Panchayat staff, 130
Taluka Panchayat, 130
Tamil Nadu, 69, 89
Tangshan, 17
Tasmania, 155
Technical Organisatoins, 64
Techno-financial framework, 82
Techno-legal, 82
Technological Needs, 44
Territory Governments, 161
Tornadoes, 19
Training and skills development, 121
Transparency, 121
Transport enable-and- control mechanism, 35
Trauma Management, 36
Tropical Cyclone (TC), 224
Tsunami Evolution, 63
Tsunami Warning Centre (TWC), 74
Tsunami Warning System, 74
Tsunami Warnings, 73
Tsunami, 17, 20, 21, 27, 73, 78, 103, 153, 160, 220, 235, 246
Turkey, 23, 52, 168

U

UN Disaster Assessment and Coordination (UNDAC) System, 66
UN Office for Coordination of Humanitarian Affairs (UNOCHA), 66
UN Secretary-General, 147, 246
UN systems, 141
Union Ministry of Agriculture and Animal Husbandry, 33
Union Ministry of Information Technology, 115
Union Territories (UTs), 224
Union Territories, 69, 220, 221, 226
Union Territory Administrations, 63
Unique geo-climatic conditions, 24, 26, 63, 92
United Nations (UN), 147

United Nations Assessment and Coordination (UNDAC), 152
United Nations Children Fund (UNICEF), 141, 151
United Nations Department of Humanitarian Affairs, 147
United Nations Development Programme (UNDP), 66, 102, 140, 147, 149, 150, 154
United Nations Disaster Management Team (UN DMT), 149
United Nations Disaster Relief Coordinator (UNDRO), 102, 149
United Nations Disaster Relief Organisation (UNDRO), 140
United Nations General Assembly, 23
United Nations High Commissioner for Refugees (UNHCR), 140
United Nations in Disaster Management, 147
United Nations Organisation, 30, 140
United Nations system, 148
United Nations, 30, 102, 140, 217
UP, 236
Urban Development, 69
Urban Flood Management, 228
Utility of HAM Operators, 78
Uttar Pradesh, 72, 229
Uttaranchal, 69, 236
Uttarkashi earthquake, 74
Uttarkashi earthquakes, 74, 221
Uttarkashi, 81
Uttranchal, 93

V

Vadodara, 126
Valukad village, 127
Venezuela, 23
Village Panchayats, 127
Volcanic eruptions, 22
Volcanoes, 25
Vulnerability Atlas, 50, 221

W

War Wastage Reserves, 198
Warning System, 34, 53, 204, 207, 220
Warnings, 59
Washington, 162
Water Resources, 69
Weather Forecast-short range/District-wise, 245
Web servers, 124
Weekly Global Climate Highlights (WGCH), 57
Wellington, 162
West Bengal, 72, 229, 236
West Pakistan, 23
Western Australia, 155
Widow Pension, 245
Wireless in Local Loop (WLL), 126
World Disaster Report, 236
World Food Programme (WFP), 141, 151
World Health Organisation (WHO), 85, 129, 141, 151, 154
World Meorological Organisation (WMO), 187
World War II, 87

Y

Yashawantrao Chavan Academy of Development Administration (YASHADA), 154